❝

This book is unique, innovative, and visually appealing.... a timely and handy reference for advertising professionals and academicians."

EDDIE C.Y. KUO, Professor and Dean,
School of Communication and Information, Nanyang Technological University

❝

Jim Aitchison has just made it a lot easier to see how great global brands are being built in Asia by leveraging local cultures, lifestyles, and values. While principles of effective advertising are universal, effective execution - getting results - is profoundly focused on what's personal. This is a wonderful contribution to strategic marketers everywhere who are looking for insights into what works in Asia."

MICHAEL ALAN HAMLIN, Author of The New Asian Corporation and Managing Director,
TeamAsia

❝

Whilst there is no fail safe formula for creating advertising that works this book is a useful, provocative survey of what is working in this diverse region...yet another invaluable contribution from Jim Aitchison."

SIMONE BARTLEY, CEO,
Saatchi & Saatchi, Singapore

❝

At a time when marketers are faced with a multitude of marketing options, it's refreshing to see the power of the big idea come through in a showcase of effective advertising campaigns. Jim Aitchison's focus on the Asia-Pacific region is sure to attract the attention of marketing decision-makers in Europe and North America, who will appreciate the multicultural mix of communication problems and creative solutions presented in this must read book."

BARRIE PARSONS, Publisher, B&T Weekly
Reed Business Information, Sydney, Australia

How Asia Advertises

The Most Successful Campaigns in Asia-Pacific and the Marketing Strategies Behind Them

How Asia Advertises

The Most Successful Campaigns in Asia-Pacific and the Marketing Strategies Behind Them

Jim Aitchison

John Wiley & Sons (Asia) Pte Ltd

Copyright © 2002 John Wiley & Sons (Asia) Pte Ltd

Published in 2002 by John Wiley & Sons (Asia) Pte Ltd
2 Clementi Loop, #02-01, Singapore 129809

Other Wiley Editorial Offices

John Wiley & Sons, Inc., 605 Third Avenue, New York, NY 10158-0012, USA
John Wiley & Sons Ltd, Baffins Lane, Chichester West Sussex PO191 UD, England
John Wiley & Sons (Canada) Ltd, 22 Worcester Road, Rexdale, Ontaario M9W ILI, Canada
John Wiley & Sons Australia Ltd, 33 Park Road (PO Box 1226), Milton, Queensland 4046, Australia
Wiley-VCH, Pappelallee 3, 69469 Weinham, Germany

Library of Congress Cataloging-in-Publication Data:

ISBN 0-470-82055-1

Typeset in 12.5/10.5 point, Mrs Eaves, by WORK
Printed in Singapore by Craft Print International Ltd
10 9 8 7 6 5 4 3 2

CONTENTS

CONTENTS   CONTENTS
CONTENTS
CONTENTS   CONTENTS
CONTENTS
CONTENTS   CONTENTS   CONTENTS
CONTENTS

PREFACE
PREFACE   PREFACE
PREFACE   PREFACE
PREFACE PREFACE
PREFACE   PREFACE PREFACE
PREFACE
PREFACE

A number of important trends are now molding and reshaping the role of advertising and marketing in today's business environment. Changes in regulation have globalized markets and exposed a large number of customers to variety, choice, and access. Product life cycles have shortened, bringing on waves of new products and services into the markets at a frenetic pace. Technology has enabled the creation of a new and sophisticated consumption culture. And the reality of the Internet Age is that all of the traditional forms of communications, such as advertising and public relations are now even more fundamental to business performance.

But the critical issue with advertising is the same as with anything else these days. In a world of mediocrity and clutter, how can you stand out from the crowd and still achieve success? Sound brand strategy and positioning, coupled with other elements such as brilliant creativity, compelling copywriting and arresting visuals have never been more significant in terms of making an advertisement work. The influence of these and other forces in the environment have made it clear that effective and innovative advertising is too crucial a discipline to ignore.

Unlike most advertising books that focus on advertising, Jim Aitchison, while showing how the fundamental principles of advertising are transferable to the Asian environment, also illustrates that the most clever and artistic ideas will travel. Importantly, he shows remarkable insight in dissecting critical business issues and linking these to successful advertising response.

Supported by a wealth of different case studies from every country, culture and category in Asia Pacific, this book offers the tools to enable practitioners to turn their creative theories into profitable realities. An invaluable reference source and eminently readable, the diverse volume of case studies and examples should convince marketers that the 21st century will need a stronger emergence of sophistication and creativity.

This book is a major contribution to the practice of marketing and branding in Asia because it successfully demonstrates two things. Firstly, that advertising can solve business problems and help build strong brands. Secondly, that Asia can produce world-class advertising.

Dr Paul Temporal
Chairman
Temporal Brand Consulting
Singapore

FOREWORD FOREWORD FOREWORD FOREWORD
REWORD **FOREWORD** FOREWORD
FOREWORD FOREWORD FOREWORD
FOREWORD

understanding asian advertising

Having spent more than 20 years in, around, about and involved in Asian advertising, I have often wondered why it has seemed so mysterious and different to western observers and analysts. To me, Asian advertising seems to reflect the psyche of the people who live and work there. At the same time, it gives some insights into the myriad cultures that make up Asia and the Asia-Pacific region, from Australia to Malaysia to Japan and India and now increasingly to China.

To me Asian advertising is not different, it's just culturally oriented. So, if you have lived, worked and been involved in Asia and in the patchwork that makes up Asia, you understand. But, not very many advertising professionals have and that's why Jim Aitchison's book on Asian advertising is so welcome. For the first time, there is a compendium of advertising examples and illustrations from across the region that not only illustrate the many cultural faces of Asia, it puts them into a common context for comparison and evaluation. Why, for example, does Petronas in Malaysia rely so heavily on cultural bonding while in Japan, Levi's reflects the country's love affair with technology. It's all here and it's all revealing, interesting and most of all, insightful about why the advertising approach was developed and why it succeeded.

I have often commented that there is a vast difference in how Asians go to market and how the western world believes marketing, advertising and communication should be conducted. In my view, western cultures are atomistic, that is, the tradition has been to try to break down every activity or event into its smallest parts and then reassemble them in an effort to explain and illustrate "how things work". That's why so much western advertising is based on such things as Unique Selling Propositions, Positioning and step-by-step, "how to" advertising copy. It's logical. It's process-oriented and in many cases, it's horribly dull and boring.

Asian advertising reflects the Asian cultures that make up the region.

It is holistic, inventive, often reflective and sometimes even whimsical, qualities that often baffle the western observer. Asian advertising is, for the most part, holistic because that's what the cultures are, holistic, from religions to everyday activities. Many Asians believe everything is connected to everything else. From feng shui to Zen, the view is that of the whole, not of the individual pieces. How things and the world fit together. How they relate. How they are seamless and consistent. And that I think, is reflected in the Asian approach to advertising and promotion. Where the western world has "contracts", Asians have "guanxi". Where the west is copy focused, Asia is visual and aural. So Asian advertising is different but it is different for a reason and therefore it works differently no matter how many western products and brands are introduced into the many markets and many cultures.

And that is why Jim Aitchison's book is so important. Jim understands Asian advertising because he has practised it…for years. But he also brings the western view of what advertising is and how it should be evaluated. It is this blending of insights and strategy. Of focus and direction. Of hard cold facts and soft, fuzzy feelings that sets this book apart.

The illustrations and examples are almost limitless. No matter what business you are in, you will find some case history that fits. Best of all, Jim takes us behind the pictures and words and sights and sounds to explain the issues the advertising was designed to address. How the strategy was developed and most importantly, the results obtained. And, given the closed nature of many Asian businesses, a recitation of results may be the most important part of the book. In other words, Jim's ability to put the advertising in a business perspective.

As you go through this book, you will likely be as surprised as I was in the variations that occur by country yet by the consistency of the thought processes, the focus on the culture and most of all, the insights into what creates successful advertising and marketing communication across a broad panoply of Asian brands and Asian businesses. In and of itself, simply having this book as a reference tool for agencies or practitioners who are attempting to understand Asian advertising for the first time or for those who are attempting to move across the various cultures, it is a treasure trove. For those of us who have observed and contributed to Asian advertising over the years, it is a welcome addition to history and legend in the making.

There is little question that with the opening of China, the fantastic economic growth of India and the recovering economies of Malaysia, Singapore, Korea and hopefully Japan, Asia will be the central focus of much economic growth and development in the next few decades. Advertising, marketing and promotion will be key elements in fuelling and driving that growth. Thus, understanding the unique natures, yet the commonalities of Asian advertising, is a critical issue for practitioner as well as academic and observer. Jim has done both in this highly readable yet fact-filled text. I would suggest you not shelve the book but keep it on your desk for ready reference. I certainly intend doing so.

DON E. SCHULTZ
Emeritus Professor-in-Service,
Northwestern University, Evanston, IL, USA
President, Agora, Inc., Evanston, IL, USA
Director, The Simon Richards Group,
Melbourne, Australia
March, 2002, Sydney, Australia

INTRODUCTION INTRODUCTION INTRODUCTION
INTRODUCTION INTRODUCTION INTRODUCTION

INTRODUCTION

INTRODUCTION INTRODUCTION INTRODUCTION
INTRODUCTION

ADVERTISING is an inseparable part of brand building. Every day, in every market of Asia-Pacific, brand owners make critical decisions to change consumer behaviour through advertising either in their own market or, as is increasingly the case, regionally.

Until now, surprisingly, there had been no single business title that contained a contemporary, category-by-category reference of what works in advertising across the major markets of Asia-Pacific — Australia, China, Hong Kong, India, Japan, Malaysia, New Zealand, the Philippines, Singapore, Sri Lanka, Taiwan, and Thailand. This book fills that gap with a broad range of work across television, print, posters, direct marketing and ambient media.

Each case history details the problems the advertising had to solve, how the strategic and creative breakthroughs were reached, and what results were actually achieved.

As Asia-Pacific's marketing becomes more sophisticated, so too will its advertising. Asia-Pacific marketers need to know what works in their product categories beyond their own borders; they need to see how other advertisers have addressed the level of consumer sophistication in other markets. How do the Singaporeans sell telecoms? How do the Chinese sell life insurance? How do the Malaysians sell petrol? How do the Taiwanese sell information technology? How do the Australians save lives on the road?

Every campaign in this book was selected because it demonstrated fresh creativity within its country context. And every campaign worked. In the majority of cases, the clients and their agencies have freely shared the results, detailing market share growth, increased sales, improved awareness levels, stronger brand recall. Others were unable to, owing to the confidentiality of their current marketing activities.

The selection is eclectic and inevitably subjective. However, it certainly enables us to glean some fascinating insights.

some learnings

there is no such thing as a "typical" asia-pacific campaign Generally, most are visually not verbally led. The best have well-focused singular themes, and present their messages in a fresh, different manner — the same qualities that distinguish effective advertising in every market of the world.

there is no such thing as a "typical" asia-pacific consumer Every market has developed its own personality. Different experiences, different exposures, have produced people with different perspectives. Does that mean advertising has to be crude and simplistic to "reach" everyone? No, because there are enough similarities, on a human level, to unite rather than divide the regional audience, whoever and wherever they are.

the best work adheres to the universal truths of advertising The universal truths of advertising — singularity of proposition, simplicity of expression, and relevance of message — always apply. Too often when global or regional campaigns are developed, the lowest common denominator in creativity wins the day. What this book will demonstrate is that uncommonly good work works as well in Asia-Pacific as it does anywhere else in the world. Even campaigns which cast a net across the region, engaging different cultures, different languages and different levels of social and economic development, work best when they contain the proven ingredients of success — some magic element of surprise or difference. Lateral thinking, too, is more evident now than it was ten or twenty years ago. Simplistic, condescending creativity pitched to the lowest common denominator can still be found in Asia, just as it can anywhere else. Thankfully, there's less of it.

the best work is true to its own culture While advertising might well have been a Western invention, the best Asia-Pacific work does not copy the West. It speaks with its own voice, appropriate to the brand, just like the best British and American work does. Malaysia's Petronas is uniquely, passionately Malaysian. The *Bugger* dog is purely, laconically Kiwi. Only Taiwan's brand of urban sophistication — a heady cocktail of Japanese and Western influences — could have produced the Stimorol Generation and the surreal Sunrise

Department Store campaign. Only Hong Kong could boast a real life icon like Tsang, the self-appointed Emperor of Kowloon; having him clean off his anti-British graffiti with Swipe was pure, local satire. Always, the best ideas go beyond mere language and style; they reflect deep characteristics of people; they come from real life.

humour Perhaps rather surprisingly, humour appeared a successful tool in more markets than might have been expected. While Thai advertising has been famous for years for its outrageous sense of humour, and Australians have always celebrated irreverence, other markets now appear more willing to sell with a smile. And the humour is even more piquant when it reflects some quirk of its local culture or society — witness *The Times of India* campaign from India.

the importance of crafting Asians certainly respond to beautiful executions and craft, not that they're alone in that. Singapore Airlines, Nippon Paint and UNICEF are proof that beautifully crafted strategic work expressing relevant, truthful brand ideas will work against all odds, anywhere. SingTel's anniversary campaign proves that crafting should be appropriate to the message — the use of almost home video executions worked perfectly for shots of ordinary Singaporeans talking about their relationships with the brand. Ideology's work in Taiwan also reminds us how production values contribute integral, yet almost indefinable, nuances to creative ideas.

Category by category, campaign by campaign, there are many other learnings in store for brand owners, marketers, advertising professionals, teachers and students. I hope this book will provide as many surprising and valuable insights for each of you, as its preparation did for me.

JIM AITCHISON
Singapore 2002

ACKNOWLEDGMENTS
ACKNOWLEDGMENTS   ACKNOWLEDGMENTS
ACKNOWLEDGMENTS

ACKNOWLEDGMENTS

ACKNOWLEDGMENTS

ACKNOWLEDGMENTS   ACKNOWLEDGMENTS

ACKNOWLEDGMENTS

MY special thanks to Theseus Chan, who designed and produced this book, and to Andie Ngoh and Evonne Ng at WORK Singapore who brought it to fruition. Thanks, too, to Johnson Tan and his team at ProColor Singapore for their care and expertise.

The driving force behind this book was Nick Wallwork, Publisher, at John Wiley & Sons (Asia); my thanks to Nick and Janis Soo for their guidance and encouragement and to Malar Manoharan, my editor, for all her patience and skill throughout the project.

To all those busy people in advertising agencies who contributed their time and talent to compile the case histories, and to their clients who gave us permission to share their brand building experiences and results, my sincere gratitude.

SONY WALKMAN   SONY WALKMAN SWATCH   SWATCH   LEVI STRAUSS JAPAN   SWATCH
LEVI STRAUSS JAPAN
SWATCH
APPAREL AND ACCESSORIES   LEVI STRAUSS JAPAN
STRAUSS JAPAN   LEVI STRAUSS JAPAN   SWATCH   SONY WALKMAN
SWATCH   SONY WALKMAN   SONY WALKMAN   LEVI STRAUSS JAPAN
SONY WALKMAN   SONY WALKMAN

Apparel
AndAccessories

THE category convention is to hold a mirror to life, a dangerous enough technique that breeds sameness and defeats indelible branding. Very often, this category is subject to rapid change, either in terms of technology or fashion. Imitation is rampant, and communications based on product features are quickly yesterday's news. The most successful campaigns avoid such obvious pitfalls. The brand's connection with the consumer is explored from a different perspective, searching for the less predictable common ground and establishing brand relationships that endure transient whims, tastes and price pressures.

category	countries	advertiser	agency
APPAREL AND ACCESSORIES	JAPAN, HONG KONG, MALAYSIA, PHILIPPINES, SINGAPORE, TAIWAN	LEVI STRAUSS JAPAN	BARTLE BOGLE HEGARTY ASIA PACIFIC, SINGAPORE

DEMONSTRATING ORIGINALITY   DEMONSTRATING ORIGINALITY   DEMONSTRATING ORIGINALITY

DEMONSTRATING ORIGINALITY DEMONSTRATING ORIGINALITY

DEMONSTRATING ORIGINALITY   DEMONSTRATING ORIGINALITY   DEMONSTRATING ORIGINALITY

DEMONSTRATING ORIGINALITY   DEMONSTRATING ORIGINALITY

the problem Levi's had successfully launched Engineered Jeans in Japan. The brand had originated the category — a new jeans product with an innovative "twisted-to-fit" design concept: the seams run over the knees rather than straight down the legs, the hip pockets slant, and the bottoms are cut so they do not trail. The new product retailed for Yen 13,000 (US$60). Levi's predicted that the Engineered Jeans category (also known as EJs or 3D jeans) would eventually occupy 20% of their core customers' wardrobes. Hailed as the new blueprint for denim, Levi's was banking on its Engineered Jeans to help win back the brand's global leadership status vis-à-vis surfwear, cargo pants and hip-hop clothing styles.

The initial launch with Japanese pop star Takuya Kimura had been tremendously successful. Next, the campaign had to roll out across Asia and combat brands such as Edwin, Uniqlo, Wrangler, Evisu and Gap, which were promoting similar products. It was important to establish that not only were Levi's the Original Jeans, but they were also the Original Engineered Jeans.

the strategy There was a strong desire to create something more than just another off-the-shelf campaign "for the kids". The jeans market was cynical about advertising. Given budget limitations and the high cost of media in Japan, the campaign would need to break the mould in terms of creativity and customer involvement.

The answer was to make the campaign physically interactive at a very inclusive street level — to hand much of it over to the people who were buying the jeans. Levi's was famous for its brand values — creativity, originality and individualism — so why not let the customers express their own originality in a pair of Levi's Engineered Jeans?

The canvas was the world's largest photocopier — a Dai Nippon scanner — *big enough, in fact, to accommodate a human being!* Pop stars and actual Levi's customers were invited to hop up onto the copier (nicknamed The Originator) and create their own completely original poster.

Instant poster printouts were individually captioned: *The Original (your name here). The Original Engineered Jeans. Levi's.*

The campaign was self-generating and each poster was unique in itself. The photocopier was located in the Original Levi's Store, Tokyo. People came in off the street, bought a pair of Levi's, climbed up onto the copier and expressed their originality. Each printout became a dramatic, instant point-of-sale poster. Takuya Kimura kicked off the campaign. Other famous stars like Karen Mok followed. The library of images grew, forming a gallery of the coolest people in town. Everyone wanted to be part of it. Suddenly, Levi's didn't have one star, but hundreds. Nor did it have just one or two executions, but countless.

The scans were digitally stored. They instantly became print ads and posters, as well as the raw material for TV advertising. Multiple scans of some people were used to make 15-second commercials. Some images were selected for other markets, for example appearing super-sized on Singapore buses. The campaign had viral potential. Images were also uploaded to a Levi's website, www.trueoriginals.levi.com forming a community of cool and original Levi's people.

the result By the end of 2000, Levi's Engineered Jeans sales had stabilised at close to 9% of total sales ex-warehouse for Levi Strauss Japan. During the launch period of the campaign, Levi's Engineered Jeans sales increased to 21.9% of sales in February 2001 and 16.9% in March 2001.

The Original Levi's Store had seen very strong sales in Levi's Engineered Jeans over the campaign period. For example, March 2001 saw an increase of almost 49% over February.

Long Term Brand Scores (end 1999-2001), measured by Millward Brown, registered particular success. Since the initial launch of Levi's Engineered Jeans in 1999, "Advertising awareness" had risen from about 27% to a peak of over 68% at the conclusion of the most recent advertising burst in 2001. Scores for "Heard something about recently" had risen from less than 26% before the initial launch to well over 55% in 2001. The all-important image attribute of "Jeans for those who set the trends" had seen constant increases from an initial 41% to over 63% in 2001. Levi's had dramatically improved its performance as a "Brand that sells innovative fashion", scoring a hefty 44% on that measure and outshining its nearest competitor Edwin by over 30%. The brand had also performed very well on many slow-changing brand image attributes including "Individual" and "Self-confident".

Campaign Brand Scores, measured from January 2001 to May 2001, chalked up many impressive increases. "Advertising awareness" for the *Original Engineered Jeans* campaign rose from 39% to a peak of 68%. "Heard something about recently" scores leapt from a pre-campaign level of 27% to 55% at the end of the campaign. Recognition as "Jeans for those who set the trends" rose from a pre-campaign 51% to 63% at the end of the burst. Asked to nominate a "Brand that sets the trends", respondents gave Levi's a 60% score, while Edwin managed 16% following its spring 2001 campaign. The total score for the brand image attribute "Individual" rose from 29% to 44% over the campaign period, while the notoriously difficult to shift score for "Self-confident" saw a solid increase of 8% — from 62% to 70% — over the campaign period.

"

We wanted an idea that truly captured the notion of self-statement. In addition, we wanted something that made the product stand out, but was also significantly different from the advertising imagery so often used by other denim brands. Once we were convinced that the 'human photocopier' was technically viable, we loved the idea. What better way to communicate that 'Everyone's Original' than by offering customers the chance to participate in a Levi's campaign?"

STEVE CASTLEDINE, Marketing Director,
Asia Pacific, Levi Strauss

"

It was ironic that to battle brands copying Levi's, the tool was the biggest copier in the world..."

STEVE ELRICK, Executive Creative Director,
BBH Asia Pacific Singapore

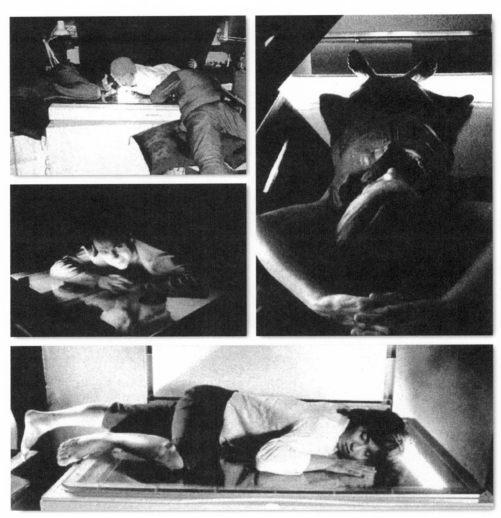

Everyone wanted to interact with the brand, thanks to the world's biggest photocopier. Suddenly, Levi's Original Engineered Jeans had hundreds of original campaign images.

THE ORIGINAL *JUN*

THE ORIGINAL **ENGINEERED JEANS**

THE ORIGINAL *CUE ZERO*

THE ORIGINAL **ENGINEERED JEANS**

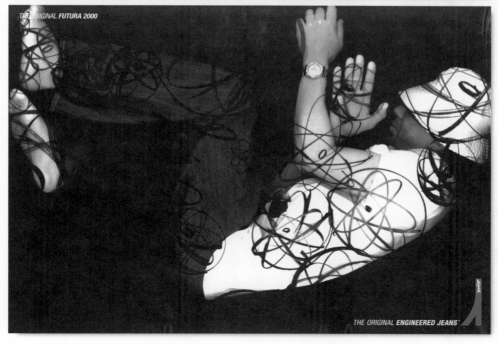

THE ORIGINAL *FUTURA 2000*

THE ORIGINAL **ENGINEERED JEANS**

category
APPAREL AND
ACCESSORIES

countries
GLOBAL

advertiser
SMH/SWATCH

agency
BATEY ADS,
SINGAPORE

A UNION OF OPPOSITES
A UNION OF OPPOSITES
A UNION OF OPPOSITES
A UNION OF OPPOSITES

A UNION OF OPPOSITES

A UNION OF OPPOSITES
A UNION OF OPPOSITES
A UNION OF OPPOSITES
A UNION OF OPPOSITES

the problem New technology developed by SMH permitted the manufacture of a watch that was just 3.9mm thick. While it wasn't the world's thinnest watch, it represented a revolution in plastic. The new product would be branded Swatch, command a premium above normal Swatch prices, and be globally distributed.

SMH's objective was to expand the Swatch family by appealing to more conservative people while retaining the loyalty of core Swatchers who valued irreverence. And therein lay the dilemma: wouldn't the more conservative audience reject the technological story as gimmicky and cheap, while core Swatchers saw the product design as boring and a significant departure from Swatch brand values?

the strategy The breakthrough came with a globally understood name, Skin, that translated the "thin" technology into a sensual, emotional message.

The campaign presented the world's top fashion names naked on the page except for a new Swatch Skin. The theme line posed the question, *Am I naked? Or am I not?*

The culturally provocative photography and nonconformist caption reassured core Swatchers that the brand values were in place. The stylish use of top fashion photography and models signalled quality and taste to an older, more conservative audience.

The campaign look was integrated globally across print advertising, collaterals and point-of-sale displays.

the result The two opposing audiences were successfully united and motivated. The initial production run of 500,000 Skin watches was sold out in 4 weeks. The second production run was underway in record time. Swatch Skin is now a permanent part of the Swatch product range.

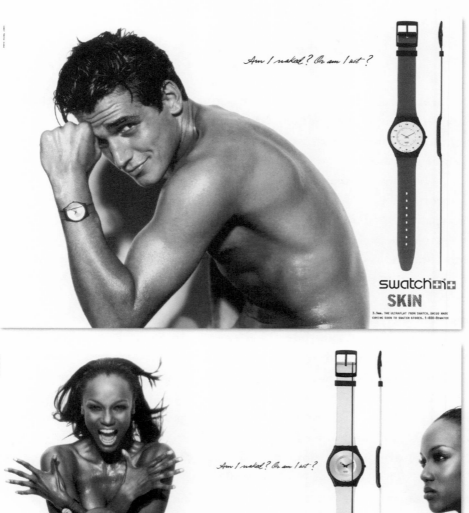

Batey Ads Singapore won the international pitch for the new thin Swatch. The agency created the name, logo, global print advertising and collaterals.

category
APPAREL AND
ACCESSORIES

countries
MALAYSIA

advertiser
SONY/WALKMAN

agency
LEO BURNETT,
KUALA LUMPUR

BRAND ENHANCEMENT BRAND ENHANCEMENT BRAND ENHANCEMENT

BRAND ENHANCEMENT BRAND ENHANCEMENT
BRAND ENHANCEMENT BRAND ENHANCEMENT
BRAND ENHANCEMENT

BRAND ENHANCEMENT

the problem Locally and globally, the Sony Walkman faced major challenges in a very competitive market. New products and gadgets proliferated, all fighting for consumer attention. Competing brands entered the market weekly with new features, new designs, all at attractive prices.

The name "Walkman" had become generic and was used by competitors and consumers to describe their portable audio products. Sony saw the need to expand its Walkman offering and reinforce its Walkman branding.

In Malaysia, Sony's brief was to communicate the many Walkman formats and enhance its existing branding. The brand targeted teenagers and young adults, aged 15 to 35, urban music lovers who are always on the go.

the strategy The key insight was that Walkman, a very personal product, was for people who self-entertain. They were primarily urban youth who did not own a car. They relied on buses and LRT (light rail transit) to get them to work and around the town. Commuting was a major, time-consuming activity. They had no choice but spend hours each day waiting for connections and riding past the same scenery. For highly energetic youths, commuting was an uncomfortable and boring part of their lives. Time passed slowly, making them feel stressed and alone. Mostly, they did not consider the need for a Walkman. They still thought of the Walkman as something that was only "cool" to have during their younger school days.

The positioning therefore involved the enhancement of the Sony Walkman branding. The Walkman had to be perceived as not only for "kids", but also for everyone. It was more than a piece of equipment. It was a means of escape, an antidote to the stress of life, and an antidote to mobile urban loneliness. Walkman offered the emotional companionship of music. And music was there for everyone, in good times and bad.

Strategically, the Sony Walkman brand personality became that of a friend, a companion. The proposition: *With Sony Walkman you're never alone.*

The creative idea was based on the notion that music is a presence that can be felt, a presence that takes the edge off loneliness. The agency humanised that thought by creating a brand icon in the form of a musical note whose presence is projected whenever one listens to a Sony Walkman. The musical note character symbolised the companionship offered by a Walkman. For the first time, Sony Walkman possessed a unique visual icon that conveyed an emotional promise — and a brand icon that separated Walkman from its competitors.

The campaign launched in Malaysia with press, magazines, outdoor posters, and ambient advertising where young people walked — like staircases at LRT stations.

the result Despite the campaign's short run, there has been an extremely positive response from the consumers and it has received overwhelming recognition from the industry as well.

BRAND ENHANCEMENT   BRAND ENHANCEMENT   BRAND ENHANCEMENT

BRAND ENHANCEMENT BRAND ENHANCEMENT

BRAND ENHANCEMENT   BRAND ENHANCEMENT

BRAND ENHANCEMENT

BRAND ENHANCEMENT

category country advertiser agency

AN CEFIRO
NISSAN CEFIRO
VOLKSWAGEN
MERCEDES-BENZ
VOLKSWAGEN
VOLKSWAGEN
NISSAN CEFIRO
RAND CAMPAIGN
AUTOMOTIVE/CARS
TOYOTA BRAND CAMPAIGN
DAEWOO
LEXUS
BMW X5 LAUNCH
BMW X5 LAUNCH
TOYOTA BRAND CAMPAIGN
DAEWOO
LEXUS

Automotive/ Cars

POWER, speed and a more stylish lifestyle are the generics. In reality, it is no longer enough to show the car on the page or run exotic driving footage on television. Skilful marketers steer their way through the competitive maze and identify more interesting opportunities to connect with consumers. Given merging technologies and a dearth of unique tangible benefits, emotional selling propositions have become crucial. Nowadays marketers demand brand propositions that can be stretched across a wide range of different models and markets. Increasingly, Asia-Pacific consumers judge high end brands on their potential for "self-expression", while younger drivers go against the category conventions altogether.

category	countries	advertiser	agency
AUTOMOTIVE/ CARS	SINGAPORE	BMW BRAND CAMPAIGN/ PERFORMANCE MOTORS LTD	M&C SAATCHI, SINGAPORE

POWERFUL PICTURES
POWERFUL PICTURES
POWERFUL PICTURES

POWERFUL PICTURES

POWERFUL PICTURESY
POWERFUL PICTURES POWERFUL PICTURES POWERFUL PICTURES
POWERFUL PICTURES POWERFUL PICTURES

the problem Despite the fact that Singapore is a multilingual market, most advertising ideas are created in English. Rarely are Chinese-educated readers addressed with campaigns created originally in Chinese, expressing thoughts in the Chinese way through the power of a pictographic language.

The Chinese-speaking segment of the market had become increasingly important for BMW. Top-end Chinese media consumers are likely to be highly successful entrepreneurs and businessmen. Traditionally they celebrated their wealth and achievements with a Mercedes-Benz.

the strategy While they are steeped in tradition, Chinese-speaking businessmen are not blindly conformist. The opportunity existed to woo them with an appropriate advertising idea. By crafting a highly original Chinese campaign, BMW stole a march on its arch-rival.

A purely typographic treatment exploited the depth and drama of Chinese characters, where every stroke has its own subtle agenda. The ads appealed to Chinese wit and one-upmanship. (Ironically, the Chinese segment is frequently described as being "literal", yet there was nothing literal in this campaign — and certainly no car shots.)

In one ad, the reader had to choose between being just another member of the crowd (众 zhòng) or being a person (人 rén) who stands out as an individualist. Literally translated, the reader was asked to look beyond the crowd instead of conforming to standard expressions of success (Mercedes-Benz).

Another ad draws a contrast between the word for earth, (土 tǔ) and the word for a worldly learned gentleman (士 shì). Which would the reader prefer to be seen as: an old-fashioned, mulish person who follows the predictable display of success, or a worldlier gentleman more inspired in his tastes?

The campaign proved so popular it was later translated into English.

the result Research conducted by the Chinese newspaper *Lián Hé Zǎo Bào* (联合早报) showed awareness recall of the campaign was very high, as was a desire to purchase. This was subsequently borne out by sales. By the end of that year, Performance Motors Ltd had achieved for Singapore BMW's highest share in the luxury car category in the world. Performance Motors Ltd went on to beat all previous years' sales.

❝

You can't think and craft in English, then package it as a campaign for Chinese readers. The beauty of this campaign was that it fully exploited the depth of the Chinese language to deliver a potent message that could only come from BMW and no other brand."

YUE CHEE GUAN, Art Director,
M&C Saatchi, Singapore

POWERFUL PICTURES
POWERFUL PICTURES   POWERFUL PICTURESY
POWERFUL PICTURES POWERFUL PICTURES
POWERFUL PICTURES   POWERFUL PICTURES   POWERFUL PICTURES
POWERFUL PICTURES

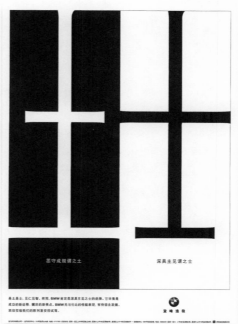

category
AUTOMOTIVE/
CARS

countries
SINGAPORE

advertiser
BMW X5 LAUNCH/
PERFORMANCE
MOTORS LTD

agency
M&C SAATCHI,
SINGAPORE

TWISTING TRADITION TWISTING TRADITION TWISTING TRADITION

TWISTING TRADITION # TWISTING TRADITION

TWISTING TRADITION TWISTING TRADITION

TWISTING TRADITION

TWISTING TRADITION

TWISTING TRADITION

the problem Chinese-educated drivers in Singapore had long favoured Mercedes-Benz as their ultimate badge of wealth and success. Having made substantial inroads into that segment, BMW was keen to again demonstrate BMW's core values to the Mandarin-speaking audience.

The new BMW X5 offered such an opportunity. It was a unique car in terms of looks and performance, and embodied many aspects of the marque.

However, given that it was an off-road vehicle being launched in a small, urbanised island nation, at a price similar to that of the BMW Series 7, uptake was expected to be small.

the strategy Chinese-educated readers opened their newspapers and found themselves looking at traditional Chinese paintings which at first glance appeared totally authentic. At second glance, however, they discerned a BMW X5 subtly illustrated somewhere within the painting. The campaign retained the style and beauty of both Chinese art and the new BMW offering.

One Chinese painting revealed the X5 perched atop the kind of forbidding cliff beloved of Chinese painters. The caption reminded readers that by reaching the peak, perfection had been attained.

A scenic view of a river and a typical Chinese bridge framed the X5 traversing the river. A poetic caption referred to an arduous trip over land and water as a test of true endurance.

In the third work the X5 emerged from the mist, making the point that it possessed the ability to move about freely despite restraints and restrictions.

While each ad communicated a fresh aspect of the X5's versatility and superior performance, the campaign as a whole reflected the brand's core positioning — *The ultimate driving machine.*

the result The first shipment of X5s imported into Singapore was sold out instantly. New orders were taken. In the process, BMW continued to raise its profile among the Mandarin-speaking audience.

category	countries	advertiser	agency
AUTOMOTIVE/	AUSTRALIA	DAEWOO	THE CAMPAIGN
CARS			PALACE,
			SYDNEY

FROM "DAE-WHO?" TO DAEWOO

FROM "DAE-WHO?" TO DAEWOO   FROM "DAE-WHO?" TO DAEWOO

FROM "DAE-WHO?" TO DAEWOO FROM "DAE-WHO?" TO DAEWOO

FROM "DAE-WHO?" TO DAEWOO   FROM "DAE-WHO?" TO DAEWOO

FROM "DAE-WHO?" TO DAEWOO

the problem Foreign marques face large barriers to successful entry and establishment in the Australian market. Cars are not an impulse purchase and the decision-making process takes weeks or months. The market has a history of marques with long-established pedigrees on one hand, as well as failed launches like Lada and Skoda on the other. Australian consumers tend to be suspicious of new marques, especially those from countries not known for car making like Korea. (Even Toyota had sold only nine vehicles when it entered the market in 1962.)

Competition is fierce and the market volatile. When Daewoo launched in 1994, car makers spent US$140 million on passenger car advertising. By the end of 1997, they had nearly doubled expenditure to US$270 million.

Unusually, Daewoo chose to launch with just one model in one market sector — the 1.5i, a small car available in 3-, 4- and 5-door versions. It was essentially a German Opel Kadett, a General Motors design of 1985 vintage. It would subsequently be replaced by the Cielo and, from March 1995, by the medium 4-door Espero sedan.

Communications were tasked with making an unfamiliar brand name familiar quickly. Not only must the advertising separate Daewoo from a host of small cars with similar positioning — the "sexy" urban run-arounds — but it also had to create a brand personality that would appeal to Australians sufficiently to overcome negative perceptions of Korean cars.

the strategy The agency's core strategy was to take an "anti-category" stance. Qualitative research suggested that Australian consumers were sated with car advertising *clichés*, whether it was the youthful lifestyle with a bouncy music track or pompous journeys up mountains to classical music. Given the basic nature of the Daewoo product, aspirational imagery was out of the question. The brand was targeted at a more pragmatic mindset — people who were looking for substance rather than glitz.

On a rational level, Daewoo was positioned as the smart, intelligent choice, a car for those who sought no-nonsense motoring value. On an emotional level, the brand was presented as fresh, different, unpretentious, cheeky and deliberately unfashionable.

The launch campaign targeted an unusual audience for the small car market: older car buyers with a male bias, reflecting the intention to attract pragmatic, "anti-image" car buyers. Over time, the Daewoo positioning and personality also appealed to the more traditional small car buyers — younger women — who were equally tired of "lifestyle" advertising hype.

Two TV commercials and various print ads were run with the theme *There's nothing you can't do in a Daewoo*. One, called *Daelinquents*, demonstrated the size of the 1.5i through the number of university students who could fit into it. The other, *Daewoof*, was more focused on the emotional positioning and demonstrated manoeuvrability, the thought being that "the Daewoo handles better than a cattle dog".

Cane the cattle dog struck a chord with Australians and became synonymous with the brand. He appeared in the launches of Espero and Cielo and various model run-out promotions. The decision to focus on Cane as the central brand property was made following qualitative research. The use of the dog had not only helped imbue Daewoo with the intended personality values, but Cane was also surprisingly powerful as a symbol of Australian reliability vis-à-vis Korean uncertainty. He could be leveraged in all communications, above and below the line.

In mid-1997 Daewoo relaunched its entire range in just six weeks on a limited budget. The Lanos, Nubira and Leganza had been designed in Britain, Italy, Germany and Korea. The brief was to build on the success of the dog and the "anti-category" tonality, and to showcase the new products.

the result Launched in August 1994, Daewoo sold over 20,000 cars in its first two years, an unprecedented sales success in Australia. By September 1998, less than four years after its launch, Daewoo had sold 60,000 cars in Australia and established a 3.9% share of the passenger car market. In that period, Daewoo's share of total car advertising expenditure never exceeded 5.2%.

No other Australian car launch had ever taken off so quickly. Daewoo's predecessors had taken anything from twice to twelve times as long to achieve comparable sales levels. Based on MARTEC/Passenger Vehicle Registration data covering all new passenger vehicle launches since 1960, Daewoo had achieved 15,000 cumulative sales in under two years; by comparison, Toyota had taken four years, Nissan six years, Mazda seven years, Honda ten years, Subaru twelve years, Suzuki eighteen years, and Daihatsu twenty-four years.

Daewoo's success was even more remarkable considering Millward Brown research in 1996 which indicated Australians' hostility towards the idea of buying a Korean car: only a quarter of those who considered buying an imported car would include Korea among the possibilities, in other words 16% of all car buyers. Yet Australians spent over US$260 million on a marque with ten-year old designs, a marque they had never heard of, from a place about which they were quite suspicious.

The initial base Daewoo model had cost only US$8,000, but competitors Holden Barina, Ford Festiva and Hyundai Excel were cheaper. In fact, Daewoo lost its initial price advantage in late 1995, when the Hyundai Excel was far more competitively priced than the Daewoo Cielo. Yet sales remained buoyant. Daewoo was an appealing brand, not merely a cheap car.

At the time of its launch, Daewoo had 65 dealer sites. But Daewoo had secondary and sometimes tertiary status. Every Daewoo dealer held another primary franchise — Ford, Holden, Nissan or Toyota — all of which sold direct competitors to the Daewoo. But by September 1994, Daewoo had become the second most desirable franchise among hardheaded Australian car dealers, based on the MTA-Howarth survey of dealers.

Cane the cattle dog conferred instant fame and credibility on the marque. The total cost of the first two years' advertising including production was US$15 million. Daewoo and its agency calculate that only the extraordinary achievement of the Cane advertising campaign can account for the brand's higher than expected sales — estimated to lie somewhere between US$88 million and US$240 million above and beyond what would have been expected from "average" advertising. Within those first two years, Daewoo advertising was better recalled than advertising for all other car brands, sharing the top honours with Toyota for television advertising awareness measured by Millward Brown from March to August 1996. In terms of recall generated per TARP, the Daewoo campaign was twice as efficient as any other car advertising in terms of memorability.

A 1996 Millward Brown tracking study of car decision makers in the US$6,000 to US$20,000 segment of the market, revealed that 93% of car buyers had heard of Daewoo. Spontaneous awareness levels indicated Daewoo was equivalent to Daihatsu, greater than Suzuki, and closing on Hyundai on the list of "brands I would consider".

Meanwhile, a Youth Scan study (Newspoll Youth Omnibus, November 1998) revealed the Daewoo Dog was nearly as "cool" as Bart Simpson and more "cool" than the Spice Girls.

❝❞

The dog was perceived as representative of both functional and emotional Daewoo attributes. Described variously as Australian, dependable, hard working, obedient, clever and man's best friend, the Daewoo dog was taken as a statement of reliability and responsiveness for the vehicle. His working dog status (or cattle dog) underscored impressions of functional effectiveness and affordability. Consumers commented favourably on the relaxed approach of the advertising... Daewoo did not take itself overly seriously. That was of interest to target consumers who often felt overwhelmed, confused or bored by technical, generic or uninspiring brand propositions..."

CHRIS ADAMS RESEARCH
January 1995

❝❞

Why do so many other makers achieve so much less with cars that are so much more interesting than a Daewoo?"

AUTOFAX REVIEW OF 1995 CAR ADVERTISING

Cane the cattle dog made his Daebut in the 1994 30-second *Daewoof* commercial when he was outperformed by a Daewoo…

A Daewoo is undergoing an obedience trial with a cattle dog. The Daewoo and the dog respond to every command.

An unseen stockman calls the instructions: *Back, back, back, stay…!*

Forward, forward, forward, forward and around, forward and around…!

Back, back, back, and forward, forward — stay…!

Now, right around, right around… Good dog, back…turn around…

Eventually the trial ends…

STOCKMAN: *Back, back, back, stay…stay…stay…*

The car stays where it has stopped. But the dog runs forward to its master.

STOCKMAN: *Why didn't you stay, boy?*

AUSSIE MALE VO: *The Daewoo. At $14,000, it handles better than a cattle dog. There's nothing you can't do in a Daewoo.*

END SUPER: *3-Year 100,000km Factory Warranty.*

An example of Cane the cattle dog at work in tactical promotions, *Dog Dae Afternoon*, from January 1995...

In his office, a car dealer tells Cane to stay while he goes outside to talk business.

DEALER: *Stay, boy...stay...*

The car dealer inspects his stock with a salesman.

DEALER: *So what are we going to do for this month's Daewoo deals?*

SALESMAN: *We could offer an extended warranty.*

DEALER: *It's got three years, 100,000k's....*

SALESMAN: *What about a stereo?*

DEALER: *It's got a powerful 4-speaker radio cassette.*

SALESMAN: *Special price?*

DEALER: *It's only $14,000...There has to be something we can give away...*

They hear a growl and turn. In the dealer's office, Cane has torn a cushion to shreds. Cut to Cane riding off in the back of a newly-sold Daewoo. The dealer waves goodbye to him.

SUPER: *4 Door Run-Out from $16,700.*

AUSSIE VO: *Daewoo deals... There's nothing a Daewoo dealer won't do for you.*

Cane became a Seeing Eye dog for a blind driver in July 1997's 45-second commercial that launched the Daewoo Nubira...

On a Sydney wharf, a blind man taps and feels his way around the newly arrived Daewoo Nubira.

BLIND MAN: *Righto, where is it... Mmm, yes, definitely European. Mmm, could be English...*

He tells Cane to get in and starts driving the Nubira around the dock.

BLIND MAN: *Engine's great. Let's see how it handles. One bark for left, two barks for right. Get it?*

Cane barks once and the car swings left. Suddenly the blind man opens her up. Cane barks once, twice, once, and the blind man swings the wheel narrowly missing containers.

THE BLIND MAN IS ENJOYING HIMSELF: *It's gotta be German.*

Suddenly the Nubira is hurtling towards the end of the jetty.

Cane barks three times.

BLIND MAN: *Three barks...? What—*

We hear a splash. Next thing we see the blind man and Cane are inspecting the new Daewoo Nubira in an ethereal Heaven-like showroom...

BLIND MAN: *I never said anything about three barks... where did that come from? You made that up...*

The launch of the Daewoo Lanos in August 1997 satirised pompous car advertising…

Open on shot of new Daewoo Lanos parked on an elegant European street.

POSH VO: *We parked Daewoo's new Lanos on one of the world's most fashionable streets…*

The locals are attracted and gather around curiously…

POSH VO: *The people here are surrounded by style and elegance every day and aren't easily impressed. Is it just the European styling of the Lanos that can turn so many heads?*

No — we see it is in fact Cane the cattle dog who is performing cute tricks behind the Lanos. The elegant locals are captivated by him.

POSH VO: *The new Daewoo Lanos.*

CUT TO END TITLE: *Daewoo Lanos from $14,250.*

POSH VO: *At $14,250, have a look.*

Citizen Cane was a tactical 15-seconder that went to air in November 1997...

Cane the cattle dog sits in a field of waving wheat.

AUSSIE VO: *A reminder that for a limited time only all new Daewoos come with air conditioning and three years scheduled servicing.*

SUPER: *New Daewoos with air. And three years scheduled servicing.*

Cane still sits there as the wheat blows in the wind.

AUSSIE VO: *See the ad...*

Suddenly a newspaper page blows into Cane's face and covers his head.

AUSSIE VO: *...in this weekend's paper.*

PICKING UP YOUNG PROFESSIONALS

CKING UP YOUNG PROFESSIONALS
PICKING UP YOUNG PROFESSIONALS
PICKING UP YOUNG PROFESSIONALS

PICKING UP YOUNG PROFESSIONALS

PICKING UP YOUNG PROFESSIONALS
PICKING UP YOUNG PROFESSIONALS
PICKING UP YOUNG PROFESSIONALS
PICKING UP YOUNG PROFESSIONALS
PICKING UP YOUNG PROFESSIONALS

the problem Mercedes-Benz has always been a status symbol in Thailand, a badge of wealth and power. However, over the years the brand had become associated with the older generation.

A younger generation of executives perceived Mercedes-Benz as expensive and conservative. They looked to other brands to express their personalities.

But with the arrival of the new C-Class, Mercedes-Benz believed it had the potential to win the loyalty of Thailand's young, rich elite. It was a case of communicating the benefits of the new model in a compelling way.

the strategy Two key messages had to be conveyed to the target audience. First, the advertising had to address the attractiveness of the new design and position the C-Class as *their* Mercedes-Benz. Second, it had to convey pride of ownership and remind the target audience that no other marque can communicate success quite like Mercedes-Benz.

Young executives became the focus of the advertising. A sophisticated female executive refused to let her chauffeur drive her new C-Class. A male executive parked his C-Class in the company president's lot. In one commercial, the car was not even shown.

the result The waiting list for the new C-Class lasted several months.

A business leader is giving a speech from a rostrum. His audience, mainly young executives both male and female, are hanging on his every word.

SPEAKER: *We probably have to spend over a decade in order to make change. In the next few years, technology will be a part of —*

A woman approaches him with a note.

SPEAKER: *The owner of licence plate no. 8373 please go to your car.*

Young executives in the audience look at each other, mystified.

SPEAKER: (repeats) *Plate no. 8373... It's a Mercedes-Benz, the new C-Class...*

The young executives are all on their feet, searching for their car keys. The speaker smiles benignly.

END SUPERS: *Suddenly things are different.*

The new C-Class.

END ON MERCEDES-BENZ LOGO.

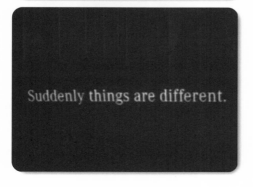

category	countries	advertiser	agency
AUTOMOTIVE/ CARS	TAIWAN	NISSAN/CEFIRO	IDEOLOGY ADVERTISING AGENCY LTD, TAIPEI

DEFEATING A DOUBLE NEGATIVE

DEFEATING A DOUBLE NEGATIVE   DEFEATING A DOUBLE NEGATIVE

DEFEATING A DOUBLE NEGATIVE   DEFEATING A DOUBLE NEGATIVE

DEFEATING A DOUBLE NEGATIVE

DEFEATING A DOUBLE NEGATIVE   DEFEATING A DOUBLE NEGATIVE   DEFEATING A DOUBLE NEGATIVE

DEFEATING A DOUBLE NEGATIVE

DEFEATING A DOUBLE NEGATIVE

the problem Nissan's brand image in the prestige sedan market was flagging. Not only was the new Cefiro tasked with rebuilding that identity, it first had to overcome the home market's prejudice against Made in Taiwan cars.

Further complicating matters, Cefiro — in 2.0 and 3.0 versions — was priced to span two market segments, M (cars that have engine capacities between 2000cc and 2999cc) and L (cars with engine capacities of 3000cc or more). At best, its positioning was ambiguous.

the strategy The battle would be won or lost on image. The campaign single-mindedly concentrated on winning recognition for Cefiro's quality. But presenting credentials alone would not capture Taiwan's discriminating, style-conscious upscale car buyers. Executional values had to separate the new era from the old. The campaign's tonality was crafted to convey challenge and disruption within the context of business and social elitism.

In one commercial, called *Wrestling with Rolls Royce*, Cefiro was juxtaposed with a Silver Spur. In another, two Caucasians debated aspects of leadership.

the result Cefiro made its debut in January 1996 and swiftly became the hottest car of the year. It was listed as one of the top ten products of the year by Taiwan's *Business Weekly* magazine and the *Liberty Times*.

Since its launch, Cefiro has consistently topped monthly sales of prestige automobiles, outdoing every car in the US$20,270–$43,440 segment. The Cefiro 2.0 has registered the highest most-preferred-car scores in the market. Cefiro also caused a sales slump of imported cars. Reportedly, 20% of all Cefiro owners had originally budgeted for either a Mercedes-Benz or a BMW, brands commanding much higher prices of at least US$72,400.

The campaign successfully redefined the branding identity of Yulon/ Nissan and changed the public's viewpoint of Taiwanese-made cars. Brand preference for Nissan was raised from 9% (4th place) to 25% (2nd place).

Nissan recorded profits over US$144,810,000 two years in a row.

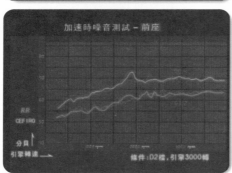

This commercial compares the legendary quietness of a Rolls Royce with that of the new Cefiro. The test is conducted both at running speed and while idling.

The new Cefiro makes its entrance. Sexy angles and lighting convey an air of style and mystery.

When the car is fully revealed, we are told that it will challenge the Rolls Royce Silver Spur.

The Rolls enters frame, a formidable gleaming behemoth.

Exterior cameras track the two cars streaking along deserted roads. We hear the rush of air and road noise.

We cut to their luxurious interiors where sensitive microphones record every second of the journey.

Audiometers register comparative sound levels.

Charts track their progress. Even when cornering, the Cefiro resolutely remains ten points quieter in noise level than the Rolls.

The winning Cefiro glides majestically into the end frame, greeted by slow motion coloured ticker tape.

Cefiro's special "Pearl" colour inspired this commercial. On one hand, it was a new automotive colour worth highlighting. On the other, it likened the value of Cefiro to that of beautiful pearls.

As the commercial opens, a woman is silhouetted with the new Cefiro.

As the commercial progresses, the woman and the Cefiro are juxtaposed with pearls.

Pearls cascade along the edges of the Cefiro, rolling over the roof, reflected in the paintwork as they tumble.

One pearl descends through the open sunroof into the woman's waiting hand.

vo: *Wear the success of Cefiro.*

category	countries	advertiser	agency
AUTOMOTIVE/ CARS	AUSTRALIA	TOYOTA/BRAND CAMPAIGN	SAATCHI & SAATCHI, SYDNEY

TURNING A "JUMP" INTO A LEAP TURNING A "JUMP" INTO A LEAP TURNING A "JUMP" INTO A LEAP

TURNING A "JUMP" INTO A LEAP

TURNING A "JUMP" INTO A LEAP   TURNING A "JUMP" INTO A LEAP   TURNING A "JUMP" INTO A LEAP

TURNING A "JUMP" INTO A LEAP

the problem Toyota was ranked the number three brand in the Australian car market. Its advertising was well established. *Oh what a feeling*, an American slogan, had been transplanted into Australia in the 1980s. With it came strict mandatories and a rigid creative formula calling for someone to jump into the air at the end of every commercial.

By 1989, when Saatchi & Saatchi was appointed in Australia, Toyota's advertising campaign had changed in most countries — except Australia. In fact, the brand owner insisted on keeping both the slogan and the "Jump" device. The question was how to drive the brand forward with a secondhand campaign that had seen better days.

the strategy The agency tapped into what was strong in the original American thought. The new creative leap came through realising that the core thought of the campaign wasn't the "Jump" at all — it was actually a campaign about feelings. The idea of selling feelings in the advertising was much more interesting than what other car manufacturers were doing, which was selling metal.

Feelings became the brand's territory. Together, brand owner and agency worked out a *different key feeling* that would be the core advertising idea for every vehicle in the Toyota range. As a result, each model would have its own personality and distinct campaign, while each campaign built on the overall range of good feelings that separated the Toyota brand from its competitors.

Better still, concentrating on feelings enabled the brand owner and agency to look at things from the customer's perspective, rather than just the manufacturer's.

Every television commercial was written backwards, starting from the emotional cause of the Toyota "Jump" — trying to work out who was jumping and why they might be compelled to act that way. Instead of the predictable finish to every Toyota TV commercial, the "Jump" then became the reason for viewers to watch the ad unfold, to try and guess who or what might jump at the end this time.

The first non-traditional jump was for Camry. A hapless chicken trying to cross the road became the victim of the car's surprisingly powerful performance. For ten years, Camry defeathered the chicken which then "Jumped" in fright. The Camry *Chicken* became one of Australia's most popular advertising icons and eventually found itself on sale as a stuffed toy.

Once the precedent was set, the executions of the "Jump" became more creative, more memorable, and more expressive of a wider range of feelings. Hats were thrown into the air. People jumped off window ledges. A cow jumped over the moon. Even a dolphin gracefully jumped skywards in the desert!

The backbone of Toyota's brand and reputation in Australia was the Landcruiser, the vehicle that helped build the monumental Snowy River Scheme back in the early 1950s and tamed the Outback for Australian farmers and miners. It had become an Australian icon, its Japanese origins all but forgotten. The key feeling for Landcruiser was defined as security, summed up in a headline: *Wherever you're crazy enough to go, you can rely on Landcruiser to bring you back alive.*

The first Landcruiser commercial was also Australia's first 3-minute roadblock commercial. It ran once on every commercial network in Australia at exactly the same time — Sunday night movie time. It was the launch of the first all-new Landcruiser model in ten years, a generational change, and Toyota wanted to communicate everything about the new vehicle in the commercial. The idea was to painstakingly reshoot one of the most famous rescue scenes from the movies — the desert rescue from David Lean's classic *Lawrence of Arabia*, subsequently nicknamed "Bruce of Australia" by the agency. The hero returned in the all-new Landcruiser rather than by camel, with all the mandatory sales features disguised as movie credits under such familiar headings as Starring, Co-starring, Grip, Locations by, and so on. Viewers were hijacked, at first mistaking the ad for the movie. Toyota sold out six months' supply of Landcruisers immediately. And when a faster turbo diesel model was introduced some years later, the original *Lawrence* commercial was run fast forward in 60 seconds, with a voice-over announcing that Landcruiser was now faster.

the result Toyota described the 1990s as its "Decade of Dominance", finishing Australia's number one auto brand more often than any competitor.

By the early 1990s, Toyota had moved from being Australia's number one spending and number three selling auto brand, to number one selling and number three spending brand after two years of its new advertising campaign.

"The reality is, you don't have to run great ads as often as you have to run good ads. Building car campaigns can be a lengthy and fraught process, but concentrating everyone's mind on a key feeling kept client, agency and the entire process on a single-minded track. In an era when customer related-marketing has become key, striving to make the ownership experience a good feeling focuses the entire company on customer service. The Toyota Feeling has permeated every aspect of the brand's interface with customers. This is an example of a brand tagline becoming much more than a piece of pithy copy; it can become a *mantra* for the brand, a mission statement for the employees, a philosophy for the company, a way to drive the whole corporation. The Feeling has become a brand property for Toyota, an invisible benefit that adds value beyond what is tangible about the product alone. Little wonder that *Oh what a feeling* is valued as an asset worth tens of millions on Toyota's balance sheet."

MICHAEL NEWMAN, Executive Creative Director Australia, Saatchi & Saatchi

TURNING A "JUMP" INTO A LEAP   TURNING A "JUMP" INTO A LEAP
TURNING A "JUMP" INTO A LEAP
TURNING A "JUMP" INTO A LEAP
TURNING A "JUMP" INTO A LEAP   TURNING A "JUMP" INTO A LEAP   TURNING A "JUMP" INTO A LEAP
TURNING A "JUMP" INTO A LEAP

Toyota turned the newspaper page into an X-ray.

The chicken became the victim of Toyota Camry's surprisingly powerful performance for over ten years...

A chicken is waiting to cross the road.

CHICKEN: *Cluck, cluck...*

We cut to a Toyota Camry.

MALE VO: *The Toyota Camry is powered by a twin cam, fuel-injected, multi-valve engine...*

Cut back to the chicken on the side of the road. It looks to the left, then to the right...

Cut to the Camry driving up the street.

MALE VO: *...so you get the fuel savings of a smaller engine, with the twin cam performance...*

The chicken steps out just as the Camry drives past. Its performance is so powerful that it completely blows all the feathers off the hapless chicken and causes an egg to drop.

CHICKEN: *Squawk!*

MALE VO: *...of a larger one.*

Shot of Toyota Camry. The naked chicken does the Toyota "Jump" in front of it.

JINGLE: *Oh what a feeling, Twin Camry...*

Suddenly we think we are watching the movie *Lawrence of Arabia*...

The familiar theme music plays as the famous rescue scene unfolds in the vast Arabian desert...

The young Arab boy rides his camel towards the distant horizon...

A silhouette comes into view...

The young boy urges his camel to go faster and faster...

Only *this* time our hero comes towards us in the all-new Toyota Landcruiser.

The dramatic 3-minute remake reaches its climax, the music swells up to the heroic crescendo and the product features roll like typical movie credits.

The commercial ends with the Toyota "Jump": the Arabs triumphantly toss Lawrence into the air.

CHORUS: *Oh what a feeling...*

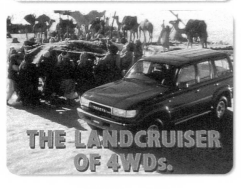

A locked off shot of a fuel gauge, with the needle pointing just below the full mark.

Our attention is riveted on the gauge, but it doesn't move.

MALE VO: *This is an announcement for all those people who bought a Toyota Camry recently. Don't worry. The fuel gauge isn't broken. It will move... eventually.*

Cut to graphic: *Toyota Twin Camry.*

Cut back to the fuel gauge. We are waiting for the Toyota "Jump" to happen.

Suddenly the needle gives a flicker.

MALE VO: *Oh, what a feeling.*

This commercial replicates *Hunt for Red October.*

We are looking at a sea of sand dunes — but hearing the distinctive sound of a submarine's radar.

"SEAN CONNERY" VO: *Until now, the only "off-road" vehicles with satellite navigation were ships — and submarines...*

Suddenly a Landcruiser emerges through the sand, rearing up like a submarine that is surfacing.

"CONNERY" VO: *Introducing the powerful Landcruiser Sahara... Wherever you're crazy enough to go, rely on Landcruiser to bring you back.*

Having surfaced, the Landcruiser drives off.

VOCAL: *Oh what a feeling... Landcruiser...*

Suddenly, out of the sand, a dolphin flips up into the air doing the Toyota "Jump".

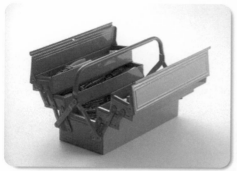

Dramatic classical-style music as we see a gleaming red tool box being closed and stood upright.

Holes are drilled in it and wheels are added.

MALE VO: *Some toolboxes are packed with power, have wheels and carry one and a quarter tonnes.*

The toolbox transforms into a Toyota Hiace van.

MALE VO: *Toyota Hiace. Building the toughest tools of the trade is our trade.*

VOCAL: *Oh what a feeling...*

Tradesman with drill performs Toyota "Jump".

category
AUTOMOTIVE/
CARS

countries
AUSTRALIA

advertiser
TOYOTA/LEXUS

agency
SAATCHI &
SAATCHI,
SYDNEY

RETAIL WITH RESTRAINT   RETAIL WITH RESTRAINT
RETAIL WITH RESTRAINT

RETAIL WITH RESTRAINT

RETAIL WITH RESTRAINT   RETAIL WITH RESTRAINT   RETAIL WITH RESTRAINT
RETAIL WITH RESTRAINT   RETAIL WITH RESTRAINT

the problem The Lexus ES300 was not the top-of-the-line model, nor was it the brand entry-level vehicle. It was caught awkwardly in the middle in terms of positioning. It was between model lives, no longer new and sexy, but not about to be replaced either.

How could some excitement be injected to generate sales?

the strategy The campaign was an agency initiative to boost traffic at dealerships. The strategy was to offer a weekend's test drive, on the basis that once the prospect had enjoyed the Lexus experience for a couple of days, it would be very hard to accept a lower standard in another vehicle.

However, creating retail ads for luxury brands is a delicate task. Brand values must be protected, particularly in a case like Lexus, which in Australia was still vying for acceptance vis-à-vis the traditional German luxury marques. Being a Japanese marque priced at the upper end of the market against long-established European brands was not an easy position.

Tonally, wit was the best option. The ads were built around the fact that people hated giving a Lexus back on Monday.

The look of the campaign was equally critical. It could not appear too "urgent". But while the ads did not look retail, they obeyed the most important retail principles: the offer was clear and the benefit integral to the idea.

the result Restraint proved a powerful ally. The one-month print campaign generated over 160 qualified leads, of which nearly 80 were converted to sales of the US$37,000 car.

...my driveway's blocked by an overturned truck.

After a 24 hour test drive, you'll find any excuse not to bring the ES300 back.

...I'm having a baby.

After a 24 hour test drive, you'll find any excuse not to bring the ES300 back.

category	countries	advertiser	agency
AUTOMOTIVE/ CARS	SINGAPORE	VOLKSWAGEN	DDB WORLDWIDE, SINGAPORE

TACTICAL CAMPAIGNS THAT BOOSTED BRAND VALUES   TACTICAL CAMPAIGNS THAT BOOSTED BRAND VALUES
TACTICAL CAMPAIGNS THAT BOOSTED BRAND VALUES

TACTICAL CAMPAIGNS THAT BOOSTED BRAND VALUES

TACTICAL CAMPAIGNS THAT BOOSTED BRAND VALUES
TACTICAL CAMPAIGNS THAT BOOSTED BRAND VALUES
TACTICAL CAMPAIGNS THAT BOOSTED BRAND VALUES   TACTICAL CAMPAIGNS THAT BOOSTED BRAND VALUES
TACTICAL CAMPAIGNS THAT BOOSTED BRAND VALUES

the problem The new Volkswagen Beetle was due to make its debut at the annual Singapore Motor Show, but thanks to global demand it wouldn't be for sale in Singapore for a further twelve months.

Volkswagen needed a tactical campaign to stimulate interest in its new model at the event. Beyond that immediate need, Volkswagen wanted to address perceptions that its brand was "expensive" vis-à-vis other German marques. Could advertising help portray its brand values in a more unique, individualistic way?

the strategy Because the new Beetle was so rare, the creative idea arose of displaying it among a priceless collection of beetles. However, issues of scale meant that the final ad could not be shot as one image.

Real beetles from a natural history museum were shot individually. Each pin was also shot individually, along with an overall background, and each shadow was individually added.

Addressing perceptions that the brand was expensive, the agency devised a range of print ads and posters that communicated brand pillars — reliability and safety. The *Clockwork* execution was utilised prior to the arrival of the new Volkswagen Passat, and the *Pollen Filter* concept ran in conjunction with the launch of the new VW Golf.

the result The tactical work lifted brand awareness. In one example, the arrival of the new Volkswagen Beetle attracted the biggest crowd at the Singapore Motor Show. Five hundred souvenir posters were produced from the *Beetle* ad, and the entire stock was gone by 11.30am on the first day of the show.

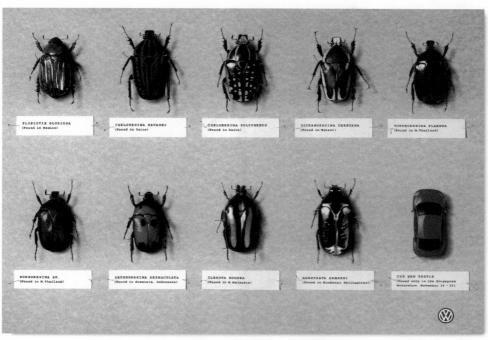

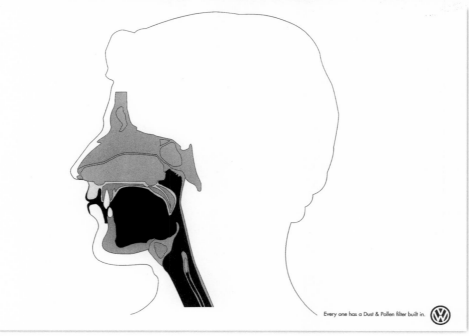

They run and run and run and ru

AUTOMOTIVE/COMMERCIAL VEHICLES

Automotive/
Commercial
Vehicles

ONCE a shopping list of features would have been adequate: buyers wanted to know about power, manoeuvrability, economy, load factors, interior space, and price. And they still do, but the means of communicating this information has changed. Lateral creative solutions have become more prevalent. However, in terms of tonality, it is still a macho man category albeit that the masculinity is more refreshingly conveyed.

NOT ANOTHER PRODUCT DEMONSTRATION

NOT ANOTHER PRODUCT DEMONSTRATION

NOT ANOTHER PRODUCT DEMONSTRATION

NOT ANOTHER PRODUCT DEMONSTRATION

NOT ANOTHER PRODUCT DEMONSTRATION

NOT ANOTHER PRODUCT DEMONSTRATION

NOT ANOTHER PRODUCT DEMONSTRATION

NOT ANOTHER PRODUCT DEMONSTRATION

the problem Toyota was planning the New Zealand launch of the most powerful Hilux ever. Hilux was already the biggest selling light truck in the country by far, and its advertising had for many years connected with everyday rural life.

Which gave rise to the problem. How could farmers be persuaded to trade up from their beloved old workhorses, with which they were perfectly happy, to the new model?

the strategy The proposition was rational: a power improvement story. The agency asked itself: what would a farmer notice if he jumped into a brand new Hilux? The answer: everything would be familiar, except for the increased power. And that is where the creative thought sprang from, by imagining all the trouble a farmer could get into if he *underestimated* the power of his new Hilux.

The unexpected power story was treated with dry, understated humour.

the result The Hilux launch was a complete sell-out within the first few months. Overnight, the campaign achieved cult status throughout the country — and not just among farmers. Originally intended to grow Hilux market share, research showed that the commercial played a huge role in increasing Toyota's overall brand preference scores in New Zealand.

Eventually the commercial made the same impact in Australia. Initial outrage and public debate fuelled free media coverage that added millions of dollars to the weight of the campaign spend. In the end, church authorities pronounced that the word "bugger" was not offensive but merely popular vernacular. Further interest was spiked by a series of tactical ideas. After the huge New Year's Eve fireworks on Sydney Harbour bridge to celebrate the new century, a full page ad ran the next morning showing the bridge in cinders with the caption: *Bugger.* In January, Toyota's giant annual Australia-wide retail event was bannered *The Big Bugger of a Sale.*

❝

Bugger became the most complained about ad in New Zealand, receiving more complaints in five days than any ad in Kiwi history. It was the lead news story in New Zealand for weeks. When the ad was threatened with being pulled off television, the country was up in arms to save it. Since then it has been measured as New Zealand's favourite commercial every month for the past two years."

JOHN FOLEY, Account Director,
Saatchi & Saatchi Wellington

❝

"The response to the ad, despite fairly low media weights, was overwhelming. We received approximately 180 letters of complaint, and yet we also received approximately 150 letters of praise (something we'd never experienced before). The ad is still being referred to in the press despite it not having run for well over 12 months. To capitalise on its success, we developed additional advertising under the *Bugger* theme... The ad injected a huge amount of personality and likeability to the entire Toyota brand..."

STEVE BRANN, Advertising Manager,
Toyota Australia

NOT ANOTHER PRODUCT DEMONSTRATION

NOT ANOTHER PRODUCT DEMONSTRATION

NOT ANOTHER PRODUCT DEMONSTRATION

NOT ANOTHER PRODUCT DEMONSTRATION

NOT ANOTHER PRODUCT DEMONSTRATION

NOT ANOTHER PRODUCT DEMONSTRATION

NOT ANOTHER PRODUCT DEMONSTRATION

NOT ANOTHER PRODUCT DEMONSTRATION

Our farming hero just can't get used to the extra power of his new Toyota Hilux. Everything he attempts with it goes wrong. After each catastrophe all he can say is "Bugger"…

He tries to straighten a sagging fence by nudging it with the bumper of his Toyota Hilux. The fence collapses.

FARMER: *Bugger…*

He tries to tow a tractor with his Hilux. Trouble is, the Hilux yanks the wheels off the tractor.

FARMER: *Bugger me…*

He pulls out a tree stump with his Hilux. It's so strong the stump is catapulted into the chicken coop, demolishing it.

FARMER: *Bugger…*

A cow is stuck in the mud. He starts towing it out with the Hilux. Suddenly he looks horrified and grimaces. We can only imagine what happened to the cow.

FARMER: *Bugger…*

The farmer's dog leaps for the Hilux but underestimates its speed. The dog plops down in the mud, splashing it onto the washing line and the farmer's wife…

WIFE: *Bugger.*

The dog just stares balefully ahead, too buggered to get up.

DOG: *Bugger…*

PETRONAS
PETRONAS   PETRONAS   PETRONAS   PETRONAS   PETRONAS
TRONAS   PETRONAS   PETRONAS   PETRONAS   PETRONAS
PETRONAS AUTOMOTIVE/PETROLEUM PRODUCTS   PETRONAS
PETRONAS   PETRONAS   PETRONAS   PETRONAS   PETRONAS
PETRONAS   PETRONAS

Automotive/ Petroleum Products

WHEN local petroleum brands compete against global rivals, purely nationalistic positioning rarely works. The consumer still seeks reassurance about quality, power and economy. Price is a dominant factor, but a fragile platform in terms of long-term brand building. Consequently, marketers require a keen insight into the emotions of their fellow countrymen to identify the most fertile ground for communications.

BUILDING A BRAND THROUGH NATIONAL UNITY

BUILDING A BRAND THROUGH NATIONAL UNITY

BUILDING A BRAND THROUGH NATIONAL UNITY

BUILDING A BRAND THROUGH NATIONAL UNITY

BUILDING A BRAND THROUGH NATIONAL UNITY   BUILDING A BRAND THROUGH NATIONAL UNITY

BUILDING A BRAND THROUGH NATIONAL UNITY

BUILDING A BRAND THROUGH NATIONAL UNITY

the problem Petronas was seen as a large, cold government oil company that was out of touch with the Malaysian community. In yuppie quarters, it was also perceived as "local", meaning "low class", a step down from foreign brands. The truth was that Petronas was extremely successful. Its upstream operations were on a par with those of large oil and gas multinationals.

Could Petronas become a brand for all Malaysians, and exemplify the spirit of the nation?

the strategy In the mid-1990s, Petronas had been running festive-styled corporate commercials. Each occasion — Hari Raya for Muslims, New Year for the Chinese, Deepavali for the Hindus — was used to drive home social messages. Leo Burnett was new to the account at that time. The agency proposed using these commercials as a means to make the corporation more likable, more human, to the general community.

The agency fashioned a new brand essence: *World Class, Yet Down to Earth Malaysian*. The first commercial, *Friends Again*, established the brand's unique story-telling style. It was the endearing tale of two young children of different ethnic backgrounds — one Malay, the other Chinese — and how they overcame a small mishap to remain the best of friends. It was particularly relevant, as it was one of the years when the major Malay and Chinese festivals of the year overlapped.

Later that year one of Malaysia's most popular commercials was developed for the National Day celebrations. It shared one man's recollections of a special day in his childhood, when he was privileged to witness the birth of his nation. Unlike most other commercials of the time, it showed real Malaysians against real Malaysian backdrops. Significantly, the hero of the commercial was a little Indian boy. Indians make up less than 10% of the Malaysian population and were seldom seem in TV commercials. The commercial demonstrated how national pride transcended race, religion or class.

In 1997, the agency took an even bolder move. May 13, 1969 is an infamous day for most Malaysians. It marks the racial tensions that led to the loss of several hundred lives. The day had become taboo for the media to talk about, let alone write a commercial about. The agency and Petronas felt differently; despite the fact it was a low point for all Malaysians, there were stories of personal bravery and compassion that needed telling. The occasion for this commercial was the joint celebration of Hari Raya and Chinese New Year. *Lee Yuen's Best Friend* told the story of two families, one Chinese and the other Malay, who helped each other out during the crisis.

Since then, the campaign has touched on many aspects of Malaysian life. Common themes have been respecting tradition and the older generation, pride in Malaysian-made products, national unity and overall tolerance towards other races and religions. In 2000, for example, viewers saw a hedge being clipped by an unseen man singing an Indian song, who turned out to be a Chinese fan of Hindi music. In another, two Chinese men were listening to a joke in the Hokkien dialect told by an unseen third person, who was later revealed as a turbaned Sikh.

the result Over the years, consumer perceptions of Petronas have changed dramatically and Malaysian motorists have developed a new relationship with the brand. The pride of being Malaysian, of having come so far together since Independence, is exemplified by the brand. Far from being "local and low class" it has become the brand Malaysians passionately regard as a symbol of national pride and unity.

Selamat Hari Raya

PETRONAS

The objective of this commercial was to get young Malaysians to re-examine their modern, superficial values. While the old world was not yet rich in worldly goods, it was far richer in compassion...

The rain is deafening as an old barefoot man in singlet, shirt and sarong, an umbrella in one hand, a sack in the other, makes his way along a narrow rural road.

A young man in a sleek, air-conditioned car with a radio playing, horns him out of the way.

Looking in the rearview mirror, the young man has a spasm of guilt. He stops his car to offer the old man a lift. But the old man can't move so quickly.

The younger man keeps looking at the dashboard clock and in the end decides to drive on.

The old man is left staring after him.

Suddenly the car skids and crashes into a ditch. The young man is saved by his airbag. The old man catches up and raps on the window. The dazed young driver struggles to get out and the old man shares his umbrella with him as they walk through the storm.

Through the drumming rain we hear a distant Muslim call to prayer.

PETRONAS LOGO AND SUPER: *Selamat Hari Raya.*

category country advertiser agency

AXA CHINA REGION DBS BANK/EIGHT OCBC BANK CREDIT CARDS CITIBANK PA INSURANCE OCBC BANK CREDIT CARDS DBS BANK/UP

S BANK/EIGHT BANKING, FINANCIAL SERVICES, INSURANCE

PA INSURANCE CITIBANK DBS BANK/EIGHT AXA CHINA REGION CITIBANK DBS BANK/UP OCBC BANK CREDIT CARDS DBS BANK/UP PA INSURANCE

Banking, Financial Services, Insurance

CONSUMERS have become particularly cynical about claims of better service and greater security. Recessions, corporate crashes and bank mergers have placed the financial sector under greater consumer scrutiny than ever before. Balancing that, "lifestyle" banking products have proliferated and redefined the category's tonality. Banks and insurance companies, once lofty and aloof, have found themselves engaged in tactical battles that would have been unheard of two decades ago.

BUILDING THE PREFERRED BRAND

BUILDING THE PREFERRED BRAND

BUILDING THE PREFERRED BRAND BUILDING THE PREFERRED BRAND BUILDING THE PREFERRED BRAND

BUILDING THE PREFERRED BRAND

JILDING THE PREFERRED BRAND   BUILDING THE PREFERRED BRAND   BUILDING THE PREFERRED BRAND

BUILDING THE PREFERRED BRAND

the problem Over the years, AXA had built very strong awareness in the Hong Kong market. Previous campaigns had clearly established the name and even the slogan, *Go Ahead*. A tracking study indicated Hong Kong people saw AXA as big, stable, reliable and global, all of the qualities needed to make it a powerful brand in the marketplace. What it missed, however, was preference in a category where no player is truly "liked".

For most people, their choice of agent ultimately dictated which company got their business. And while the stability and size of the insuring company is important, most brands could provide that basic reassurance. To help their agents, AXA wanted to put the brand back into the equation. The more people who specifically preferred AXA, the more business their agents would write.

the strategy Given that people already accepted AXA's credentials, the agency sought a communications lever that would drive preference. In the Hong Kong context, an interesting insight emerged — liberation. There is a moment when people first buy insurance when they feel free of worry, fully protected and are able to relax and enjoy themselves. Sadly, in stressful Hong Kong, that split second passes by all too quickly. Yet, while Hong Kongers apparently like to worry, they also enjoy their moments of fun.

Creatively, this insight opened the door for a campaign that captured that moment of liberation. The idea was simply, you can worry about things in life or you can just get on with it. Expressed in communications terms, *What have you got to lose? Go ahead with AXA.*

Two executions, *Donkey* and *Kids* were pretested in focus groups. The *Donkey* concept was radical, especially in the conservative area of insurance. Scenes of sleepwalkers emerging from toilets and a man in bed with a donkey were hardly the category norm. *Kids* was a safer bet, wherein adults exhibited moments of childlike exuberance. Predictably enough, 100% of respondents favoured the *Kids* execution, while *Donkey* generated mixed reactions. Interpreting the results, it was felt that people are more critical in a focus group environment than they might otherwise be. While *Kids* had scored well, there was concern that once on air it might not stand out as well as *Donkey*. Wisely, both executions were produced and aired.

the result The commercials cut through and registered high recall. Interestingly enough, immediately after the launch, awareness of *Donkey* (69%) was twice that of *Kids* (32%).

Based on a series of four qualitative focus groups conducted by NFO WorldGroup, AXA's image had become younger, more professional and progressive. AXA was seen as a life partner, not just an insurance company. AXA was perceived as more relevant and closer to its audience. Respondents confirmed that when buying insurance they would think of AXA first.

AXA's tracking study revealed advertising awareness was now twice that of its closest competitor. After the initial launch, the campaign was driving preference for the brand with fewer respondents having "no opinion".

Overall, AXA had gained a stronger share of preference at the expense of its competitors.

BUILDING THE PREFERRED BRAND

BUILDING THE PREFERRED BRAND

BUILDING THE PREFERRED BRAND   BUILDING THE PREFERRED BRAND

BUILDING THE PREFERRED BRAND

BUILDING THE PREFERRED BRAND

BUILDING THE PREFERRED BRAND   BUILDING THE PREFERRED BRAND   BUILDING THE PREFERRED BRAND

BUILDING THE PREFERRED BRAND

A woman pushing a barrow collides with a donkey.

MALE VO (MATTER-OF-FACTLY): *Every year, donkeys cause more injuries than aeroplanes.*

A man finds himself the victim of coconuts.

MALE VO: *You are more likely to be struck by falling coconuts than lightning.*

A sleepwalker comes to grief and we see him emerging from a toilet bowl.

MALE VO: *Sleepwalkers have more accidents than joggers.*

A man wakes up in bed with a donkey.

MALE VO: *And most mishaps happen at home.*

The donkey gives the man a lugubrious smile.

MALE VO: *But hey, be positive. What have you got to lose? Go ahead with AXA.*

AXA LOGO AND END SUPER: *Go ahead.*

category
BANKING,
FINANCIAL
SERVICES,
INSURANCE

countries
SINGAPORE

advertiser
CITIBANK

agency
DENTSU YOUNG
& RUBICAM,
SINGAPORE

NEW REASONS TO USE CREDIT

NEW REASONS TO USE CREDIT   NEW REASONS TO USE CREDIT

NEW REASONS TO USE CREDIT

NEW REASONS TO USE CREDIT

NEW REASONS TO USE CREDIT

NEW REASONS TO USE CREDIT   NEW REASONS TO USE CREDIT   NEW REASONS TO USE CREDIT

NEW REASONS TO USE CREDIT

the problem Revolving credit line products had been on the Singapore banking scene for years. Owing to product parity, bank clients perceived no differences among the key players.

The banks themselves exacerbated the situation. Rather than building brands, the category focused on short-term promotional activities to attract clients.

Citibank, already established as a high ground player, believed its Citibank Ready Credit product had an opportunity to become the dominant brand.

the strategy A fresh consumer insight shaped the campaign strategy. Absolute necessity was no longer the motivation to use Citibank Ready Credit. A new trend saw Citibank clients more inclined towards self-actualisation.

Clearly the campaign needed to break away from category parameters. Rather than a proposition based on the "nuts-and-bolts" of product deliverables, Citibank Ready Credit addressed the emotions associated with consumer empowerment and indulgence.

Creatively, Citibank Ready Credit was portrayed as solving less prosaic problems. The tonality demonstrated wit and charm, further bending the rules of the category.

the result Citibank Ready Credit became the preferred brand among existing and non-users of revolving credit lines.

We open on a wide shot of old Singapore *Peranakan* terrace houses. A young man jogs through frame.

Suddenly he returns. Something has caught his eye. He stands transfixed outside a gate. Behind it we see a Volkswagen Beetle.

He makes an offer for it, but the owner isn't interested and shuts his front door.

The young man doggedly waits, refusing to take "no" for an answer. Even a rainstorm doesn't deter him. Impressed and puzzled by the younger man's persistence, the owner relents and sells him the old car.

The elated young man has it towed away to a workshop where we assume he will have it faithfully restored.

But not quite...when next we see the Beetle, it has been sliced in half, sprayed yellow and converted into a huge armchair for his surreal apartment.

MALE VO: *With the power of ready cash, you'll always be ready to make the right moves. Citibank Ready Credit.*

A young man and his wife are standing outside a derelict house. A sign on the fence announces its impending demolition. Their attention is focused on a big old tree standing in the overgrown garden.

As the film dissolves back into the past, we soon understand why. We see the old house in all its former glory when the young couple played there as children... Then, as teenagers, they fell in love and carved their initials on the tree.

Returning to the present, the woman reluctantly leaves her memories. But when they reach their modern home, we catch a glimpse of her husband on the phone. He seems to be organising something.

The next morning when the woman awakes, she looks down from her balcony to discover the old tree has been transplanted into their courtyard.

MALE VO: *With the power of ready cash, you'll always be ready to make the right moves. Citibank Ready Credit.*

category	countries	advertiser	agency
BANKING, FINANCIAL SERVICES, INSURANCE	SINGAPORE	DBS BANK/ EIGHT	SAATCHI & SAATCHI, SINGAPORE

REBRANDING A UNIT TRUST
REBRANDING A UNIT TRUST
REBRANDING A UNIT TRUST

REBRANDING A UNIT TRUST

REBRANDING A UNIT TRUST
REBRANDING A UNIT TRUST   REBRANDING A UNIT TRUST   REBRANDING A UNIT TRUST
REBRANDING A UNIT TRUST   REBRANDING A UNIT TRUST

the problem The 1997 economic downturn left its legacy in Singapore. Many consumers had been burnt, or knew someone else who had been. Anything considered an "investment" was automatically equated with high risk. Most Singaporeans were happy to leave their money in savings accounts; at least with a savings account, "you know your money is secure".

Not surprisingly, the unit trust category was stagnant. And conventional advertising didn't help:complicated communications with bank talk, pie charts and graphs only confirmed consumers' prevailing fears.

Against this scenario, DBS Bank planned the rebranding and relaunch of what had been previously communicated as a unit trust product. Frank Russell, one of the world's largest investment strategy consultants, managed the fund. It was distributed by the bank and leveraged the DBS brand. The business objective was to have 30,000 Singaporeans each invest US$6,000 in the fund over a 12-month period.

the strategy Despite their fears, Singaporeans did want to be wealthier. They didn't want to hear about investing. Rather, they wanted to know how to save more.

Armed with that insight, the agency developed the campaign proposition: *A smarter way to save*. The fund was branded "eight", the luckiest Chinese number of all. Amusing situations in TV commercials and print ads portrayed Singaporeans and their dreams of wealth, each execution tagged with the positive injunction *Get ready for a better life*. A Walter Mitty-esque man is seen with his son, dreaming of the day when he can afford a lavishly-stocked wine cellar. A girl flying Economy fantasises about being in Business Class. A young executive imagines being chauffeur-driven to work — much to the puzzlement of a bus driver.

The tonality was light and engaging. Consumers were directed to pick up the prospectus, itself a refreshing change from previous unit trust publications. "eight" was explained in a colourful outsized book, written in consumer language and uncluttered by jargon.

the result 100,000 copies of the prospectus were moved in the first week of the campaign. "eight" attracted US$130 million in the first 4 weeks. The 12-month business objective — US$180 million — was achieved in 8 weeks. "eight" had re-stimulated the category, which it now leads.

REBRANDING A UNIT TRUST

REBRANDING A UNIT TRUST   REBRANDING A UNIT TRUST

REBRANDING A UNIT TRUST   REBRANDING A UNIT TRUST

REBRANDING A UNIT TRUST   REBRANDING A UNIT TRUST   REBRANDING A UNIT TRUST

REBRANDING A UNIT TRUST   REBRANDING A UNIT TRUST

Watched by his curious son, a man holds up a wineglass of water. He examines it critically.

MAN: *Brilliant ruby colour...*

He sniffs it and gives his assessment...

MAN: *A forward nose of cherry, tobacco and cedar...*

He takes a considered sip and, like an expert wine taster, spits it out.

MAN: *Such power and finesse, unmistakably the '82 Chateau Margaux.*

He pours bottled water into the next glass.

MAN: *Ah, and what do we have here?*

He savours its bouquet appreciatively.

MAN: *Plums, pepper and earth...*

SUPER: *Get ready for a better life.*

DISSOLVE TO LOGO AND END SUPERS: *eight.*

*The smarter way to save.
Call 1800-8811188.*

A young businessman is on his way to work. Settled comfortably in his seat, he converses with his "chauffeur" as the world passes by in the background.

BUSINESSMAN: *James, after this send the kids to school and help madam with the shopping...*

We see the driver's eyes studying him in the rearview mirror.

BUSINESSMAN CONTINUES: *At 3pm, collect my suit from the tailor's. As for me...*

The driver's eyes look puzzled.

The businessman puts on his glasses and consults the blank pages of his diary.

BUSINESSMAN CONTINUES: *Looks like I have a busy day today, so be prepared to wait for me this evening...*

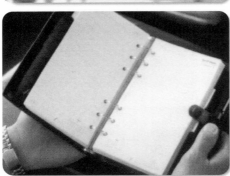

The shot widens as the businessman stands up and we realise he is merely a passenger on a public bus.

As he alights, he tells the driver: *Same time, same place... Carry on, James...*

SUPER: *Get ready for a better life.*

DISSOLVE TO LOGO AND END SUPERS: *eight.*

The smarter way to save.
Call 1800-8811188.

A young woman seated in the front row of Economy Class reaches into a bag at her feet. First, she produces a cloth and spreads it neatly on her tray table.

Next she carefully lays out her silver cutlery, then her salt and pepper shakers. She examines her wine glass to ensure it is spotless. A baffled male passenger watches her.

When the food trolley arrives, the stewardess can't believe her eyes. Shrugging, she places the plastic dish of airline food into the elegant setting.

Just at that moment the curtains separating the classes are drawn. A sign clearly states: *Business Class Only Beyond This Point.*

The girl ruefully starts her meal.

SUPER: *Get ready for a better life.*

DISSOLVE TO LOGO AND END SUPERS: *eight.*

The smarter way to save.
Call 1800-8811188.

category	countries	advertiser	agency
BANKING, FINANCIAL SERVICES, INSURANCE	SINGAPORE	DBS BANK/UP	TBWA, SINGAPORE

UP AND UP

the problem The Singapore public is quite averse to investment funds and unit trusts. In fact, only 3% of Singaporeans invest in managed funds compared with 40% of Americans.

Singaporeans still prefer to keep the bulk of their funds in low risk, low interest savings accounts at high street banks. At present, some US$100 billion is held in fixed deposits in Singapore earning, on average, 2% interest.

Consequently, DBS Bank and TBWA faced an awesome marketing challenge: how does a bank woo risk-averse customers away from the security blanket of savings accounts into more sophisticated banking products?

When the bank wanted to launch a unit trust into the market, the conventional approach would have been to create a highly technical product, formal and authoritative, aimed at current sophisticates. It would be advertised only in the business pages of the press and would compete with the existing range of unit trusts in a market worth around US$1 billion.

Had DBS Bank gone down the traditional unit trust marketing route, its target customers would have tuned out. It became clear that the bank had to break free of the usual technical specifications and intimidating jargon and go to market with a truly populist financial product. Positioning and tonality would be everything.

It was decided to reframe the competitive context: rather than trying to win a 10% share of the existing US$1 billion unit trust market, agency and client pursued a 5% share of the US$100 billion fixed deposit market instead.

Knowing that its customers would need a lot of reassurance, the bank decided to market a product that offered some certainties — a guaranteed fund that protected the capital invested, offered a guaranteed return of 4% on that investment, and above that, promised the potential to earn up to 5% more. The new fund would be released in bursts, each capped by a fixed limit for subscriptions.

the strategy Given the cautious nature of the target market the tonality had to be simple and transparent, but not frivolous or patronising. It was a fine line, and the choice of product name and iconography was critical.

A brand with personality was needed, not just a product with an interest rate. The name had to be easy and friendly sounding so it could unlock the market opportunity.

In research, names based on the auspicious colour red — including "Red Star" and "Red Egg" — did not sound contemporary or progressive enough. Instead, respondents warmed to the simplicity, straightforwardness and quirkiness of the name "Up".

Preliminary concepts were explored. An idea using arrows on signs, all turned out of context so that they pointed up, appeared in a brochure. Then came other visual ways of expressing "Up", such as people's uplifted hair, even a mole whisker pointing upwards. But the image of a dog whose ears lifted up, rendered with scrap art for a workshop meeting with the bank's managing director of group marketing, won the day. The client fell in love with the idea of the dog, and the same dog was ultimately used in the campaign. Interestingly, consumers agreed; there was more "humanity" in the dog's face than human faces.

The dog became the brand icon. Strategically, it made sense. With each new "window" for "Up" lasting only 4 to 5 weeks, there would be no time to waste reinventing the wheel. "Up" needed to establish itself as a brand in its own right.

"Up" was launched with print, outdoor and in-bank advertising. The dog with the upwardly pointing ears was everywhere: accessible and approachable, deliberately light, whether he appeared in the early general news section of the morning paper or on a mobile hanging from the bank's ceiling.

Television came later, acting as the accelerator. The dog's ears lifted up as it listened to the voice-over message.

the result Had DBS Bank adopted a conventional strategy, it would have been happy to pull in US$100 million.

Instead, "Up" has attracted nearly US$0.5 billion through three tranches in less than a year.

The first tranche was officially capped at US$75 million and was marketed from November 13 to December 20, 2000. It required an all-cash investment. Approximately US$1.5-2 million a day was drawn in from subscribers generally aged 35 years and over. The total media budget was less than US$250,000.

A second tranche was offered from January 12 to April 30, 2001, and subscribers could invest using savings from their Central Provident Fund accounts. The second tranche performed even better than the first.

"Up" has pulled in five times the amount of funds that conventional unit trusts attract. By not accepting things on face value, the bank was able to dictate tomorrow's market.

❝

We have a uniquely collaborative working system, both inside the agency and with clients, and we are always looking to step outside conventional lines. We collapse the system, so we can brainstorm up front, and the client is brought into the process. The client fell in love with the idea of the dog at a workshop meeting..."

JOHAN FOURIE, Chief Executive Officer/Regional Director Asia Pacific, TBWA (Singapore)

UP AND UP   UP AND UP
UP AND UP **UP AND UP** UP AND UP
                                              UP AND UP
UP AND UP
        UP AND UP   UP AND UP

PAINLESSLY SHIFTING PERCEPTIONS

PAINLESSLY SHIFTING PERCEPTIONS
PAINLESSLY SHIFTING PERCEPTIONS
PAINLESSLY SHIFTING PERCEPTIONS
PAINLESSLY SHIFTING PERCEPTIONS
PAINLESSLY SHIFTING PERCEPTIONS
PAINLESSLY SHIFTING PERCEPTIONS
PAINLESSLY SHIFTING PERCEPTIONS
PAINLESSLY SHIFTING PERCEPTIONS

PAINLESSLY SHIFTING PERCEPTIONS

the problem The Oversea-Chinese Banking Corporation had its roots deeply planted in the soil of Singapore's Chinatown. It had established a proud reputation for prudence and stability that appealed to thrifty Chinese families and business folk. Its long established slogan, *Solid as a rock*, communicated timelessness and conservatism.

By the 1990s, Singapore banking had changed dramatically. Western marketing methods had come to town. It was no longer enough to be a traditional banking institution. Banks became brands, reaching out to a younger, more Western-oriented generation. Sensibly, OCBC did not want to discard its heritage. Nevertheless, times were changing and the bank had to relate to a new target audience.

the strategy The bank's credit cards operation offered a perfect opportunity to target younger customers without alienating older ones.

The first phase saw the bank align itself with the upsurge of interest in culture — concerts, plays, opera and ballet — and the rapidly growing Singapore Arts Festival. The launch of the OCBC Arts Card, an international MasterCard credit card with arts-related privileges, positioned the bank at the heart of the vibrant arts scene. Cardmembers enjoyed first choice of the best seats as well as special discounts, while helping to support the arts in Singapore. The advertising reflected the bank's new aspirations. The visual dynamics and typographic treatment broke new ground and conveyed a fresh tonality relevant to the target audience. A national free-standing insert in the *Sunday Times* (400,000 copies) was supported by subscription leaflets.

Then, in 2000, the dynamics of the OCBC Credit Card Porsche promotion carried the bank further into the aspiring younger executive mass market. The lucky draw prize was not a conservative car, but a sporting Porsche Boxster S. Creatively, full-page, full-colour print ads, magazine ads, full bus exteriors and interiors, exterior and in-bank posters and collaterals presented a fresh face of the bank to the Singapore public. Significantly, a young woman won the Porsche.

the result The shift in consumer perception had an immediate impact on the brand. For example, the Porsche promotion ran from 15 May to 31 October 2000. During that five and a half months, card spend increased 8%, or by over US$12 million, while the number of new applications for OCBC credit cards totalled 5,800.

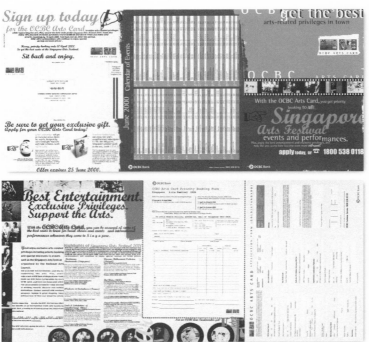

category	countries	advertiser	agency
BANKING, FINANCIAL SERVICES, INSURANCE	CHINA	PA INSURANCE	McCANN-ERICKSON GUANGMING LTD, BEIJING AND GUANGZHOU

BRANDING PEACE OF MIND BRANDING PEACE OF MIND BRANDING PEACE OF MIND
BRANDING PEACE OF MIND

BRANDING PEACE OF MIND

BRANDING PEACE OF MIND
BRANDING PEACE OF MIND BRANDING PEACE OF MIND
BRANDING PEACE OF MIND

the problem Established in 1991, PA Insurance is China's third-ranked insurance company with premium income exceeding US$1.56 billion. The PA Group spans life and property insurance, securities, trust and investment, overseas holdings and information management.

To achieve new marketing goals and become more competitive when China joined the WTO, PA identified the need to enhance perception as market leaders.

the strategy Using its proprietary brand tool McCann Pulse™, the agency refined the core brand values and explored the company's connection with consumers. Ongoing dialogue with consumers explored the contexts and connections for new creative ideas.

The brand name itself offered immediate opportunities. In Chinese, PA is *Píng'ān* (平安), a disyllabic word meaning peace. However, a single Chinese word can often have many subtle meanings and *ān* is no exception: calm, tranquil, safe, secure, in good health, setting one's mind at ease. All the connotations are positive.

PA's connection with consumers was built around added security in life and a service guarantee. A 60-second commercial called *Peace* showcased different parts of China bearing the name Peace, underscoring the fact that PA Insurance is everywhere in China. The theme line *Zhōng Guó Píng'ān, Píng'ān Zhōng Guó* juxtaposed the thought of a peaceful China with the brand name.

the strategy Regular consumer dialogue through McCann Pulse™ indicated that consumers positively reacted to the spirit of PA Insurance. The campaign enabled PA to improve sales performance and delivery of its "3A" service concept — *Anytime, Anywhere, Any Way*.

PA increased premium income by 23.22% to US$3.29 billion in 2000. The campaign also helped PA reach its target of a 35% incremental increase in annual premiums and secure its position as China's third biggest insurance brand in 2001.

In September 2000, when *Asiaweek* charted the share values of 25 insurance companies in Asia, PA Insurance was ranked second.

BRANDING PEACE OF MIND   BRANDING PEACE OF MIND   BRANDING PEACE OF MIND

BRANDING PEACE OF MIND **BRANDING PEACE OF MIND** BRANDING PEACE OF MIND

BRANDING PEACE OF MIND   BRANDING PEACE OF MIND

BRANDING PEACE OF MIND

People are at peace across all the different regions of China.

Peace County, Qinghai: Awe inspiring views of the mountain people.

Peace Avenue, Beijing: A young couple with their newly born baby; an elderly couple with a photo of their children.

Peace Town, Guangxi: Beautiful images of bridges and village life.

Peace Village, Harbin: Children play in the snow.

Peace Lane, Shanghai: An old man holds up a photo of the street when it was derelict, then looks at the fine new skyscrapers around him.

All the faces of China wish us peace.

MALE VO: *Wherever and whenever we are, whatever we do, we sincerely pray for peace of mind for China.*

LOGO: *Peace Insurance.*

COCA-COLA   GATORADE   VITASOY
TIGER BEER   ASIA BREWERY/ABSOLUTE DISTILLED WATER
GATORADE   BEVERAGES   COCA-COLA   TIGER BEER
WERY/ABSOLUTE DISTILLED WATER   VITASOY   GATORADE   VITASOY
TIGER BEER   COCA-COLA

Beverages

IN Asia-Pacific, this category has witnessed more change in the past ten years than the last hundred. A dazzling array of new age drinks has swamped the market. Consumer tastes and preferences have changed overnight. Old-established icons have found themselves challenged on several fronts. Maintaining market leadership has become the shrewdest game in town. For marketers in this category, the lyrics of a song put it quite aptly: *If you can make it here, you can make it anywhere...*

category	countries	advertiser	agency
BEVERAGES	PHILIPPINES	ASIA BREWERY/ ABSOLUTE DISTILLED WATER	OGILVY & MATHER, MANILA

SIMPLIFYING PURITY
SIMPLIFYING PURITY SIMPLIFYING PURITY
SIMPLIFYING PURITY **SIMPLIFYING PURITY** SIMPLIFYING PURITY
SIMPLIFYING PURITY SIMPLIFYING PURITY
SIMPLIFYING PURITY SIMPLIFYING PURITY

the problem Absolute Pure Distilled Water had no significant brand image. The key player, in terms of distribution and media advertising, was Wilkin's, followed by Viva from the San Miguel group and a cluster of smaller brands.

Consumers were growing more confused. The market was flooded with brands, each claiming to be the cleanest, the safest, the purest. The end result was that bottled waters had become commoditised.

the strategy A review of competitive advertising showed that virtually every brand supplied the "how" and "why" of purity. A battery of scientific claims, laboratory tests, and the benefits of one filtration process over another assaulted consumers. The agency reached the conclusion that demonstrating something as simple as purity had ironically become contrived and complicated.

Consumer research led to a strategic breakthrough. People were not picking up on the scientific angle at all, and no single brand was perceived as "purest" or "safest". It was an advertising environment where all the brands were saying the same thing, which was neither relevant to consumers nor had any bearing on their brand choices. The category was waiting for a brand that differentiated itself. And to do that, the brand would need to communicate something interesting and relevant.

The agency knew that the creative leap had to be "extreme"; it had to take something as mundane as water and identify a simple, fresh perspective. Pure water is exactly that — pure. Pure and unadulterated, the agency rationalised, meant none of the bad stuff, only the good stuff of water, and nothing but. This led to executions where the outline of the Absolute bottle was rendered "invisibly" — all the viewer saw were the green bottle cap and the green paper label, and nothing but. A snail that appeared to be crawling on air, and a shadow seemingly from nowhere, underscored the fact that there was a bottle in the picture.

the result Three months after the campaign launched, top-of-mind brand awareness increased by 250%. Sales rose by around 30% and Absolute became the number two bottled water brand in the Philippines.

Absolutely clear. Absolutely pure.

Open on a pure, clear screen. Suddenly lettering travels across it, mysteriously magnified by some unseen presence. A choral track is heard throughout.

THE MOVING WORDS READ: *Absolutely clear. Absolutely pure.*

The Absolute green bottle cap and label appear, but no bottle, followed by the exaggerated sound of a water droplet. The moving lettering reduces in size to become the end title.

Open on a pure, clear screen. Two animated goldfish swim around.

Underwater fish sounds are heard with harmonica music throughout.

The goldfish swim towards each other, but suddenly collide with something invisible.

The fish swim off, leaving the Absolute green bottle cap and label on screen. Absolute is so clear and pure even fish can't see it.

SUPER: *Absolutely clear. Absolutely pure.*

A LESSON IN LEADERSHIP
A LESSON IN LEADERSHIP
A LESSON IN LEADERSHIP
A LESSON IN LEADERSHIP

A LESSON IN LEADERSHIP

A LESSON IN LEADERSHIP
A LESSON IN LEADERSHIP
A LESSON IN LEADERSHIP
A LESSON IN LEADERSHIP
A LESSON IN LEADERSHIP

the problem Coca-Cola is, and always has been, the largest selling soft drink in New Zealand. The on-going challenge for a well established brand is to continue its strong relevance with teens, especially with the emergence of a wide variety of new products in recent years.

the strategy Qualitative and quantitative consumer research conducted by **Coca-Cola** in New Zealand showed that 40 percent of the New Zealand population are under the age of 25 years, and also a part of the youth target market for **Coca-Cola**.

Further, the research highlighted that New Zealand youth were jaded and constantly wanted new stimulus to keep them interested in a brand and wanted advertising to address them on their own terms.

The communication tactics involved **Coca-Cola** in New Zealand engaging the global strategy of "think local, act local" to create locally relevant and innovative advertising, which would communicate with New Zealand youth in their own language. Messages were created so only teenagers could decode them. The "street" style language demanded youth had to work to understand the message which created engaging advertising.

Subtle cues enhanced the targeted communication. For example, the *Mr. Grumpy* character – like the youth **Coca-Cola** were talking to – was born in the 1980's. They had identified with him since childhood.

The leadership of **Coca-Cola** in teen pop culture was also exemplified in the *Getting Off* commercial. The retro styled animation was leading edge as was the music. New Zealand's leading DJ and king of the dance club scene, DJ Roger Perry composed the track specifically for the TV commercial. Perry saw the potential of the music and extended it into a full 7-minute dance track, had it released under the title *That Coke Track*, and took it to a gathering of the world's hippest DJ's in Miami.

Goths, an advertisement starring members of the New Zealand Gothic community, a distinct group recognised for their dark coloured dress and downbeat approach, are seen hyped up and having a great time at a bowling alley. Again the advertisement needs youth to decode the communication to understand the message. The brand tagline followed the decoding strategy with the word *'Enjoy'* appearing over a red bottle cap at the end of each advertisement. The **Coca-Cola** logo did not appear at all.

the result As well as growing New Zealand sales of **Coca-Cola**, the campaign drove positive increases in brand equity, measured through both qualitative and quantitative consumer research.

Qualitative results confirmed a positive reaction to advertising with the youth audience responding positively to the localisation of communication, the quirkiness of the advertisements and the edgy, youth focussed execution.

Quantitative results established the high "likeability" of the ads relative to the normative data of other fast moving consumer goods. In particular, *Goths* scored very well in the key scores, both with mainstream youth and those known as "early adopters" of trends, and was the single highest scoring commercial across a wide range of product categories.

Coca-Cola is a registered trade mark of The Coca-Cola Company.

A LESSON IN LEADERSHIP

A LESSON IN LEADERSHIP

A LESSON IN LEADERSHIP

A LESSON IN LEADERSHIP A LESSON IN LEADERSHIP

A LESSON IN LEADERSHIP A LESSON IN LEADERSHIP A LESSON IN LEADERSHIP

A LESSON IN LEADERSHIP

MR.GRUMPY

Mr. Men and Little Miss™ & © 2000 Mrs. Roger Hargreaves.

Mr. Men and Little Miss™ & © 2000 Mrs. Roger Hargreaves.

Swing

We are staring at a swing, its chains tangled around the crossbar, the empty seat dangling high above the ground.

Street ambience is heard.

This locked-off shot continues for 12 seconds. Absolutely nothing happens.

Suddenly an upside down, empty **Coca-Cola** bottle appears on a **Coca-Cola** red background. The bottle makes a final plastic popping sound and vanishes.

SUPER: *Enjoy*

Owl

We see an owl sitting against a vivid blue sky with a bright yellow sun.

Nothing happens for 9 seconds.

Then the owl blinks once.

Nothing happens for another 4 seconds.

Suddenly we see the inverted **Coca-Cola** bottle on the familiar **Coca-Cola** red background. With a plastic popping sound it vanishes.

SUPER: *Enjoy*

Getting Off

A typical diagram on an aircraft safety leaflet has come to life using retro animation.

We see the plane in the water. The evacuation slide has inflated.

Some very hip dance club music kicks in as two young males start performing all kinds of cool moves up and down the slide.

One of the young men hands his bottle of **Coca-Cola** to the aircrew and passengers who have gathered in life jackets at the emergency exit. A crewmember stares at it.

Cut to inverted empty **Coca-Cola** bottle on red background. It pops off.

SUPER: *Enjoy*

Goths

We are watching a group of Goths at a bowling alley. For those in the know, their behaviour doesn't ring true. Instead of being downbeat and depressive, they are exuberant and vital.

Whenever a Goth bowls, wild screaming and yelling breaks out.

A typical suburban male bowler looks at them curiously.

If we'd been watching carefully, we would have seen one of the Goths holding a bottle of **Coca-Cola**.

A Goth girl arrives and stares disbelievingly at her friends. Cut to inverted empty **Coca-Cola** bottle on red background. It pops off.

SUPER: *Enjoy*

A BRAND RECLAIMS ITS BIRTHRIGHT

A BRAND RECLAIMS ITS BIRTHRIGHT   A BRAND RECLAIMS ITS BIRTHRIGHT   A BRAND RECLAIMS ITS BIRTHRIGHT

A BRAND RECLAIMS ITS BIRTHRIGHT

A BRAND RECLAIMS ITS BIRTHRIGHT   A BRAND RECLAIMS ITS BIRTHRIGHT
A BRAND RECLAIMS ITS BIRTHRIGHT
A BRAND RECLAIMS ITS BIRTHRIGHT

the problem Gatorade is a sports drink brand launched in the US by Quaker Oats in the 1960s. It dominates its category with a volume share in excess of 80% and generates a retail turnover of US$1,500 million annually. American consumers have an unquestioning belief in Gatorade's re-hydration and energising properties — on average, they drink between 6 to 7 litres per person a year. Gatorade is part of America's sporting ritual. Most NFL games end with the coach of the winning team being immersed in Gatorade.

Australia is a different story. From 1991 to 1993, retail sales of sports drinks increased from US$1.7 million to US$28 million, with males accounting for 70% of consumption. Gatorade launched in October 1993 with the *Be Like Mike* campaign featuring Michael Jordan, at the time voted the most admired sports star by Australian teenagers. After four weeks, Gatorade took market leadership with a 40% share. Unfortunately, many "new age" beverage brands entered the market at the same time. Most were short lived. Unlike the US where its sports history and word-of-mouth support helped build the brand, Gatorade's scientific story was largely lost. Many consumers dismissed it as simply "another new drink". Nor did negative publicity about sports drinks help. Leading nutritionists came out questioning the value of sports drinks, damning them as "no better than water", "high in sugar" and "a cause of tooth decay".

In 1994 the similarly named PowerAde was launched with a significant distribution advantage. And when PowerAde was relaunched in the summer of 1995 with a new pack and a new blue flavour — Mountain Blast — it took category leadership in July 1996.

Between early 1994 and August 1998, Gatorade's total volume share of the sports drink category fell from 55% to 26%. Collectively, others players like Lucozade, Isosport, Sport Plus and Adams Ale held another third. Prices remained at relative parity. By February 1999, PowerAde commanded a weighted distribution level of 75% versus Gatorade's 48%, as measured by the AC Nielsen 6 City Route Distribution.

Meanwhile, sports drinks and bottled water had achieved high market penetration. 89% of 13- to 39-year olds claimed to consume bottled drink during sport. The category drove interest and trial, but not brand loyalty. Consumer trial of sports drinks was around 60%, but repeat purchase was low at 19%.

With 80% of 13- to 39-year olds claiming to participate in some form of sport every week, a major opportunity existed to build brand commitment and belief.

It would not be easy, however. Australians perceived water as the legitimate thirst quencher, the drink by which all others are judged. Beer was the reward for a hard-earned thirst; in fact, more Australians ritually consumed beer after sport and exercise than sports drinks. Branding was not a driver; as far as Australians were concerned, there was little difference between sports drink brands. If their preferred drink was not available, another brand would do. It was a low risk impulse purchase.

With a change of bottler to Bonlac Foods in March 1998, Gatorade was relaunched. The objective was to drive a 20% increase in Gatorade volume from September 1998 to February 1999.

the strategy If long-term growth were ever to be achieved, the agency believed that the category's lack of legitimacy had to be addressed. Low repeat purchase levels, consumer cynicism and negative media publicity all pointed to the need to rebuild belief in sports drinks. It was in Gatorade's interest to take a leadership stance. But as qualitative research had shown, Gatorade was perceived as simply one of the "Ades". The brand lacked substance, depth and personality.

Gatorade had to win the loyalty of the core consumer group, males aged 15 to 25. Thanks to their education, these young men were highly marketing literate. They could see through blatant attempts to "market to them". Brand advertising had to be based on brand truth.

The Campaign Palace drilled into the brand. Four pillars emerged. Gatorade was the first sports drink and had created the category. It was based on science; over 25 years of research proved it worked. Its formulation had stood the test of time. And it was part of the fabric of sport and genuinely committed to sport. (Its Sports Science Manager was a former Olympic and Commonwealth Games athlete; its Managing Director was a triathlon participant.)

During this process, the agency discovered how Gatorade had been invented. Dr. Robert Cade of the University of Florida wanted to help the "wooden-spooners" of American college football — the Florida Gators. The drink he formulated became the team's secret weapon. Soon the Gators became known as the "second half" team, because Dr. Cade's drink replaced the energy that they expended in the first half. Their performance improved throughout 1965 and 1966 until they made it to their first ever Orange Bowl against rivals Georgia Tech in 1967. The research unearthed a quote from the coach of Georgia Tech: "We didn't have Gatorade, that made the difference..."

Suddenly the brand had a unique proposition: *Gatorade is legendary sport fuel.* The question then was, how should the legend be brought to life for young Australian men?

The creative solution was a 2 1/2-minute documentary retelling the story of that historic Orange Bowl. It was not to be seen as advertising, but as a Gatorade film.

Real footage of the game was used, including a shot of Richard Nixon who attended the '67 Orange Bowl. Original participants of the game were tracked down. The documentary commercial integrated interviews with Dr Robert Cade, Gators coach Ray Graves, a Gators cheerleader who was at the game, as well as opposing quarterbacks from both teams. Authenticity was achieved by contrasting past and present shots of these people. Adding contemporary Australian relevance, the closing sequence featured shots of Aussie sports heroes drinking Gatorade. The campaign line was, *What legends are made of.*

A total media spend of US$1.7 million was invested from September 1998 to February 1999. The commercial launched during "live" telecasts of the AFL and NRL Grand Finals, quickly building reach, momentum and scale. 20% of the buy went on off-peak programmes. The 2 1/2-minute commercial took up an entire ad break, giving Gatorade a dominant leadership presence and enabling it to break through the advertising clutter. Television advertising ran for the first four weeks, reaching 77% of males aged 16 to 24 at a frequency of one plus. Cinema and PAY-TV extended the life of the commercial through the summer. Targeted men's magazines followed, with ads focused on the science behind Gatorade. Transit and static outdoor posters blitzed point of purchase.

the result Ex-factory sales rose 28% over the previous year. In grocery, Gatorade achieved a 6-point share increase directly following the launch. Strong share gains were made in convenience stores.

Unaided advertising awareness increased from 36% to 50% following the campaign, with top-of-mind brand awareness growing by 22.5%. Gatorade became the most salient brand in the category, with total unaided brand awareness up by 10.5% to 74% versus PowerAde at 44%. Overall familiarity with the brand was up 17%. Key image attributes recorded significant growth: "Worth the money you pay" increased by 26%, "Used by top athletes" by 34%, "Scientifically proven" by 42%, and "Advertising that's meaningful" by 74%.

❝

The *Legends* TVC is a category breaking ad which has successfully differentiated the Gatorade brand. As a result of this, key awareness and imagery measures have significantly increased post the campaign. Key recall from the creative was extremely rich — some of the richest unaided recall I have ever seen in the many tracking studies I have worked on."

ADRIAN GONZALEZ, **Managing Director,**
Millward Brown Australia

A BRAND RECLAIMS ITS BIRTHRIGHT

A BRAND RECLAIMS ITS BIRTHRIGHT   A BRAND RECLAIMS ITS BIRTHRIGHT   A BRAND RECLAIMS ITS BIRTHRIGHT

A BRAND RECLAIMS ITS BIRTHRIGHT

A BRAND RECLAIMS ITS BIRTHRIGHT   A BRAND RECLAIMS ITS BIRTHRIGHT

A BRAND RECLAIMS ITS BIRTHRIGHT

A BRAND RECLAIMS ITS BIRTHRIGHT

TITLE: *What you are about to see is a true story.*

Open on shot of deserted Florida
Gators football stadium.

SUPER: *Miami Orange Bowl.*

Sitting in one of the dugouts is an old
man who begins to narrate the story.

OLD MAN: *It all happened more than 30 years
ago, but I remember it as though it was just
yesterday.*

Cut to footage of 1967 and the
atmosphere inside the stadium. We
catch a glimpse of Richard Nixon in
the old newsreel footage. Snatches of
'60s music are heard throughout.

Cut to bone-crunching action as the
Gators are bombarded by their
opponents, Georgia Tech.

OLD MAN: *It was 1967, it was the summer of
love, but somehow someone forgot to tell these
guys. The Florida Gators were doing it tough
against the favourites Georgia Tech, in their
first ever Orange Bowl.*

Cut to ex-Gator defence Steve Spurrier
in the empty stadium.

SPURRIER: *In the first quarter it seemed
like Georgia Tech had all the answers. My
teammates, they were blocking their hearts out,
but it seemed like nothing was working.*

Cut to Donna Kay Berger, Gators'
cheerleader 1967-68. As she talks, cut
away to original newsreel footage as
she was at the Orange Bowl.

CONTINUED ON NEXT PAGE...

WHAT
LEGENDS ARE
MADE OF.

Gatorade

...CONTINUED

DONNA: *The guys were getting hammered. We did everything we could to try and lift them.*

OLD MAN: *By the end of the first quarter, me and just about everybody else in the place never gave 'em a chance.*

ORIGINAL COMMENTARY: *The Gators are not looking good...*

Cut to Dr. Robert Cade, Professor of Medicine, University of Florida.

DR. CADE: *The problem for the Gators was that they expended so much energy early in the game, that they had none left for the end. So we devised a drink of carbohydrate and electrolytes that speeds into the system and supplies everything they need for energy production. Naturally we named it Gatorade...*

OLD MAN: *Whatever it was these guys came up with worked, because when the Gators came out the second half, they were a different team.*

ORIGINAL COMMENTARY: *Well, folks, I reckon the Gators' coach had some stern words to say to his players, because they're playing the third quarter as if their life depended on it.*

Cut to Kim King, Georgia Tech quarterback 1965-67.

KING: *In the second half our guys seemed to get more tired, but those Gators, they just kept on coming...*

OLD MAN: *The final nail in Georgia's coffin came when Larry Smith set an Orange Bowl record by running 94 yards for a Gators' touchdown. So the Gators, with a little help from the doctors at the University of Florida, won the 1967 Orange Bowl for the first time ever.*

A super is added, identifying our old narrator as none other than Ray Graves, Gators coach 1960-69.

GRAVES: *After the game, the Georgia Tech's coach Bobby Dodge said to me, "We didn't have Gatorade, that made the difference..."*

HE PAUSES TO REFLECT: *I believed that then, and I still believe that to this day.*

Newsreel shots of the victorious Gators are intercut with today's Aussie sports heroes drinking Gatorade.

END TITLE AND LOGO: *Gatorade. What legends are made of.*

category	countries	advertiser	agency
BEVERAGES	UNITED KINGDOM	TIGER BEER	M&C SAATCHI, SINGAPORE

STALKING THE BRITISH BEER DRINKER

STALKING THE BRITISH BEER DRINKER   STALKING THE BRITISH BEER DRINKER

STALKING THE BRITISH BEER DRINKER   STALKING THE BRITISH BEER DRINKER

STALKING THE BRITISH BEER DRINKER

STALKING THE BRITISH BEER DRINKER   STALKING THE BRITISH BEER DRINKER   STALKING THE BRITISH BEER DRINKER

STALKING THE BRITISH BEER DRINKER

the problem Asia Pacific Breweries dominates its Singapore home market with Tiger Beer. In 1997, APB launched Tiger in the UK, targeting mainstream British beer drinkers. Previously, Tiger had been a niche product, and APB was keen to disassociate it from Chinatown and curry restaurants. The perception of Tiger had to shift from an Asian beer to drink with Asian food to a great beer to enjoy in clubs and pubs.

the strategy Research in the British market indicated many of the old perceptions of the Far East were still firmly in place — Asia was mysterious, sexually intriguing, dangerous even. The Tiger Beer launch couldn't have been better timed: Michelle Yeoh was appearing in a James Bond movie.

Three waves of print ads were crafted with exotic detail, inviting the reader to *Discover the Tiger*. The Oriental woman challenged the British beer drinker to forsake the familiar and try a new experience. In one execution, an Oriental beauty carrying a lantern leads us into a cave of Chinese opera masks with a question rendered in authentic Chinese Calligraphy: *Nǐ pà mǎ?* (你怕吗?) meaning "Are you frightened?"

Acupuncture, tattoos and shaving were explored in magazines like *The Face*, *GQ* and *Arena*. The campaign was later extended to Ireland and Europe.

the result Distribution in the UK exceeded APB's targets, with Tiger Beer achieving double-digit growth.

category	countries	advertiser	agency
BEVERAGES	**HONG KONG**	**VITASOY**	**SAATCHI & SAATCHI, HONG KONG**

MAKING IT COOL TO BE WHOLESOME
MAKING IT COOL TO BE WHOLESOME
MAKING IT COOL TO BE WHOLESOME
MAKING IT COOL TO BE WHOLESOME

MAKING IT COOL TO BE WHOLESOME

MAKING IT COOL TO BE WHOLESOME
MAKING IT COOL TO BE WHOLESOME
MAKING IT COOL TO BE WHOLESOME
MAKING IT COOL TO BE WHOLESOME

the problem Vitasoy is a Hong Kong icon, a well-established, much-loved brand that has been around for over 60 years. Everyone from age 3 upwards happily consumes it. But with more alternative health drinks entering the younger end of the market, Vitasoy took steps to secure its leadership with Hong Kong youth aged 18-25.

the strategy The agency researched Hong Kong youth in its own environment — homes, schools, shopping malls — rather than in the usual one-way mirrored focus group. Young consumers were frank about the issues that concerned them. They also stressed that their relationships with brands were changing. They wanted to express their own opinions, and deal with brands that spoke their language and understood their issues.

Somehow, Vitasoy had to develop communications that were specifically relevant to youth without jeopardising the loyalty of its other consumers. Wholesomeness was Vitasoy's brand equity. But should that platform be abandoned in favour of a younger, more hip image? Obviously not.

The creative solution made wholesomeness even more compelling by subverting it and being "too wholesome". The brand's equity was exaggerated in a series of television class tutorials. Each commercial had a class bell and Vitasoy tutorial title as opening mnemonics, summoning young viewers to partake another quick lesson in social graces and interpersonal relationships. Each concluded with classroom voices singing the tag line off-key.

The advertising held a slightly cracked mirror to life and teenage situations. Hong Kong youth could engage with the brand, while older consumers could share the tongue-in-cheek humour.

the result Sales exceeded Vitasoy's already high consumption levels. Vitasoy commissioned a tracking study by NFO WorldGroup. Top-of-mind brand awareness grew from 85% to 90%, while ad awareness leapt from 19% to 40%.

In 2000, Vitasoy appeared 31 times on *Media & Marketing* magazine's Top 10 advertising recall chart, and in 7 out of 8 editions in 2001. The study was compiled from telephone interviews with a random sample of n=100 respondents stratified to be representative of the Hong Kong population.

On the street, core target respondents could recall television commercials verbatim, line-by-line.

MAKING IT COOL TO BE WHOLESOME

MAKING IT COOL TO BE WHOLESOME   MAKING IT COOL TO BE WHOLESOME   MAKING IT COOL TO BE WHOLESOME

MAKING IT COOL TO BE WHOLESOME

MAKING IT COOL TO BE WHOLESOME   MAKING IT COOL TO BE WHOLESOME

MAKING IT COOL TO BE WHOLESOME   MAKING IT COOL TO BE WHOLESOME

OPENING MNEMONIC: The *Vitasoy Tutorial Class* title frames a shot of teenagers at school. A class bell rings.

Two girls stroll along a school path. One is curious about her hair.

GIRL: *Should I have short hair?*

HER FRIEND: *No, you look good in long hair.*

Suddenly a boy interrupts them.

BOY: *I think a perm is better.*

The boy becomes the subject of the tutorial.

GIRL VO: *Guys, getting into other people's conversation is unpopular behaviour.*

He is seen in old, black-and-white documentary footage, boarding a bus and a ferry, labouring on a construction site, as the girl's voice corrects his unwholesome behaviour.

GIRL VO: *Instead you can choose getting into the bus, getting into the boat, getting into a construction site, or getting into other people's dinner table.*

The two girls walk away from him.

GIRL VO: *But remember, don't get into other people's conversation.*

END PRODUCT SHOT, CLASSROOM SINGERS AND SUPER: *Always good for you. Vitasoy.*

The classbell heralds another tutorial. It opens with people coming out of a sad movie show.

A young man turns to his friend.

GUY: *Are you crying?*

HIS FRIEND: *You're a nut. No, it's the sand.*

Suddenly he becomes the subject of the tutorial.

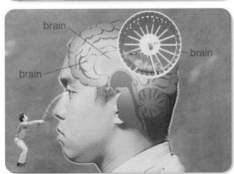

GIRL VO: *Guys, crying is actually good for our health.*

Our male friend now resembles a bizarre medical chart. A safe opens in his chest revealing a shiny red heart, which promptly breaks in two.

GIRL VO: *When your heart breaks...*

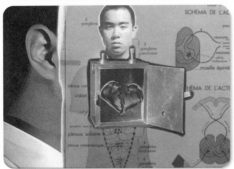

Next his skull lifts back revealing his brain. Soon, tears pour from his eyes and are caught by another man in a bucket.

GIRL VO: *...the brain will order the lachrymal gland to produce tears to rapidly soothe your emotions. So if you want to cry, just cry.*

We see our male hero crying on his friend's shoulder.

GIRL VO: *Don't try to hold it back.*

END PRODUCT SHOT, CLASSROOM SINGERS AND SUPER: *Always good for you. Vitasoy.*

The class bell rings for another Vitasoy tutorial. This time, a young man aims a basketball for an easy shot and misses.

HIS FRIEND JEERS: *Hey, you are so crap.*

Immediately his crude language makes him the subject of the tutorial. 1950s canned music plays cheerily in the background.

GIRL VO: *Guys, the word crap is not appropriate. Let's try to use some other words.*

The basketballer's friend holds up one finger.

SUPER: *Example 1.*

When the basketballer misses the shot, his friend says: *Hey, you are not up to standard.*

The friend now holds up two fingers.

SUPER: *Example 2.*

When the basketballer misses yet again, his friend says: *Hey, you are below average.*

GIRL VO: *Guys, from now on remember to mind your wordings.*

END PRODUCT SHOT, CLASSROOM SINGERS AND SUPER: *Always good for you. Vitasoy.*

UNILEVER/CLINIC
EXIT DEODORANT   UNILEVER/CLINIC
UNILEVER/HARMONY   RECKITT & COLEMAN/VEET   PROCTER & GAMBLE/OIL OF OLAY   UNILEVER/CLINIC
& COLEMAN/VEET COSMETICS, TOILETRIES, PERSONAL HYGIENE
T DEODORANT   JOHNSON & JOHNSON/BAND-AID   EXIT DEODORANT   JOHNSON & JOHNSON/BAND-AID
PROCTER & GAMBLE/OIL OF OLAY   UNILEVER/HARMONY   UNILEVER/HARMONY

Cosmetics, Toiletries, PersonalHygiene

EFFICACY was everything once. And while demonstrations are still an important part of brand communications, emotional connections offer the richest opportunities. Improved ad literacy has empowered Asia-Pacific consumers. Long-established brands have searched their armouries for new marketing strategies and communication techniques. More compelling and innovative advertising has been one result, as these case studies will demonstrate.

category	countries	advertiser	agency
COSMETICS, TOILETRIES, PERSONAL HYGIENE	THAILAND	EXIT DEODORANT	DENTSU YOUNG & RUBICAM, THAILAND

ENTER THE REBEL   ENTER THE REBEL

ENTER THE REBEL

ENTER THE REBEL   ENTER THE REBEL   ENTER THE REBEL   ENTER THE REBEL   ENTER THE REBEL   ENTER THE REBEL

the problem Thailand's deo spray market was highly competitive, dominated by strong brands like Axe and Tros. If Exit were going to break through and position itself as a major player, it would need strong differentiation and high relevance.

the strategy Exit's strategy stemmed from a consumer insight: 15-year old boys sought self-identity and self-satisfaction. They were "transitionals", caught between the rebellion of youth and the desire to appeal to the opposite sex. Exit could stake its claim for their loyalty by adopting a "bad" attitude.

While the category norm was "sexy, masculine, cool and charming", Exit would be the "bad boy" of the market. Its brand values would be youth, chaos and rebellion — highly relevant to 15-year old males who sought outlets for self-expression in conservative Thai society.

the result Exit gained 8% share of market within five months of its launch. It became the number two brand after Axe in the deo spray segment.

Research with 200 respondents indicated that Exit, with its distinctive and appealing personality, was their preferred brand.

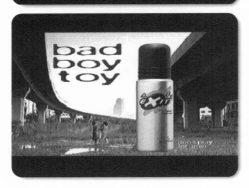

Two enraged teenage girls wearing boxing gloves are fighting each other on vacant land beneath a flyover. Their bleeding noses and lips attest to the seriousness of their fight.

With blood-curdling screams they charge each other and fists fly.

A third girl runs in. She shouts for them to stop.

SHE ASKS: *Why on earth are you doing this?*

Suddenly she sniffs something in the air.

We cut to discover a geeky 15-year old boy in glasses spraying his skinny body with Exit deodorant.

Now the third girl takes on the other two, slamming her fists into their faces.

END PRODUCT SHOT AND SUPER: *Bad boy toy.*

category	countries	advertiser	agency
COSMETICS, TOILETRIES, PERSONAL HYGIENE	CHINA	JOHNSON & JOHNSON/ BAND-AID	McCANN-ERICKSON GUANGMING LTD, SHANGHAI

FROM THE FUNCTIONAL TO THE EMOTIONAL

FROM THE FUNCTIONAL TO THE EMOTIONAL

FROM THE FUNCTIONAL TO THE EMOTIONAL

FROM THE FUNCTIONAL TO THE EMOTIONAL FROM THE FUNCTIONAL TO THE EMOTIONAL

FROM THE FUNCTIONAL TO THE EMOTIONAL

FROM THE FUNCTIONAL TO THE EMOTIONAL

the problem Band-Aid has long been established in China. The category is not new and there are many imitators. The imperative was to shift away from selling the functional aspects of the product and enrich the brand's *emotional* appeal.

the strategy Band-Aid was reframed through a series of familiar yet painful situations. The campaign — under the theme *Growing up hurts* — portrayed those moments that everyone suffers, those emotional wounds that no one can avoid.

The little boy crying for the toy he can't have; the little ballerina snubbed by her peers; a young man's broken heart — each scenario was crafted in sepia photography with the only colour provided by an actual Band-Aid strip. Innovative typography and graphic design treatment broke category conventions.

And seizing the moment to make the world a less painful place, the brand celebrated the historic meeting of the Presidents of North and South Korea and the first reunification talks. The headline read: *Band-Aid strongly believes there's no wound that can't be healed.*

the result Band-Aid continues to lead its category.

邦迪坚信
没有愈合不了的伤口。

BAND-AID 邦迪 创可贴

category	countries	advertiser	agency
COSMETICS, TOILETRIES, PERSONAL HYGIENE	AUSTRALIA	PROCTER & GAMBLE/ OIL OF OLAY	SAATCHI & SAATCHI, SYDNEY

AL WOMEN, REALLY CONVINCING   REAL WOMEN, REALLY CONVINCING   REAL WOMEN, REALLY CONVINCING

REAL WOMEN, REALLY CONVINCING

REAL WOMEN, REALLY CONVINCING   REAL WOMEN, REALLY CONVINCING   REAL WOMEN, REALLY CONVINCING
REAL WOMEN, REALLY CONVINCING

the problem Given Australia's harsh, dry climate, skin care products proliferate. Yet, most claims are greeted with natural Aussie scepticism.

One exception was Oil of Olay, a tried and trusted brand that had been around for 50 years. But its market share was declining slowly, as its core users grew older. While there remained a positive side to the Olay image— "Unpretentious", "Down to Earth", "Trustworthy"— negative brand comments were being sounded more frequently in research groups: "Nana uses it" and "Daggy" being at the extreme end. Further exacerbating the problem, Olay's traditional testimonial ads weren't cutting through any more and it was being outspent by major competitors.

In advertising terms, the beauty category is mind numbing. While products claim secret formulas, their advertising sticks to the predictable ones. The sameness defeats differentiation. Clearly, staid, old-fashioned Oil of Olay needed a brand a new face.

the strategy The opportunity came with a new formulation. The product news was: Your favourite Oil of Olay moisturiser now comes with a sun protection factor of 15+.

Australian women were no longer so relaxed about living in a sunburnt country. They saw the sun as a problem, something that inhibited their lifestyle. The single-worded brief for the advertising was: Freedom.

The creative theme empowered women: *Get out and live.* The idea was to feature real Australian women in the ads — not English roses or overdubbed American models — who faced the Aussie elements in their everyday lives. The product proposition was interpreted with photojournalistic, almost documentary, realism. Six women told it like it was, preserving Oil of Olay's traditional testimonial approach, but subtly shifting the brand to a more natural, younger, Australian face without jeopardising the existing loyal customer base. The three women featured in the television spoke from the heart about their real lives, not mouthing the usual scripted spiel. A champion in-line skateboarder confessed she'd "like to come back as a bird". A farmer was adamant she loved cows ("I'd much rather sit round a boardroom table with 20 cows than 20 men in suits"). A building contractor admitted to enjoying the scenery on the job ("Some of the boys I work with, they're more like body builders"). Meanwhile, the print ads showed a sailing instructor, a truck driver at a gold mine, and a police officer. In every case the women conveyed genuine passion for living life outdoors and living out their own choices.

But it was still advertising and showing "beauty" was mandatory. Rather than anything posed or "set up", the entire ad was infused with the woman's natural beauty. Significantly, production was in female hands. Print was shot by photojournalist Penny Clay and the TV directed by Diana Leach.

the result Oil of Olay SPF 15 products showed a substantial 14% uplift in volume sales during the campaign period.

"

Maybe our creative 'leap' was to jump out of the way and let people tell their own stories. The ads really stood out for their authenticity and emotion in a world of outlandish claims, silly pseudo-science and garish over-airbrushed beauty shots. The casting brief was to find suitable women in the appropriate age group for each product. Our 'secret ingredient' was real emotion."

SUE CAREY, Senior Writer,
Saatchi & Saatchi Sydney

REAL WOMEN, REALLY CONVINCING   REAL WOMEN, REALLY CONVINCING
REAL WOMEN, REALLY CONVINCING

REAL WOMEN, REALLY CONVINCING

REAL WOMEN, REALLY CONVINCING   REAL WOMEN, REALLY CONVINCING   REAL WOMEN, REALLY CONVINCING

REAL WOMEN, REALLY CONVINCING

GET OUT AND LIVE.

OIL of OLAY SPF 15 RANGE.

Driving heavy vehicles at the Kidston gold mine, thirty-four year old Louise Wione faces the sun every day. Age Defying Series Lotion, from Olay's range of SPF moisturisers, contains Beta Hydroxy to restore radiance to her skin, and SPF 15 to protect it from the sun's harmful effects. Wherever you're at in life, Olay has an SPF 15 moisturiser for you.   Proof we can help you feel younger.

GET OUT AND LIVE.

OIL of OLAY SPF 15 RANGE.

As a sailing instructor, thirty-three year old Amanda Laithwaite faces the sun every day. Age Defying Series Lotion, from Olay's range of SPF moisturisers, contains Beta Hydroxy to restore radiance to her skin, and SPF 15 to protect it from the sun's harmful effects. Wherever you're at in life, Olay has an SPF 15 moisturiser for you.   Proof we can help you feel younger.

The camera as journalist observes Jodie Tyler in training.

SUPER: *Jodie Tyler, 25, Pro In-Line Skater.*

JODIE VO: *When I started I was working in an office wearing suits every day and I would never ever have dreamed that I would end up in skating. I've always liked to go fast and I would always say to my dad, 'Come on, Dad, go faster, make the carbies roar!'. There's nothing better than looking out the window in the morning and seeing a beautiful day and knowing that you can go outside and enjoy it.*

Jodie is literally airborne on her skates.

JODIE VO: *If I had another chance at life, I'd come back as a bird.*

It becomes so much part of your life, that it is your life.

END DISPLAY: *Oil of Olay SPF 15 Range.*

We explore Joanne's passion for farm life, the open skies and rolling countryside that she calls "her office".

SUPER: *Joanne Cimbaljevic, 32, Cattle Breeder.*

JOANNE VO: *The farm is my life. It's my office out there. I just love the freedom, the sun, the sweat, the physical side of it. If you can't drive a tractor, and if you can't cut the hay, and if you can't chase the cows, then you can't be a farmer.*

Joanne brushes one of her beloved cows.

JOANNE VO: *I could never give up my life on the farm. I'd much rather sit around a boardroom table with 20 cows than 20 men in suits. I love cows...*

END DISPLAY: *Oil of Olay SPF 15 Range.*

We share a day in the life of Karen, a builder. How does she handle her male counterparts on tough construction sites without compromising her identity?

SUPER: *Karen Jacobs, 46, Building Contractor.*

KAREN VO: *I use a lot of psychology in life. I speak the language that they speak. The ones who I work with, some of them are absolutely gorgeous, I mean they're like body builders. It's very pleasant to be doing a really hard labouring job and you've got something nice to look at. When it's sunny it's beautiful, when it's windy it's awful. You can't survive in the building game being a fairy princess. I mean, I don't demand respect, I expect it.*

END DISPLAY: *Oil of Olay SPF 15 Range.*

category	countries	advertiser	agency
COSMETICS, TOILETRIES, PERSONAL HYGIENE	AUSTRALIA	RECKITT & COLMAN/VEET	EURO RSCG PARTNERSHIP, SYDNEY

LATERAL LEAP

LATERAL LEAP

LATERAL LEAP

LATERAL LEAP

LATERAL LEAP

LATERAL LEAP

LATERAL LEAP

LATERAL LEAP

LATERAL LEAP

LATERAL LEAP

the problem Veet Warm Wax is a waxing product traditionally used by women. Microwavable, it is a fast and effective way to silky smooth skin. The question was, could Veet be sold to Sydney's gay male population as they prepared themselves for the annual Mardi Gras?

the strategy Mardi Gras is a huge festival, attracting visitors from all over the world. Gay Sydneysiders spend a lot of time and money making sure their bodies are in top shape for the event. Unwanted hair removal is high on the agenda. Logically, Veet Warm Wax stood an excellent chance of becoming the preferred male waxing product.

Creatively, though, the risk was that advertising addressed at gay communities often "tries too hard" and becomes condescending.

The campaign adopted an open, honest tonality in print and outdoor executions. Meanwhile, interactive outdoor featured a male stripper performing in front of the Veet *Male Stripper* poster as it travelled up and down Oxford Street, the main gay thoroughfare.

the result Veet achieved over a 60% increase in sales during the campaign period. The campaign was talked about in local newspapers and magazines, while the posters were mysteriously stolen off the streets. It was applauded by the gay community for speaking their language and won official recognition for Positive Portrayal of Minority Groups.

Getting under the skin of Sydney's gay community. Veet posters were mysteriously stolen off the streets.

category	countries	advertiser	agency
COSMETICS, TOILETRIES, PERSONAL HYGIENE	THAILAND	UNILEVER/ CLINIC	LOWE & PARTNERS WORLDWIDE, THAILAND

COMBINING BEAUTY WITH EFFICACY
COMBINING BEAUTY WITH EFFICACY
COMBINING BEAUTY WITH EFFICACY
COMBINING BEAUTY WITH EFFICACY

COMBINING BEAUTY WITH EFFICACY

COMBINING BEAUTY WITH EFFICACY
COMBINING BEAUTY WITH EFFICACY
COMBINING BEAUTY WITH EFFICACY
COMBINING BEAUTY WITH EFFICACY

the problem Until 1999, the value of the anti-dandruff segment accounted for about 20% of the total hair care category. Although the incidence of dandruff was reportedly as high as 65%, the total anti-dandruff segment had been stagnant.

Clinic, the market leader in anti-dandruff shampoos, had 9% of the total shampoo market. But the prevailing consumer mindset was the biggest obstacle to building the brand. Consumers perceived the chemicals in anti-dandruff shampoos were too harsh and did not want to use such products even for preventive purposes. Clinic had not only to establish itself as the best brand to ward off competitors, but also to establish its relevance to a wider group of users. Nothing revolutionary had been developed by any manufacturer in the segment so there was really nothing new to offer consumers. The brand had to find a way of communicating its benefits in a more impactful way, and to project its superiority without any breakthrough in terms of formulation.

the strategy A key consumer insight showed that consumers were not prepared to compromise their hair. They might want to get rid of dandruff, but not if it meant having dry, difficult-to-manage hair. Beauty mattered above everything, even more than being dandruff-free.

Based on that insight, the communications objectives were twofold: Clinic had to improve consumer perceptions that it was an effective way to stop dandruff — while it left soft, beautiful, easy-to-manage hair. The dual benefits were rational. The emotional benefit was *confidence*.

In terms of execution, however, Clinic faced even greater obstacles. The creative had to go beyond the traditional "slice of life" approach. The campaign had to distance the brand from any competitor, in terms of both image and market share. Competition from major beauty brands Sunsilk and Pantene was fierce; both continuously brought new advertising on air, backed with big media budgets. Consumers were often confused by what the brands were saying; executional styles were similar with beautiful girls and beautiful hair shots. Not only did the creative have to break through this clutter, but also inject a modern, contemporary feel — portraying Clinic as anything but a boring, medicinal brand.

The advertising idea busted the category: *When having dandruff-free, soft, beautiful hair can be a matter of life and death, Clinic is the only answer.* Two commercials were developed: *Theme* and *Beauty*. Both were based on the spy movie genre.

the result Clinic's share of the total shampoo market rose from 9% in 1999 to 12% by third quarter 2000. Its share of the hair conditioner market rose from 2.9% to 4.2%. Spontaneous unaided brand awareness leapt from 34% to 45%, with ad awareness driven from 26% to 36%.

Unilever's quantitative research checked the effectiveness of each piece of communication. The new campaign achieved high impact — well above the average of attention getting and memorability on air. Viewers found the commercials distinctive, highly interesting and involving. Message take-out for the dual benefits of dandruff-free and beautiful hair was exceptionally strong. The *Theme* commercial proved more enjoyable than the *Beauty* execution. And while both commercials scored well in terms of engaging viewer attention, *Theme* proved the stronger of the two — registering a mean score of 6.53% against 5.47%, in a category where scores usually averaged 4.60%.

COMBINING BEAUTY WITH EFFICACY
COMBINING BEAUTY WITH EFFICACY
COMBINING BEAUTY WITH EFFICACY
COMBINING BEAUTY WITH EFFICACY

COMBINING BEAUTY WITH EFFICACY

COMBINING BEAUTY WITH EFFICACY
COMBINING BEAUTY WITH EFFICACY
COMBINING BEAUTY WITH EFFICACY
COMBINING BEAUTY WITH EFFICACY

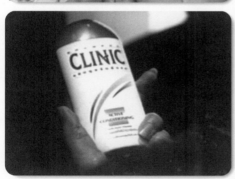

In *Theme*, our heroine is being pursued along dark city streets. *James Bond*-style music adds to the spy movie atmosphere. She tries to escape into a nightclub, but the bouncers take one look at her unkempt hair and dandruff and stop her.

It's a matter of life and death. She darts into a washroom and shampoos her hair with Clinic.

vo: *With unbeatable anti-dandruff action from Zinc PTO technology, the new Clinic immediately removes dandruff with the first wash.*

When she emerges, her hair is shiny, soft and swinging, with no trace of dandruff.

vo: *Plus, increased multi-vitamins make hair softer than ever.*

The bouncers take one look at her and immediately welcome her inside…

vo: *Change into a new you instantly.*

…but stop her two evil-looking pursuers from following her.

vo: *New Clinic! Beautifully soft, dandruff-free hair.*

End on Clinic range shot.

128

category	countries	advertiser	agency
COSMETICS, TOILETRIES, PERSONAL HYGIENE	THAILAND	UNILEVER/ HARMONY	LOWE & PARTNERS WORLDWIDE, THAILAND

TIME TO DIFFERENTIATE
TIME TO DIFFERENTIATE
TIME TO DIFFERENTIATE   TIME TO DIFFERENTIATE
TIME TO DIFFERENTIATE **TIME TO DIFFERENTIATE** TIME TO DIFFERENTIATE
TIME TO DIFFERENTIATE   TIME TO DIFFERENTIATE   TIME TO DIFFERENTIATE
TIME TO DIFFERENTIATE

the problem Being third to enter Thailand's health soap category — following Protex from Colgate Palmolive and P&G's Safeguard — Harmony needed a distinctive point of difference. Previous campaigns followed in the footsteps of competitors: a family health soap that provided effective bacterial cleanliness, usually told through the eyes of a concerned mother.

As Harmony would always be fighting on the same threshold, under the same brand positioning, it needed an execution that differentiated it from competitors. Its new brand saliency had to make consumers feel that Harmony was closer, more relevant to their lives.

the strategy The agency's consumer insight was that getting dirty or grimy is no big deal — it's just part of leading a fulfilling life, and everyone knows they can get really clean again.

From there, the advertising idea took shape: *Whatever life throws at you, you can bounce back confidently*. Executionally, commercials were developed around interesting, engaging everyday examples of the times when Harmony is needed most. The situations were typical accidents or mishaps in life, unpleasant and unhygienic, and the people caught in them were likable and real.

The desired response being sought: bad things may happen to you, but thanks to Harmony you don't have to let them get you down.

the result For 14 straight weeks from its launch, Harmony was ranked among Thailand's top fifteen most-liked advertising campaigns, reaching as high as third. The research was conducted with 1,000 Bangkok respondents by an Assumption College poll and Than Sethakit Research Design Company.

Harmony also garnered a dramatic increase in top-of-mind advertising recall within the total soap category, as measured by the agency's monthly pulse analysis.

Currently, sales are at their highest with Harmony enjoying 6% share of the health soap category, double its share prior to the campaign launch.

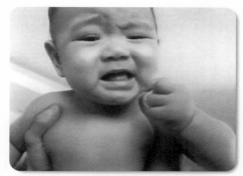

A father rushes to pick up his crying baby. The father holds the baby in the air and pulls all kinds of funny faces to entertain his child.

FATHER: *Easy...don't cry...Oh no!*

Suddenly the baby urinates all over him.

Cut to the father washing away animated bacteria with Harmony soap.

SUPER: *Helps retard 99% of bacteria.*

MVO: *It's time for Harmony, which helps retard 99% of bacteria.*

Cut to smiling father and his family with Harmony pack shot.

MVO: *Harmony gives confidence back to your skin.*

END SUPER: *Harmony gives confidence back to your skin.*

A woman is listening to a song, swaying to the music, her face turned skywards.

SONG: *If I could fly like a bird, I would fly high up in the sky…*

Suddenly a passing bird drops something unwelcome on her face, spoiling her mood entirely.

WOMAN: *Yach!*

The woman is seen showering, washing away animated bacteria with Harmony soap.

SUPER: *Helps retard 99% of bacteria.*

MVO: *It's time for Harmony, which helps retard 99% of bacteria.*

Cut to smiling woman and Harmony pack shot.

MVO: *Harmony gives confidence back to your skin.*

END SUPER: *Harmony gives confidence back to your skin.*

A beautiful woman steps from her car — and straight into an open drain. We hear a distant splash!

The woman is seen showering, washing away animated bacteria with Harmony soap.

SUPER: *Helps retard 99% of bacteria.*

MVO: *It's time for Harmony, which helps retard 99% of bacteria.*

Cut to smiling woman with Harmony pack shot.

MVO: *Harmony gives confidence back to your skin.*

END SUPER: *Harmony gives confidence back to your skin.*

A teenage boy is cycling along, whistling, calling out to some girls.

BOY: *Hi there, girls — oops!*

He was so distracted by the girls that he has ridden his bike straight into the jaws of the garbage truck!

Teenage boy showering, washing away animated bacteria with Harmony soap.

SUPER: *Helps retard 99% of bacteria.*

MVO: *It's time for Harmony, which helps retard 99% of bacteria.*

Teenage boy, happy and confident again, with Harmony pack shot.

MVO: *Harmony gives confidence back to your skin.*

END SUPER: *Harmony gives confidence back to your skin.*

category country advertiser agency

McDONALD'S/THAILAND
cDONALD'S/THAILAND McDONALD'S/HONG KONG McDONALD'S/HONG KONG
PIZZA HUT FAST FOOD PIZZA HUT PIZZA HUT
McDONALD'S/THAILAND
IcDONALD'S/HONG KONG McDONALD'S/HONG KONG
McDONALD'S/THAILAND PIZZA HUT

FastFood

THE cut and thrust of tactical communications frequently overshadows the maintenance of long-term brand building. However, the major fast food players recognise the need for an ongoing strategic presence, and are adept at leveraging their images for short-term retail advertising. The lessons from this category are relevant in others.

COLLECTING RECORD SALES

COLLECTING RECORD SALES

LECTING RECORD SALES

COLLECTING RECORD SALES

COLLECTING RECORD SALES   COLLECTING RECORD SALES   COLLECTING RECORD SALES

COLLECTING RECORD SALES   COLLECTING RECORD SALES

the problem In 1998 McDonald's launched a Snoopy Happy Meal promotion in various countries around the world to drive sales. There were 28 different Snoopys to collect, each version coming with a Happy Meal for kids.

the strategy While the promotion was globally targeted at kids, Leo Burnett's insight told them that in Hong Kong it was adults rather than kids who have grown up with Snoopy. And Hong Kong adults are crazy for collectibles!

Which is why the agency chose a very different approach by targeting adults: buy an Extra Value Meal and get a Snoopy collectible for HK$10. With 28 different versions of Snoopy available, the advertising would announce a different Snoopy collectible every day. The advertising idea: *Every dog has his day.*

By focusing on the value of owning the full collection of 28 Snoopies, the advertising could highlight the uniqueness of each Snoopy. Continuous promotional reinvention meant 28 different TV executions each day for 28 days.

the result Business results showed record daily sales for four weeks in a row, with Extra Value Meal units increasing by 80% during the promotional period — equalling virtually one meal sold for every person living in Hong Kong!

The public relations results were equally impressive: ten mentions on CNN and CNBC, 30 radio mentions, and 567 press clippings including foreign publications around the world. With everyone from officials to ordinary people fighting to get their own McDonald's Snoopy collection, the event ranked in the top ten Hong Kong news stories in several publications.

EXCITING CONSUMERS

EXCITING CONSUMERS

EXCITING CONSUMERS

EXCITING CONSUMERS EXCITING CONSUMERS

EXCITING CONSUMERS   EXCITING CONSUMERS   EXCITING CONSUMERS

EXCITING CONSUMERS

the problem Thailand experienced a flat GDP in 1999, but the quick-serve restaurant category remained highly competitive. McDonald's looked for a way to stimulate sales, generate profitable incremental transactions and create business momentum.

the strategy Consumers needed a jolt of excitement in the midst of an economic recession. The price component of the value equation had to be delivered in an unexpected manner and it was decided to limit the time of each promotional offer to one week only. Core McDonald's products — including Chicken McCrispy, Big Mac, McNuggets, Filet-O-Fish and McChicken — were all promoted at a reduced price of 29 Baht. And by limiting each offer to one week, the call to action became more irresistible and urgent.

Creatively, the one-week-only offers sparked a very fresh concept: *Every second counts*. The agency started thinking of real life activities where consumers wanted to make the most of their time, being able to eat anywhere, anytime, to take advantage of each offer. The breakthrough came by thinking of unusual activities that created strong visual impacts and stayed in the consumer's mind. Television commercials, print and point-of-sale posters developed executions where people consumed McDonald's products in exaggerated situations. A Thai boxer was half way through a crucial boxing match, a swimmer was in the midst of swimming, a bride was in the middle of her most important day, and a drummer during his concert.

In each case, every second counted in order to enjoy the savings.

the result Sales far exceeded expectations. McDonald's Samurai sales rose by 345%, McChicken by 355%, Filet-O-Fish by 500%, Big Mac by 530% and McNuggets by 553%.

A bride and groom stand at the altar.

A church choir sings the hymn *Jerusalem*:
"And did those feet,
"In ancient times…"

As the shot slowly tightens on the bride, we can see through her veil. She appears to be chewing.

Next minute, she lifts a McDonald's burger to her mouth and takes a bite. Then she takes another, her eyes remaining intently fixed on the preacher.

SUPER: *Pork Burger Baht 29, one week only.*

Dissolve to black, retaining the white super, then add McDonald's logo in lower right corner of the screen.

We are at a swimming carnival.
People are cheering.

The swimmers come into frame.
Suddenly, the swimmer nearest to
camera takes a bite from a McDonald's
burger, which he deftly holds clear of
the water without losing concentration.

After each stroke he takes another
bite, the burger held away from the
splashing water.

SUPER: *Filet-O-Fish Baht 29, one week only.*

Dissolve to black, retaining the white
super, then add McDonald's logo in
lower right corner of the screen.

category	countries	advertiser	agency
FAST FOOD	THAILAND	PIZZA HUT	BBDO BANGKOK LIMITED

PIZZA ONLINE   PIZZA ONLINE

PIZZA ONLINE   **PIZZA ONLINE**   PIZZA ONLINE

PIZZA ONLINE

PIZZA ONLINE   PIZZA ONLINE   PIZZA ONLINE

the problem In the early 1990s, Pizza Hut became the first fast food brand to introduce a delivery service to Thai consumers. In order to maintain its leadership image in a fast growing business, Pizza Hut launched an online delivery service.

At that time though, the Internet represented a niche market in Thailand. Mostly affluent Thais, fixated on everything related to computers and the Net, were in a position to use the service. The issue was how to cost effectively deliver the message — with the appropriate leadership tonality.

the strategy Print was tasked with the launch. The widely recognised Pizza Hut delivery box was used to symbolise a laptop computer, making the connection with Pizza Hut's new online delivery service.

It was a simple, visual execution with which the target audience immediately identified.

the result Pizza Hut's delivery sales via the Internet have increased steadily since the launch of the *Laptop* campaign.

HOMECARE INTERNATIONAL/SWIPE   PROCTER & GAMBLE/TIDE

PROCTER & GAMBLE/TIDE   SELLEYS CHEMICAL/TALON   PROCTER & GAMBLE/BOUNTY

ER & GAMBLE/TIDE FAST MOVING CONSUMER GOODS   SELLEYS CHEMICAL/TALON

CARE INTERNATIONAL/SWIPE   SELLEYS CHEMICAL/TALON   PROCTER & GAMBLE/BOUNTY

PROCTER & GAMBLE/TIDE   HOMECARE INTERNATIONAL/SWIPE   PROCTER & GAMBLE/BOUNTY

FastMoving Consumer Goods

UNIQUE product differences, once the central focus of advertising, have become fewer. Perceived differences, emotional differences, have become the order of the day. While not exactly crafting a brand "out of thin air", the average FMCG brand builder assumes the role of detective: finding where a brand fits into the consumer's life, discerning the nuances of brand relationships, understanding the rhythm of product life cycles. Life and death in the fast lane of marketing calls for sharp analytical skills and a keen knowledge of human behaviour. The following case studies present the fruits of fresh thinking.

category	countries	advertiser	agency
FAST MOVING CONSUMER GOODS	HONG KONG	HOMECARE INTERNATIONAL/ SWIPE	EURO RSCG PARTNERSHIP, HONG KONG

REJUVENATING THE BRAND
REJUVENATING THE BRAND
REJUVENATING THE BRAND
VENATING THE BRAND
REJUVENATING THE BRAND

REJUVENATING THE BRAND

REJUVENATING THE BRAND
REJUVENATING THE BRAND
REJUVENATING THE BRAND
REJUVENATING THE BRAND

the problem Swipe is one of the oldest domestic cleaners in Hong Kong. While competitors targeted young housewives with more attractive packaging and fresh, contemporary advertising, Blue Swipe appealed to older generation housewives and even light industrial operators. How could Swipe target young housewives without changing the pack and without offending existing users?

the strategy Younger housewives are more adventurous, more receptive to creative executions with something different to say. The strategy was to reinforce Swipe's local heritage and trade on its permanency — but to do it in a way that would break new ground in the category.

A local "celebrity" was engaged for the campaign — not a Hong Kong movie star, not a Cantonese pop singer, but Tsang, the bizarre, self-proclaimed Emperor of Kowloon. This eccentric old man was a Hong Kong icon, famous for defacing public property with claims of how the British Empire had stolen all his family's properties over the past century. His graffiti was a distinctive landmark all over Hong Kong and had supposedly inspired several local fashion designers.

What if Tsang wanted to reform and clean up his act across the entire city — what cleaner would he trust?

The campaign used 45- and 30-second TV commercials and full page, full colour newspaper ads. The highly irreverent tonality busted the category.

the result Sales data is confidential. However, the campaign generated so much interest that local channel TVB profiled Tsang after the commercials had aired.

On anything and anyplace. Kowloon City. Grenade Hill.

Clean the kitchen. Clean the toilet.

And even clean the two space shuttles.

Our camera follows Tsang, the Emperor of Kowloon, as he scrawls his graffiti all over the city, then cleans it off with Blue Swipe.

The demonstration proves Swipe's efficacy — Tsang is an old man yet his graffiti vanishes as effortlessly as it was applied!

TSANG VO: *My ancestors came here 2,700 years ago. I clean whatever I write, on anything and anyplace. Kowloon City, Grenade Hill, everything is clean. Hong Kong is clean. The Sau Mau Ping district, the Choi Hung Estate, the Tsui Lok Building, cleaning until everything is spotless. Clean the kitchen, clean the toilet, and even clean the two space shuttles. Blue Swipe cleaner cleans your house no matter how big it is. I suppose your house is not as big as mine...*

TURNING A LUXURY INTO A NECESSITY
TURNING A LUXURY INTO A NECESSITY   TURNING A LUXURY INTO A NECESSITY   TURNING A LUXURY INTO A NECESSITY

TURNING A LUXURY INTO A NECESSITY

TURNING A LUXURY INTO A NECESSITY   TURNING A LUXURY INTO A NECESSITY   TURNING A LUXURY INTO A NECESSITY
TURNING A LUXURY INTO A NECESSITY

the problem During tough economic times, Japanese women choose to remain faithful to products they trust. In the case of cleaning, most women use the traditional, economical cleaning cloth — the *zokin*. Changing to a disposable paper product like Bounty would seem unacceptably extravagant.

The challenge was to change women's buying behaviour, and get them to switch to what was perceived as a luxury item.

the strategy The campaign was no ordinary slice-of-life concept. Quite the opposite, it was based on slices of very fractured life. The advertising idea derived from the universal belief that men are unable to look after themselves, while women are perceived to be the ones who know what works best when it comes to household products.

The campaign ran as a serial, from February to December 2000 and told the story of a Japanese woman who left her husband. Although she is no longer there to clean for him, she ensures that he has the strongest and most resilient paper towel to help him in his daily household tasks. Bounty, as she tells him, is "perfect for someone graceless like you".

Each commercial was another episode in the unfolding drama. Beginning with the husband's voice telling us how long his wife has been gone, his wife's voice was introduced through her letters home, advising, admonishing and encouraging him. Her postcard from Hawaii tells him she went to the fire dance, while he burns up with fever in a typical Japanese winter. She sends their daughter to visit, who ends up looking after her father. After five months she comes home and their passion flares — but it was all a dream!

Because she continued sending her husband Bounty paper towels, the audience knew that she still cared for him. Bounty not only became his dependable household partner, but also offered him hope that his wife would return. Each episode contained a P&G side-by-side demonstration, strong branding, and a powerful mnemonic that demonstrated how Bounty was strong even when it's wet — water is wrung out of a Bounty paper towel, which then springs back to life full-screen.

the result Three weeks after the product was launched, sales well exceeded P&G's target. Bounty took up to a 30% market share. The campaign successfully communicated Bounty's key strategic message, changing the perception of the product; because of its durability and dependability, Japanese consumers could justify Bounty economically.

TURNING A LUXURY INTO A NECESSITY

TURNING A LUXURY INTO A NECESSITY   TURNING A LUXURY INTO A NECESSITY   TURNING A LUXURY INTO A NECESSITY

TURNING A LUXURY INTO A NECESSITY

TURNING A LUXURY INTO A NECESSITY   TURNING A LUXURY INTO A NECESSITY   TURNING A LUXURY INTO A NECESSITY

TURNING A LUXURY INTO A NECESSITY

A young, mournful husband dons an apron.

HUSBAND VO: *My wife left me last night.*

He opens her farewell letter, placed near pack of Bounty.

HIS WIFE VO: *I'm sorry, but I must leave you. But as long as there's Bounty, I'm sure you will survive. It's not just any paper towel.*

The husband pours hot water into a cup. He spills it and scalds his hand.

HIS WIFE VO: *The sheets are quilted, so big spills can be wiped quickly.*

The husband opens the fridge with a bandaged hand.

HIS WIFE VO: *Also, Bounty is so strong it will hold strawberries under running water without tearing.*

Cut to side-by-side demonstration: an ordinary paper towel caves in under the water, while the wet Bounty firmly contains the strawberries.

WIFE VO: *As for me, I've reached my limit. I hope you understand. Be strong.*

The husband sits alone eating strawberries while he watches a nature programme on TV.

TELEVISION COMMENTATOR: *The mother kangaroo spends all her time with the infant. The father becomes unimportant.*

Bounty towel wrings out and springs back to life. Pack shot and logo.

FEMALE VO: *Strong, even when it's wet. The all-round paper. Bounty, from P&G.*

The husband wearily steps from the toilet in the middle of the night.

HUSBAND VO: *It's been a week since my wife left me.*

He picks up her letter and reads it.

HIS WIFE VO: *You never seemed to notice the important things. And you probably don't even notice now that Bounty also comes in a box.*

He is deeply asleep when the alarm clock rings. He knocks over a carton of milk and reaches for the box of Bounty beside the bed.

HIS WIFE VO: *Because the sheets are quilted, it absorbs so much.*

Having wiped up the milk, he falls asleep again.

HIS WIFE VO: *One needs to always keep life's important things close by.*

He wakes suddenly, looks at the clock, and panics. He struggles into his trousers, knocking over a vase in the process.

HIS WIFE VO: *Before I left, I placed the Bounty boxes around the house where I'm sure you'd spill something.*

Cut to side-by-side demonstration of paper towels scrubbing a carpet: one wears through and disintegrates, but Bounty remains intact.

HIS WIFE VO: *It's perfect for someone graceless like you.*

Bounty towel wrings out and springs back to life. Product shot and logo.

FEMALE VO: *Strong even when it's wet. The all-round paper. Bounty, from P&G.*

The husband returns home, carrying a big delivery box.

HUSBAND VO: *It's been a month since my wife left me.*

He opens her musical birthday card, then inspects his two presents: a birthday cake from his daughter, and rolls of Bounty from his wife.

HIS WIFE VO: *Happy birthday. Your daughter baked this cake for you, and the Bounty Designer Prints are from me.*

The husband sits alone, candles burning on his cake, a Bounty Designer Print towel serving as a napkin.

HIS WIFE VO: *You can choose from a variety of designs and make your tabletop bright and exciting. This will help liven up your party. Of course, if someone spills something, you can use it to scrub away the mess.*

The husband accidentally knocks over a cup. He uses Bounty to clean it up.

Cut to side-by-side demonstration: an ordinary paper towel shreds itself on a carpet, while Bounty remains strongly intact.

The husband leans on his balcony, clutching a Bounty teddy bear towel.

HIS WIFE VO: *Your daughter loves the teddy bear print. She says you're like a teddy bear.*

Bounty towel wrings out and springs back to life. Product shot and logo.

FEMALE VO: *Strong even when it's wet. The all-round paper. Bounty, from P&G.*

STAYING AHEAD WITHOUT LOWERING PRICES

STAYING AHEAD WITHOUT LOWERING PRICES

STAYING AHEAD WITHOUT LOWERING PRICES

STAYING AHEAD WITHOUT LOWERING PRICES   STAYING AHEAD WITHOUT LOWERING PRICES

STAYING AHEAD WITHOUT LOWERING PRICES

the problem The Philippines is a market where consumer response to an economic crisis is to downscale to cheaper brands. Tide is priced twice that of its closest competitor, Surf. The question was, how should Tide respond to the pressure to lower its prices while maintaining market leadership built on its performance?

the strategy Against the economic crisis, Tide decided to set a leadership example and remain at the heart of every Filipino household. It chose to build its brand by creating an emotional bond with the consumer — a bond that transcended price — and, in the process, encourage brand loyalty. To achieve this, its advertising would have to bust the category and reach out to consumers with fresh, irresistible relevance.

The agency developed a campaign that paid tribute to all mothers by showing how their love shines through in their whitest wash. Each subject had to be treated with sensitivity and credibility, avoiding the obvious pitfalls of crass commercialism. Storylines went beyond the predictable slice-of-life: a mother's never-ending love extended to her grandchild, a street child experienced a mother's love for the first time, and a washerwoman became a second mother to a child.

But perhaps the most poignant commercial was *Choir*, about mother-daughter bonding forged when a little girl has her first period. The execution was subtle yet powerful. Tide was an integral part of the story as it unfolded.

the result Despite the onslaught of competitive detergent advertising in the past three years, Tide consumers continue to be loyal. Tide has retained a significant core of its consumers, enabling it to maintain market leadership in value share.

Paying tribute to the campaign, non-advertising groups have commended it for promoting Filipino family values.

Watched by her mother, a girl sings in her church choir. Suddenly she becomes agitated, looks down, then across to her mother with a silent plea for help. She slips away from the choir and meets her mother outside.

GIRL: *Mom...there's a bloodstain.*

Her mother leads her from the church, covering the stain on her daughter's choir uniform with her fan.

In their back garden, the girl stares at her stained uniform.

GIRL: *It dried up... it may not come off.*

MOTHER: *Yes, it dried up...but I can remove this with Tide.*

Her mother pours Tide into a bucket and gently handwashes the stained garment. The little girl watches.

GIRL: *Mom, why?*

MOTHER: *It's a natural thing. You're a lady now.*

The girl takes her turn washing. Eventually she holds up the sparkling white garment.

GIRL: *Mom, it's gone...*

Dissolve to the little girl once again confidently singing in the choir.

MALE VO: *You'll be facing more challenges, but you'll make it. Mom will always be there.*

The girl looks across to her mother and sings the final *Amen.*

MALE VO: *Tide. Cleanliness you can always depend on.*

POSITIVE BRANDING IN A NEGATIVE CATEGORY
POSITIVE BRANDING IN A NEGATIVE CATEGORY
POSITIVE BRANDING IN A NEGATIVE CATEGORY
POSITIVE BRANDING IN A NEGATIVE CATEGORY

POSITIVE BRANDING IN A NEGATIVE CATEGORY

POSITIVE BRANDING IN A NEGATIVE CATEGORY
POSITIVE BRANDING IN A NEGATIVE CATEGORY
POSITIVE BRANDING IN A NEGATIVE CATEGORY
POSITIVE BRANDING IN A NEGATIVE CATEGORY

the problem Talon is a brand of rat bait marketed in Australia by Selleys Chemical Company on behalf of Crop Care Australasia. Until 1997, Talon had never received consumer advertising support.

Rat baits, known officially as rodenticides, had been introduced commercially into Australia in the 1940s. In recent years the market had grown erratically, with fluctuations in rat bait demand determined by the effect of rat plagues in any given year. Sales are heavily seasonal; up to 50% of annual volume is usually concentrated in the April to June quarter when the warm, wet conditions of late summer cause a prevalence of rats pre-winter. 80% of all rat bait sales are through grocery outlets. The Ratsak brand dominated the market.

Talon had been launched in 1982 and grew to a brand share ranging from 15—20%. Selleys acquired the marketing and distribution rights in 1991. According to AC Nielsen, Talon had then achieved a higher brand share of 20—25%. Over the years Talon had enjoyed exclusive use of an ingredient called Broudifacoum that helped deliver a product performance 40 times more effective than Ratsak. Its cost meant that Talon's retail price was considerably higher than Ratsak's. But in 1996 this window of marketing opportunity was closed when the famous Australian insecticide brand Mortein also acquired the rights to Broudifacoum for its rat bait product.

Complicating matters further, The Leading Edge Market Sizing Study of 1996 showed that 52% of Australians had never experienced a problem with rats, while another 12% had infrequent problems. Of those with rat problems, 46% favoured the use of a well-known brand. It was obvious that higher levels of awareness equated to higher brand sales. With 93% brand awareness, and 47.8% brand share, Ratsak was almost the generic name in the category.

When Selleys decided to advertise Talon for the first time, the objectives were to increase the level of Talon's awareness among consumers, and establish a position of superiority over Ratsak that would justify Talon's premium pricing — while keeping Mortein at bay.

the strategy Advertising's task looked simple enough on the surface: make a direct product comparison, leveraging the fact Talon is 40 times more effective than the market leader, possibly with a degree of horror or shock value.

But because consumers fell into two groups — those with a rat problem and those without — a deeper understanding of the consumer's emotional state was necessary. Those without a rat problem would dismiss the advertising on a rational level; worse, they might reject the message outright, without making any emotional connection with the brand. On the other hand, unless the advertising reached those with a rat problem at precisely the time they had the problem, they were more likely to reach for the brand they were most familiar with — Ratsak.

Rats are an emotional subject. People don't like to think about them; they're a problem that "other people" have. Logical arguments or shock tactics will merely raise their defences. The advertising had to strike a delicate balance: engender positive feelings towards the *brand*, without provoking negative feelings associated with the *category*.

A simple shift in focus addressed this challenge. Instead of viewing the problem through consumers' eyes, the advertising looked at the issue from the rat's point of view. Instead of highlighting consumers' fear of rats, it highlighted the rat's fear of Talon. The proposition: *The one rats fear most.* Product superiority was implied, but in a less confrontational way, by delivering a brand-based story with broad appeal. It also provided opportunities for distinctive creative work capable of cutting through consumers' lack of interest in the category and establishing higher awareness for the brand.

Creatively, the classic image of "woman-standing-on-chair-screaming-at-rat" was subverted. Instead, have "rat-standing-on-chair-screaming-at-pack-of-Talon". The 15-second commercial was called *Scaredy Cat*.

Executional values were also given a twist to overcome consumer resistance. A stop-frame animation technique created a caricature rat, sparing consumers' revulsion at seeing real rats, dead or alive, and ensuring the commercial — and therefore the brand — didn't turn them off.

Media strategy contributed on three levels. Despite having a US$200,000 budget normally considered below the threshold in the household category, it recommended television as essential to deliver the emotional point of difference to drive brand awareness. Secondly, it recommended running 15-

seconders only to maintain greater continuity across the key pre-winter period. Thirdly, it recommended diverting virtually all funds into regional areas where the budget would work harder and where rat plagues were more likely to occur. It delivered Talon a 42% share of voice for the year. However, while Talon outspent Ratsak in 1997, Mortein outspent Talon 3 to 1.

the result The campaign achieved a lift in brand share of 8 share points, equivalent to a 40% increase in business. AC Nielsen data confirmed that Talon was less than 3 share points behind Ratsak, with Talon retaining the same price premium over Ratsak.

Based on a comparison of ex-factory sales in the peak April to June quarters of 1996 and 1997, Talon enjoyed an increase of around 58% in both unit and dollar sales.

Talon's brand awareness rose 28% — from 50% to 64% over the campaign period — according to The Leading Edge/Newspoll tracking studies of 1996 and 1997. It was achieved despite heavy marketing activity from Mortein and against the almost generic Ratsak.

Brand preference increased by 38% while Ratsak declined by 26%. Ratsak's loyalty base was eroded with Talon being the competitor that gained most — 5 percentage points. 46% of Talon brand preferrers responded that they "only started using the brand recently" and 74% of these recent Talon brand preferrers responded that their previous brand had been Ratsak.

Brand usage increased by 19%. Talon achieved a 10-point turnaround versus Ratsak and exceeded 30% penetration for the first time in the brand's history.

The total investment on advertising, including media and production, was US$275,000, which helped generate a 42% uplift in sales. The payback for the advertising investment was around eight months, after which it began returning additional profit to the brand.

Open on a pack of Talon sitting on a kitchen floor. In the foreground, a chair is shaking. We hear what we assume is a woman screaming.

MALE VO: *If you have problems with rats, then you need Talon.*

Suddenly we see why the chair is shaking. A stop-frame animated rat is perched on it, looking down at the Talon pack and screaming.

MALE VO: *It's the bait professional pest controllers use. So it's no wonder...*

Cut to wide shot with Talon pack in foreground, and the rat screaming on the chair in the background.

MALE VO: *...that Talon is the one rats fear most.*

END SUPER: *The one rats fear most.*

NONG PHO MILK   TOBLERONE   PILLSBURY/HÄAGEN-DAZS

NEW ZEALAND CHEESE PROMOTIONS LTD   NEW ZEALAND CHEESE PROMOTIONS LTD

STIMOROL   FOOD, CONFECTIONERY   NONG PHO MILK   STIMOROL

RALIAN MEAT & LIVESTOCK CORPORATION/BEEF   NEW ZEALAND CHEESE PROMOTIONS LTD

MEAT & LIVESTOCK AUSTRALIA LTD/LAMB   TOBLERONE

PILLSBURY/HÄAGEN-DAZS

Food, Confectionery

CLASSIC marketing case histories often originate in this category, and the following studies are no exception. When major foods like meat and cheese are in jeopardy, it takes exceptional strategies to arrest their decline. Food and confectionery brands, too, offer many instructive studies in survival and growth. The selected communications demonstrate acute insights into consumer expectations, tastes and habits. As we have seen in other categories, it is not simply a case of holding a mirror to life; rather, if the mirror is slightly cracked, life can be seen from a more interesting or unpredictable perspective.

BEEFING UP SALES

BEEFING UP SALES   BEEFING UP SALES

EFING UP SALES

BEEFING UP SALES

BEEFING UP SALES   BEEFING UP SALES   BEEFING UP SALES

BEEFING UP SALES

the problem The Australian Meat and Livestock Corporation (AMLC) had fought the decline in red meat consumption for many years. Between 1976/77 and 1987/88, average annual per capita consumption fell from 69kg to 40kg. A short recovery followed, but by 1992 a further four-year decline led AMLC to seek a new, radical strategy.

Women, who traditionally made 80% of all meat purchases, were turning against red meat. Red meat was perceived as the cause of health problems. Despite the availability of lean beef, red meat was still associated with fat and cholesterol. Beef was seen as heavy, hard to digest, and a cause of lethargy, quite the opposite of the well being and energy derived from "lighter" foods. While aware of beef's nutritional role as a source of protein and iron, only 18% of women considered beef a true dietary essential. Even then it came after chicken and fish, and was well behind fruit and vegetables. Younger women turning to vegetarianism — a trend supported by the media, aspirational role models and the growth in vegetarian restaurants — exacerbated beef's fate. What started as a fringe trend had become a mainstream fashion.

Fragmented eating habits, more variety in eating habits, and new cuisines like Thai which placed less emphasis on beef were all taking their toll. From red meat's sacred position as the centre of the meal surrounded by three vegetables, beef had become no more than a potential ingredient.

How could AMLC put beef back on Australian tables?

the strategy Women were the core target group. 17% were defined as appreciators of red meat, those who believed beef was essential to healthy living. Another 42% were termed acceptors; they liked red meat, but enjoyed other foods just as much. However, resisters who believed meat was not essential to a healthy diet accounted for 29% of women, while outright rejecters made up the balance.

Strategically the resisters, generally younger women, were the greatest concern. Their interest in meat was diminishing quickly and they needed positive reasons to eat it. It would not be enough to imply that meat "wasn't bad for you".

Of all beef's nutritional attributes — protein, zinc, vitamin B12 — its role as a source of iron offered the most compelling opportunity to forge a real emotional bond between women and red meat. All women understood the fundamental female need for iron in terms of menstruation and loss of blood. Iron transports oxygen through the blood; insufficient iron leads to lethargy, frequent infections and poor stamina. The notion of feeling tired and lethargic due to lack of iron would strike a chord of recognition and introduce real doubts about the wisdom of reducing red meat consumption. Iron would become the prime rationale for eating beef in the same way that calcium provides a reason to drink milk. In fact beef emerged as a better source of iron than consumers realised; gram-for-gram it is a richer source than spinach, while the body absorbs the iron in lean beef more easily than iron from many other natural sources.

But because of women's emotional distance from beef, the message could not be hammered home without losing credibility. So the campaign deployed two distinct phases: in 1993, it raised the issue of iron deficiency; in 1994, it confirmed beef as the best daily source of iron.

Working with the Australian Iron Advisory Panel, the CSIRO Division of Human Nutrition compiled a report that was launched in April 1993. It revealed that 70% of Australian women fell short in their recommended daily intake of iron. The findings were circulated to health professionals and doctors, and formed the basis of a public relations campaign conducted through selected women's groups, leading nutritionists and media personalities. From April to May, the report generated a lot of media coverage and provided a receptive environment for the subsequent advertising. 60% of consumers had prompted knowledge of iron as an issue even before the advertising rolled out.

The first commercial, *Faces 1*, ran in June 1993 and sought to raise the thought in women's minds that they could be "one of the 70%". It was based on the fact that women were aware of the importance of iron, but were inclined to attribute the symptoms of iron deficiency to other causes. The women featured on air were not professional actors. They talked credibly and emphatically about feeling tired and run down. Tonally, the commercial was unselfconsciously feminine, completely independent of traditional family and male dominated imagery, and tapped into the holistic perspective of how many women view their own health. Lean beef was presented as a "possible" solution — without any hard sell. Three black-and-white print ads provided further information on the iron issue and the relevance of lean beef.

A second commercial, *Faces 2*, ran in August/September 1993, featuring staff from well-known women's magazines explaining why they believed their iron intake was adequate. Their subsequent iron tests showed that one in five had sufficiently depleted iron stores to warrant medical attention. The take-out was that no one could afford to be complacent about iron deficiency.

Having sown doubt in 1993, the 1994 campaign provided the solution. The campaign promise was, *Your best source of essential daily iron*. In February 1994 three 15-second commercials highlighted the iron absorption capabilities of a little lean beef in side-by-side comparisons with other natural dietary sources of iron such as spinach, fish and pork. The commercials made the point that 25% of the iron in lean beef is absorbed, versus 2% of the iron in other sources like vegetables. Visually, the idea was demonstrated with a lens that enabled objects of different sizes to appear the same when shot at different distances. For example, a piece of lean beef looked equal to a fish. It was only when someone placed the fish alongside the beef that consumers realised how big the fish actually was.

Magazine executions echoed the television. Interestingly, the use of designer pastel background colours not normally employed in food advertising gave beef a contemporary image.

In 1993, media advertising ran in bursts to shake up entrenched attitudes, while a subtle, slower "drip" flighting pattern was used in 1994.

the result Between July 1993 and June 1994, Australian beef consumption rose for the first time in 12 years coinciding exactly with the iron campaign. Lean beef consumption rose to 36.4kg per capita. The increase in consumption of 1.5kg per capita represented an additional volume of 32,300 tonnes per annum. At saleyard prices, these extra sales were worth an additional US$49 million to Australia's meat producers. Based on retail prices monitored by AC Nielsen, consumers had spent an additional US$140 million on beef than they did the year before — despite a 5.2% price rise, the largest increase in retail beef prices for many years. The iron campaign had been the principal agent of change for an investment of only US$2.8 million, which was more than recouped in just one year.

Three stages of tracking research were conducted, a pre-advertising benchmark study, a second survey after three weeks of *Faces 1*, and a third following *Faces 2*. Awareness of publicity about the iron issue rose from the high level of 60% achieved pre-advertising to 92% after three weeks, and stood at 95% in the third wave of fieldwork. Advertising awareness was extremely high, especially for *Faces 1* at 74% unprompted and 88% prompted after just three weeks. By September, post-Faces 2, these levels had risen to 89% unprompted and 94% prompted.

The advertising succeeded in raising doubts among women about the adequacy of their own iron intake. As many as 68% agreed that the advertising had made them consider having more iron in their diet. The proportion of women who were not confident that their diet contained enough iron rose from 37% to 46%.

The *Faces* advertising shifted fundamental attitudes faster than had been expected. In just three weeks, lean beef overtook spinach as the best source of iron in the eyes of women. Pre-advertising, 48% had voted for spinach and 44% for lean beef. Post-*Faces 2*, 63% chose lean beef and only 32% nominated spinach.

In November 1994, following a year-long "drip" campaign, awareness of the side-by-side commercials was very high. 75% of women recalled the *Spinach* commercial, and 72% recalled *Fish*. A number of attitudinal measures showed enhanced perception of red meat as a healthy food and lean beef as a source of iron. 66% of respondents agreed that "Lean beef is the single best source of iron".

❝❝

It generated the strongest tracking results
I've ever seen in such a short period."

ELIZABETH DANGAR, Dangar Research Ltd,
Business Review Weekly

7 out of 10 Australian
women don't get
their recommended
intake of iron.

Source: National Dietary Survey, 1983. (Women Aged 25–54.)

In 1993, *Faces 1* communicated that 70% of women did not get their recommended intake of iron. Shot in stark black-and-white, it was a "Public Service" message more than a commercial…

A series of women, seen in close up, talk about feeling tired and run down. We cut from one face to another — younger women, older women, women from different ethnic backgrounds.

Sometimes each face speaks only one or two words of each statement.

WOMEN: *Why do I feel tired and run down? Why? Because I've got a child, and I work, and I run a household. Just family problems, relationships. I think it's environmental, I think it's to do with living in a big city, I think it's lifestyle. Because I'm overworked. Trying to do too much, I suppose. Oh, I'm a single mum with a daughter. Well, sometimes the weather…*

CUT TO TITLE: *7 out of 10 Australian women don't get their recommended intake of iron.*

WOMEN: *I suppose I just don't get enough sleep.*

TITLE: *Iron is essential to carry oxygen in your blood.*

WOMEN: *Um, actually, I really don't know.*

TITLE: *Lack of iron could well be the reason so many women feel run down.*

DISSOLVE TO END TITLE: *In a balanced diet, lean beef is one of the richest sources of iron.*

ADD LOGO: *Supported by Australian Nutrition Foundation.*

In 1994, lean beef was communicated as the solution to iron deficiency in a series of 15-second commercials and print ads...

Open on what appears to be a split screen, horizontally divided into two pastel halves. In the top left corner is a steamed snapper on a plate.

vo: *This steamed snapper...*

A plate of steak is placed in the bottom right corner.

vo: *Or this grilled lean rump steak will give you half your daily iron needs. So let's see them side by side.*

Suddenly a woman steps into frame and picks up the plate of snapper. As she lifts it, we realise that the fish and steak aren't on a split screen. The fish is actually a metre long and had been on the floor while the steak was on the tabletop. When they are side by side, the snapper totally dwarfs the steak.

SUPER UNDER THE STEAK: *122 grams*

SUPER UNDER THE FISH: *7.9 kilograms*

VO WITH END SUPER: *Lean Beef. Your best source of essential daily iron.*

LAMB: FROM LOST CAUSE TO NATIONAL ICON

LAMB: FROM LOST CAUSE TO NATIONAL ICON

LAMB: FROM LOST CAUSE TO NATIONAL ICON

LAMB: FROM LOST CAUSE TO NATIONAL ICON

LAMB: FROM LOST CAUSE TO NATIONAL ICON

LAMB: FROM LOST CAUSE TO NATIONAL ICON

LAMB: FROM LOST CAUSE TO NATIONAL ICON

LAMB: FROM LOST CAUSE TO NATIONAL ICON

the problem One of Australia's core primary industries, sheep farming had almost been written off as a lost cause. Lamb consumption had been in continual decline since 1986 — a 30% reduction in volume over 12 years.

Younger households saw chicken and beef as healthier, more modern alternatives to lamb. Lamb lacked interest; chops and legs were the only well-known cuts, and the decline in cooking skills among younger women exacerbated the situation. Lamb was more popular with older households, indicating further reductions as these segments aged.

Meat and Livestock Australia could not change the product offering, price or distribution, and nothing on the horizon seemed likely to reverse the decline. In fact, the final nail in lamb's coffin looked to have arrived in July 1999 when the US Government introduced steep tariffs on imported Australian lamb.

The MLA's short-term goal was to arrest the decline and maintain current market share. The longer-term goal was to increase fortnightly lamb servings by 10%. But only fundamental shifts in perceived brand attributes of lamb could sustain long-term growth and income for the industry.

the strategy Previous lamb campaigns had addressed younger households without children, while lamb needed the consumption volume of family households. Strategically, lamb had to recapture the hearts and stomachs of Australian families with children aged 6-17.

Interestingly, consumer insights revealed an underlying patriotic appeal and affinity with lamb that could be harnessed to drive consumption. The creative strategy was defined. Lamb would be identified as an icon of Australian life, and given a cheeky, irreverent personality. Promoted as *The flavour of Australia*, brand activity would modify the consumer mindset towards lamb, while tactical activity spikes added interest and delivered high profile calls to action.

But in July 1999, the introduction of US tariffs on Australian lamb threatened to bring about major losses for the US$60 million export market.

This meant it was all the more important to reverse the domestic decline of lamb. Within 48 hours of President Clinton's announcement, the agency had produced a tactical campaign encouraging Australians to eat one more lamb meal a week to help soften the blow. America had declared war on Aussie farmers, argued one ad, and Aussie families had to defend them at the dinner table. And anyhow, eating the world's most flavoursome lamb was not what you'd call a sacrifice. Butchers' windows became campaign real estate, and lamb had started to fight back.

From September to October 1999, Australia's traditional season for Spring Lamb, brand activity kicked in. *We Love Our Lamb — The Flavour of Australia* included "larrikin" scenarios like a truckie cooking a lamb casserole in foil under the bonnet of his rig.

Tactical activity built consumption opportunities outside of the traditional Spring Lamb season. For Australia Day in January 2000, lamb was positioned as Australia's National Meat for barbecues. Shortly after, Valentine's Day saw lamb cheekily invite consumers to *Enjoy a leg over dinner*. When Australia's controversial GST was introduced, public interest was leveraged for lamb with ads that announced, *Garlic Spuds and Thyme: The only GST on Lamb*. The August football finals and the 2000 Olympic games delivered even more patriotic reasons to eat lamb.

Total category spend from July 1999 to December 2000 was US$8 million; total lamb expenditure was US$1.5 million. Share of voice over this period was chicken 36%, pork 31%, lamb 18%, beef 10%, and turkey 5%.

Media adopted a slow-burn drip strategy leading to tactical events. A continual daytime brand presence was secured. After each burst of brand activity, one week of "clean air" provided the necessary distance between the brand and the tactical ads in order to avoid any confusion of messages. Tactical bursts ran for between one week and ten days. A peak presence of 70% enabled the acute emotional trigger to impact a broader audience in time for the long weekend or festive barbecue occasions.

the result Ten years of continual decline were reversed. National lamb servings in August 1999 increased by 8% over the previous month. Lamb servings increased 29% over the period August 1998 to August 1999.

Volume growth continued throughout the next twelve months, with lamb servings increasing 25% from July 1999 to July 2000, more than double the campaign's original target.

Tactical campaigns achieved peak penetration and consumption, with new users continuing to purchase lamb as well as consolidating usage by existing consumers. Lamb's appeal broadened with the average number of serves purchased per buy increasing from 5 to 7 across all market lifecycles. A particularly strong response came from Young Parents and Mid-life Households.

Lamb became the only meat to have significantly increased its per capita consumption — 1.2% from 1999 to 2000. According to Roy Morgan Research, "People who bought lamb in the last seven days" from July 1998 to December 2000 grew 19% whilst "People who bought meat in the last seven days" grew only 11%. Lamb accounted for nearly 30% of fresh meat growth.

Positive brand attributes were registered in tracking studies from August 1999 to December 1999. "It's very versatile" improved from 40% to 52%, "It's easy to cook" from 39% to 52%, "I'm proud to buy and serve this" from 49% to 59%. Recognition as "The Australian Meat" increased from 46% to 57%.

Above all, the campaign demonstrated how multiple strategic and tactical executions could be deployed on a low budget across a wide range of media for effective year-round brand enhancement and retail-driving support.

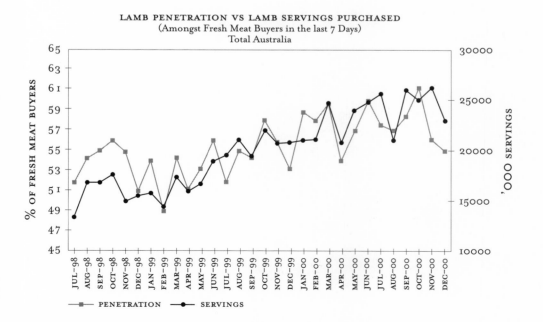

LAMB PENETRATION VS LAMB SERVINGS PURCHASED
(Amongst Fresh Meat Buyers in the last 7 Days)
Total Australia

AMERICA HAS PUT TARIFFS ON OUR LAMB, WE SUGGEST ROSEMARY AND GARLIC

Australian Lamb
HAVE YOU HAD YOURS THIS WEEK?
MEAT & LIVESTOCK AUSTRALIA

OUR LAMB IS SO GOOD, MR CLINTON WANTS IT RARE

Australian Lamb
HAVE YOU HAD YOURS THIS WEEK?
MEAT & LIVESTOCK AUSTRALIA

Garlic Spuds and Thyme. The only GST on Lamb.

THE FLAVOUR OF AUSTRALIA

We love our GST-free Lamb

MEAT & LIVESTOCK

FOOTY FINAL TIP: REMOVE MOUTHGUARD BEFORE EATING BBQ LAMB

THE FLAVOUR OF AUSTRALIA

We love our Lamb at Footy Finals time

In tough times, Aussies always give a hand. Today, try a leg.

President Clinton's new tariffs on Australian lamb came into effect this week. They're about as far from the Australian sense of 'fair go' as you can get. We can't reverse the US decision but we can all do something to help the producers of our tender lamb through these tough times. If every one of us has just one more lamb meal a week we can guarantee a future for an industry that's the backbone of Australia. Start today. Invite the family over for a roast dinner of the most flavoursome lamb in the world. Not only will they thank you but our farmers will, too.

Australian Lamb
HAVE YOU HAD YOURS THIS WEEK?
MEAT & LIVESTOCK AUSTRALIA

America has declared war on our lamb producers. Use these weapons to defend them.

President Clinton's tariffs on Australian lamb come into effect today. They are clearly unfair. Our farmers won their share of the US market with a better product at better value; but it seems 'fair go' doesn't mean much to the Americans. We can't reverse the US decision but we can do something to help the producers of our tender lamb through tough times. If every one of us has just one more lamb meal a week we can guarantee a future for an industry that's the backbone of Australia. Chops, racks, roasts, curries; one more lamb meal a week is all it takes. And with the most flavoursome lamb in the world now in your butcher and supermarket, it's not what you'd call a sacrifice.

Australian Lamb
HAVE YOU HAD YOURS THIS WEEK?
MEAT & LIVESTOCK AUSTRALIA

A teenage boy has brought his Goth girl friend home for dinner. His mum enters and sets down a plate of lamb chops before her.

MUM: *We've been so looking forward to meeting you.*

The Goth girl stares at her plate.

MUM: *It's lamb.*

THE GOTH GIRL: *I'm vegetarian.*

For a moment the tension is palpable. The father and mother are speechless.

Their son suddenly grins and breaks the silence.

BOY: *No worries.*

He grabs his girl friend's plate, scrapes her lamb chops onto his, and returns her just the vegies.

END VO: *We love our Lamb. It's the flavour of Australia.*

The corner butcher is setting trays of fresh lamb in his window. Suddenly he looks up.

He grins when he recognises a dog with its nose pressed against the glass eyeing the meat.

BUTCHER: *You again. It's for Mother's Day.*

Suddenly he stares in disbelief. We cut to his point of view. Lots of puppies are crowded around their mother, all staring in at his lamb.

END VO: *We love our Lamb on Mother's Day.*

MAKING PEOPLE SAY CHEESE MORE OFTEN
MAKING PEOPLE SAY CHEESE MORE OFTEN
MAKING PEOPLE SAY CHEESE MORE OFTEN

MAKING PEOPLE SAY CHEESE MORE OFTEN

NG PEOPLE SAY CHEESE MORE OFTEN
MAKING PEOPLE SAY CHEESE MORE OFTEN
MAKING PEOPLE SAY CHEESE MORE OFTEN

the problem Cheese consumption in New Zealand took a 19% dive — from 31,000 tonnes in 1987 to 25,000 tonnes in 1992. At the same time, the Dairy Board was being shut out of overseas markets. In order to maintain acceptable returns to dairy farmers, domestic cheese consumption had to be stimulated. New Zealand Cheese Promotions was established with one mission: increase domestic cheese consumption by 10,000 tonnes in five years — a lift of 40%.

The odds against succeeding were enormous. There was no ready source of new customers. Cheese was already found in 96% of all New Zealand homes; those without it were Asian and Polynesian families traditionally averse to dairy products. 90% of all people aged 10 and over ate cheese every week, with an annual per capita consumption of 7.1 kg, and the vast majority of New Zealanders (85%) already knew cheese was an essential food item. There were no health problems associated with cheese — although it contained fat, it was perceived as a naturally healthy product rich in calcium and protein. Nor was price a factor. Cheese was regarded as an economical food, and cheese prices were on par with overall food price fluctuations.

There were no gains to be made from distribution; cheese was already in every supermarket and corner store. However, cheese manufacturers, who had control over all elements of the marketing mix, and whose support was critical, had little faith in generic cheese promotion.

The core problem was that other foods had overtaken cheese. While cheese had stayed pretty much the same, other foods had become more innovative, more dynamic and more contemporary. New Zealanders had more choices: non-traditional foods like pasta, prepared foods like Chicken Tonight, convenience microwavable foods, ethnic foods like Mexican and Thai, not to mention a revolution in snack foods and more eating-out options.

Cheese was boring and too back-of-mind. Consumer feedback was negative: "Cheese is just cheese", "It's a means to an end", "The unexciting yellow brick", and "It's just part of the fridge". And while they still bought cheese, they were buying less of it while other foods attracted more of the weekly grocery dollar. It was a trend that was likely to worsen.

the strategy The task was to get New Zealanders to take another look at cheese. Drilling into the research, people still had positive things to say. Cheese was perceived as a tasty, versatile, naturally healthy product that everyone enjoyed, offered good value and was economical. But if the advertising merely reinforced what people already thought, it would not deliver the scale of growth required.

Cheese had to be shifted from the back of people's minds to the front by making it more compelling. Cheese needed a powerful personality so people would feel better about it — and feel like eating more of it more often.

The creative breakthrough came by taking an everyday expression used whenever mum took the family photos and wanted people to smile: "say cheese". From there, the campaign theme was developed: *If you want to make 'em smile, Say Cheese.* From being the boring yellow brick, cheese could evolve into the food that made people light up with a big cheesy grin.

the result From 1992 to 1997, the market volume of cheese sold domestically increased by a massive 30%, well on the way to achieving the targeted increase of 40%. Natural block cheese rose 70% in market volume, processed cheese by 19% and specialty cheeses by 11%, reported Pricewaterhouse and AC Nielsen.

The total value of retail and wholesale cheese sales increased in four years by a massive 32%. According to Statistics New Zealand, the price of cheese remained stable throughout that period and did not deviate significantly from the overall Food Price Index.

New Zealanders were eating more cheese. Pricewaterhouse reported that per capita consumption had been lifted by 31% in four years — from 7.1 kg in 1992 to 9.3 kg in 1996. This represented growth in the domestic market from 25,000 tonnes pre-campaign to 32,500 tonnes post-campaign.

There was good news for dairy farmers: the increase in the domestic market had delivered an additional US$25 million to the dairy industry.

The *Say Cheese* campaign displayed a consistently strong market presence over the four years from 1993, delivering a level of cut-through well in excess of its relative spend. The cost of maintaining the campaign became cheaper and more efficient as time went by.

The consumer mindset had changed. CM Research indicated 38% of consumers now "felt better" about cheese. MRL Research reported the preference for cheese as a food increased from 82% to 95%, with cheese rising from 6th to 4th place in terms of the most essential food, outranking eggs, meat and butter.

Retailers endorsed the campaign, pointing out that cheese was doing "really well" and "we are now making more money out of cheese than we used to". Supermarkets saw cheese as a more profitable category worthy of investment in more chiller space.

The campaign rose into the realm of social currency. It was repeatedly hijacked beyond the advertising context by TV comedians, cartoonists and magazine columnists.

With New Zealand Cheese Promotions having no control over product, no say over distribution and no influence over pricing, success had rested entirely on the advertising to change consumer behaviour.

❞❞

We were highly optimistic when we set the growth targets for domestic consumption. The *Say Cheese* campaign has well and truly exceeded our wildest expectations."

CHRIS MOLLER, formerly Group General Manager,
Finance & Corporate Development, New Zealand Dairy Board

MAKING PEOPLE SAY CHEESE MORE OFTEN
MAKING PEOPLE SAY CHEESE MORE OFTEN
MAKING PEOPLE SAY CHEESE MORE OFTEN
MAKING PEOPLE SAY CHEESE MORE OFTEN
MAKING PEOPLE SAY CHEESE MORE OFTEN
MAKING PEOPLE SAY CHEESE MORE OFTEN
MAKING PEOPLE SAY CHEESE MORE OFTEN

Open on tight close-up of a French chef who reacts to the VO's requests with mounting distaste...

vo: *Say "English cooking".*

French chef: *English cooking.*

vo: *Say "Well done steak".*

French chef: *Well done steak.*

vo: *Say "Spanish champagne".*

French chef (almost choking on the words): *Spanish champagne.*

vo: *Say "Cheese".*

The chef breaks out into a grin.

French chef: *Cheese...*

chorus over animated title: *If you want to make 'em smile, Say Cheese...*

Cut to beaming chef sniffing a platter of cheeses.

Open on tight close-up of a little girl. The VO's requests get an increasingly sour response…

VO: *Say "Snail dumplings".*

LITTLE GIRL: *Snail dumplings.*

VO: *Say "Spider stew".*

LITTLE GIRL: *Spider stew.*

VO: *Say "Slug soup".*

LITTLE GIRL: *Slug soup.*

VO: *Say "Cheese".*

The little girl breaks into a big, cheesy, toothless grin.

LITTLE GIRL: *Cheese…*

CHORUS WITH ANIMATED TITLE: *If you want to make 'em smile, Say Cheese…*

Cut to little girl eating gooey cheese savouries.

A topical twist to the campaign idea, capitalising on New Zealand's defeat at the hands of the Australian Wallabies led by skipper David Campese.

Open on close-up of a rather distressed-looking New Zealand footballer. He gets even more distressed as the VO continues...

VO: *Say "David Campese".*

FOOTBALLER (RELUCTANTLY): *David Campese.*

VO: *Say "We lost".*

FOOTBALLER: *We lost.*

VO: *Say "World champion Wallabies".*

The footballer refuses and remains silent.

VO: *Say "Cheese".*

The footballer's face lights up.

FOOTBALLER: *Cheese...*

CHORUS WITH ANIMATED TITLE: *If you want to make 'em smile, Say Cheese...*

Footballer bites into a huge bun with cheese.

Open on game show hostess. She listens intently to the VO, gradually becoming more confused as he continues...

VO: *Lana, say "I'm absolutely sick and tired of being thought of as just some pretty-faced game show hostess because what I really want is to pursue a more serious career in television".*

LANA (FROWNING): *Is there an A in that?*

VO: *Say "Cheese".*

LANA: *Cheese...*

CHORUS WITH ANIMATED TITLE: *If you want to make 'em smile, Say Cheese...*

Lana happily eating an open cheese sandwich.

category FOOD, CONFECTIONERY

countries THAILAND

advertiser NONG PHO MILK

agency BBDO BANGKOK LIMITED

FINDING A STRONGER BENEFIT
FINDING A STRONGER BENEFIT
FINDING A STRONGER BENEFIT
FINDING A STRONGER BENEFIT

FINDING A STRONGER BENEFIT

FINDING A STRONGER BENEFIT
FINDING A STRONGER BENEFIT
FINDING A STRONGER BENEFIT
FINDING A STRONGER BENEFIT

the problem Nong Pho had less than 10% share of the milk market. Bigger brands bombarded consumers with messages that milk helped kids grow taller. Other high calcium milks hammered the generic benefit of strong bones. If the Nong Pho brand were to grow, it had to find a point of difference. Or was there nothing new left to say?

the strategy One benefit that milk advertising had not addressed before was building stronger teeth. In addition, research from the Health Department revealed that oral diseases were a major concern for the authorities.

Nong Pho high calcium milk used strong teeth as its separator. Print and television executions focused on a row of glasses filled with milk and shot on a black background, replicating a row of perfectly healthy teeth. The message was stark and simple. Drink more Nong Pho, or else.

the result After the launch of the new advertising, Nong Pho's market share went up from 9% to 16% and is still growing.

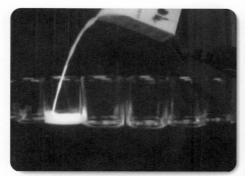

Eight empty glasses are lined up against a black backdrop. Milk is poured into three of them and we begin to see that the glasses have been arranged like a row of teeth.

The other glasses are left empty, conveying the impression of missing teeth.

MALE VO: *These are your kids' teeth if they don't get enough calcium.*

The remaining glasses are now filled so they replicate a row of perfectly healthy teeth.

MALE VO: *For stronger teeth, drink more milk.*

END PACK SHOT: *Nong Pho High Calcium Milk.*

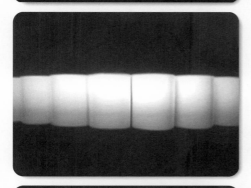

| category | countries | advertiser | agency |
| FOOD, CONFECTIONERY | AUSTRALIA | PILLSBURY/ HÄAGEN-DAZS | LEO BURNETT CONNAGHAN & MAY, MELBOURNE |

REINVENTING SENSUALITY

REINVENTING SENSUALITY   REINVENTING SENSUALITY   REINVENTING SENSUALITY

REINVENTING SENSUALITY

REINVENTING SENSUALITY   REINVENTING SENSUALITY   REINVENTING SENSUALITY

REINVENTING SENSUALITY   REINVENTING SENSUALITY

the problem Australia is the world's third biggest ice cream market. Through its Häagen-Dazs brand, Pillsbury wanted to become leader in the super-premium ice cream segment.

The agency was given the global strategy and brand essence. At its core, Häagen-Dazs stands for sensuality, a brand so indulgent, so satisfying, so exceptional, that the only experience comparable to eating it is a sexual one. The brand's international advertising presented Häagen-Dazs as part of a couple's sexual experience — with the ice cream precipitating the ultimate sexual moment.

All well and good, except that by 1999 a plethora of super-premium ice cream brands had already crowded the segment in Australia, each claiming to deliver the ultimate ice cream experience and many copying the Häagen-Dazs formula wholesale. Australian consumers had been exposed to dozens of cavorting couples in sex-and-ice-cream scenarios. In fact, sensuality and sexuality didn't easily impress young Australian adults, the prime initial prospects. Being advertising savvy, they viewed commercials critically and demanded to be engaged, entertained and inspired. Their sentiment rang the alarm bells in focus groups.

How then could Häagen-Dazs — at *twice* the price of its well-entrenched competitors and with very little money — create a cachet for itself that made the brand seem not just special, but *extraordinary*?

the strategy The agency knew that sensuality and sexuality had to be given a new, unexpected treatment. Literally executing the Häagen-Dazs "Couples" theme would not elevate the brand. Nor would it surprise and intrigue the cynical target audience. The brief had to be reinterpreted. Sexuality had to be reframed.

A new strategy took Häagen-Dazs beyond the category and into the realm of fashion. The concept combined body sculpture with cutting edge photographic art. The artistic look, and not blatant sexuality, gave the brand an identity and point of difference that was fresh and relevant for the times.

The agency worked with American photographer Howard Schatz to shoot and "colourise" bodies that put a new slant on sensuality. The radical colouration process communicated the brand's unique flavours. Ad layouts were kept as simple and focused as possible, replicating the feel of "hung" art.

the result Despite significant competition and a huge price premium, the turn rate per store has been twice that of the international average. The brand has achieved 12.3% market share in Victoria, the Australian state where distribution has been highest.

Recently, distribution has been further strengthened.

REINVENTING SENSUALITY
REINVENTING SENSUALITY   REINVENTING SENSUALITY   REINVENTING SENSUALITY
REINVENTING SENSUALITY
REINVENTING SENSUALITY   REINVENTING SENSUALITY   REINVENTING SENSUALITY
REINVENTING SENSUALITY   REINVENTING SENSUALITY

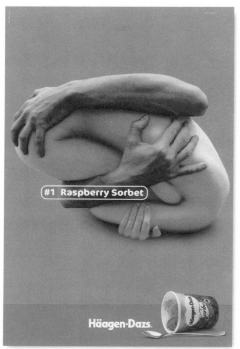

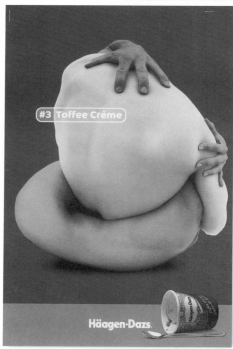

CREATING A GENERATION
CREATING A GENERATION CREATING A GENERATION CREATING A GENERATION

CREATING A GENERATION

CREATING A GENERATION CREATING A GENERATION CREATING A GENERATION
CREATING A GENERATION
CREATING A GENERATION

the problem Wrigley's Doublemint dominated the chewing gum market. With a very limited budget, how could a new brand put itself on the map?

the strategy Ideology defied the advertising conventions in the category and disregarded the grammar of commercial filmmaking. The context of chewing gum was redefined. Stimorol developed a new advertising "language" to challenge the leading brand.

The campaign reached out to the younger generation and echoed their voices within each execution.

the result Over the years, with an adspend averaging only 11% of Doublemint's budget, Stimorol at its height had 20% share of the market. (For example, in the Rainmaker 1998 Ad Spend Ranking by Product, Doublemint spent US$1.9 million compared to Stimorol's US$328,702.)

The Stimorol campaign has bred a so-called "Stimorol Generation" in Taiwan, much as MTV and the Internet have done around the world. Many Stimorol commercials, even those aired years ago, have become cult videos. The campaign's impact has become a cultural issue, frequently debated by scholars and researchers in the fields of mass communications and cultural studies.

The Stimorol project is generally considered one of the most successful local advertising campaigns created in Taiwan.

Old typewriter keys are pounding out letters. We soon realise we are seeing the same words, repeated endlessly:

Green is beautiful. Green is beautiful.

A tribal song is heard through the clatter of the typewriter. A shot of a street in a mountain village. Two naked children race into a barren field.

The typewriter continues its mission: *Green is beautiful. Green is beautiful.*

The screen is a sea of black-and-white words on which are two pellets of Stimorol, also monochromatic.

The typewriter is on a road. Paper streams out of it into the distance.

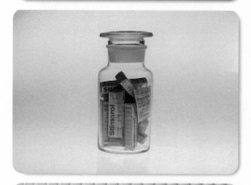

The commercial is titled: *The Drug.*

Paper clips, capsules and pellets of Stimorol gum are juxtaposed and mixed, a surreal cocktail that melts on a spoon.

Bizarre, uptempo music becomes more and more frenzied.

A juggler performs outside a featureless modern building.

We see Stimorol in a jar.

vo: *Legal to use in a public place. Stimorol.*

Scenarios of beautiful young males, fresh faced and innocent, like members of a boy band.

They are garbed in Elizabethan costumes with elegant wigs, seated astride motor cycles, reclining on lounges, reading books, holding a violin.

MALE VO IN ENGLISH: *Right men in the wrong place.*

One young male regards us with interest from a bed of Stimorol.

As the commercial ends, another young male is wrapping himself in cloth.

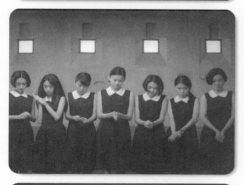

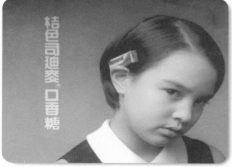

Stark shots of crying children.

Schoolgirls hold out their hands for caning.

Bizarre sketches of children being hit with rulers.

One girl has a bleeding nose.

Girls study their hands.

SCHOOLGIRL VO: *Excuse me, Mr. Minister, could you please tell me which hand cream works better?*

Another girl rebels, wearing a pack of Stimorol behind her ear like a cigarette.

Men and women with black-and-white hair and minimalist costumes parade with their perfumes.

The visuals imply androgyny.

Everyone moves with languid yet carefully choreographed precision, spraying perfume and sniffing their wrists.

MALE VO: *What perfume are you wearing?*

FEMALE VO: *Stimorol.*

One girl chews Stimorol.

FEMALE VOCAL: *What are you wearing now?*

category	countries	advertiser	agency
FOOD, CONFECTIONERY	SINGAPORE	TOBLERONE	DENTSU YOUNG & RUBICAM, SINGAPORE

LOW BUDGET LAUNCH LOW BUDGET LAUNCH LOW BUDGET LAUNCH
LOW BUDGET LAUNCH **LOW BUDGET LAUNCH** LOW BUDGET LAUNCH
LOW BUDGET LAUNCH LOW BUDGET LAUNCH
LOW BUDGET LAUNCH
LOW BUDGET LAUNCH

the problem Introduce a product variation — dark chocolate — on a very restricted budget.

the strategy Toblerone Blue faced an uphill battle. The budget could only afford colour magazines and bus shelters. Everything hinged on the creative work extending the impact of the advertising.

The brand was famous for its distinctive shape. That shape, married with the colour blue, became the basis for the creative idea. Chickens, dinosaurs, ostriches, camels, and other creatures were cast in the role of the villain. *Who ate my Toblerone Blue?* was the question. The easily recognisable Toblerone shape and the colour blue betrayed the guilty party. The new product was contained within a blue frame.

the result The successful introduction was completed well ahead of budget.

category	countries	advertiser	agency
FOOD, CONFECTIONERY	HONG KONG	WINNER FOOD PRODUCTS/ DOLL BOWL NOODLE	EURO RSCG PARTNERSHIP, HONG KONG

RELAUNCHING THE NOODLE RELAUNCHING THE NOODLE

RELAUNCHING THE NOODLE

RELAUNCHING THE NOODLE

AUNCHING THE NOODLE   RELAUNCHING THE NOODLE   RELAUNCHING THE NOODLE
RELAUNCHING THE NOODLE   RELAUNCHING THE NOODLE

the problem Doll brand was the first instant noodle launched in Hong Kong in the 1960s. It had become the generic. In 1983, new packaging — the instant bowl noodle — was developed to combat increasing competition from Japanese brand Nissin Cup Noodle. In 1999, two new Japanese-flavoured soup bases were created to expand Doll Bowl Noodle's market share in the youth segment.

the strategy The Japanese flavours catered to the trendy young Hong Kong audience that appreciated most things Japanese — music, pop culture, fashion and food. The target youths understood that slurping is the traditional way a Japanese eats his noodles — the more he slurps, the tastier the noodle!

Most advertising shows either what happens with the product or what happens without the product, and in the case of Doll, the importance of slurping provided the creative breakthrough. What if the product was so good, so tasty, so slurpable, that it left a permanent trademark — incredibly extended lips!

A 20-second TV commercial spearheaded point-of-sale posters, Floor Vision in selected supermarkets and in-store tasting. Special price reductions were offered during the trial period.

the result The slurping visual generated high awareness among the target youth. Sales data is confidential.

A young couple are embracing in a Laundromat, their backs towards us. Only when they turn do we see their weirdly extended lips. Strange music throughout.

Cut to two girls on a beach, their lips jutting forward from their faces.

Cut to schoolchildren, their lips permanently locked in a sucking motion.

Cut to a young man in a shower, his prominent lips angled at camera.

Cut to a boxer recoiling from a savage punch. His lips poke out like a snout.

VO AND SUPER: *It's so delicious, don't tell me you haven't tried it!*

Finish on product shot establishing the new Doll Bowl Noodle packs.

SUPER: *Slurp...*

VO: *The brand new Doll Bowl Noodle.*

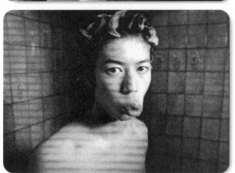

It's so delicius, don't tell me you haven't tried it!

NIPPON PAINT   NIPPON PAINT   NIPPON PAINT   NIPPON PAINT   NIPPON PAINT   NIPPON PAINT   NIPPON PAINT

HOME IMPROVEMENT AND DECORATION

NIPPON PAINT   NIPPON PAINT   NIPPON PAINT   NIPPON PAINT   NIPPON PAINT   NIPPON PAINT   NIPPON PAINT

Home Improvement AndDecoration

LEADERSHIP was once founded on product efficacy. Today, given swift imitation and severe price pressure, brands have to connect at a variety of levels. Defensive strategies are never a serious option; it is far wiser to seize a more positive opportunity to build brand equity, then aim for the jugular.

NIPPON PAINT: BUILDING A BRAND BY BONDING WITH A NATION

NIPPON PAINT: BUILDING A BRAND BY BONDING WITH A NATION

NIPPON PAINT:
NIPPON PAINT: BUILDING A BRAND BY BONDING WITH A NATION

BUILDING A BRAND BY BONDING WITH A NATION

NIPPON PAINT: BUILDING A BRAND BY BONDING WITH A NATION

PPON PAINT: BUILDING A BRAND BY BONDING WITH A NATION

NIPPON PAINT: BUILDING A BRAND BY BONDING WITH A NATION

the problem China presented a special challenge for Nippon Paint. Scores of low-priced, locally made paints dominated the market. Nippon Paint was going to be the first international brand to compete against them.

First, the worldwide slogan, *Working beautifully everywhere*, had to be translated into Chinese. Like so many English slogans, it was impossible to translate literally, word-for-word. Clearly, the proposition had to capture the essence of the English original, while resonating with Chinese consumers. The line 处处放光彩 (*Chùchù fàng guāngcǎi*) conveyed an evocative message to the people of China — "radiance bursts forth everywhere".

The brand was launched on television. The first commercial depicted Nippon Paint painting things that are part of people's lives, everything from toys to cars to oil rigs and buildings. A second commercial showed Nippon Paint protecting famous icons around the world like the Sydney Opera House, the Taj Mahal and the Great Wall of China. Progress was made, and even traditional rival ICI Paints remained a relatively small player in China.

After addressing city dwellers, Nippon Paint's strategy was to bond with the heartland of China. Was there a way to show how Nippon Paint touched the lives of people around China by adding even more colour and beauty to the already beautiful surroundings?

the strategy The idea was to paint the *impossible* places in China. Nippon Paint would be seen performing miracles in the poorest, most remote parts of China, improving the quality of life wherever it went. The premise was that if Nippon Paint could paint a rustic environment, what more a city environment. Production values had to stress authenticity.

Mongolia was chosen as the shoot venue because of the simplicity of people's lifestyles, the natural beauty of the countryside, and the rustic houses made of mud. Nippon Paint sponsored the painting and repair of an entire village of 45 houses. All the paint along with teams of carpenters and painters were brought hundreds of miles from Beijing. In fact, a special paint was formulated for use on mud walls; even the paint colours were specially developed to reflect ethnic fabrics and costumes.

The actual villagers, their wives and children were the talent. The choice of indigenous people and not actors stemmed from Nippon Paint's positioning to be part of the lives of the people of China from the most insignificant village to the biggest city.

Beautiful natural cinematography recorded the natural beauty of the paint against a spectacular landscape. Little post-production work was used. It was a case of real people, real houses, real paint.

The music was authentic in every detail. The chanting of the Mongolian A-B-C was recorded in the village classroom. A small German orchestra that specialised in Mongolian music played the emotive Mongolian melody, *Tal Nutag*.

the result The commercial became an overnight sensation. It turned an already well-known brand into a well-liked one, extending not merely the breadth of awareness but more importantly the *depth*.

The Mongolian commercial also ran in Singapore and Thailand, a country that boasts many ethnic communities of its own.

Four years after its first screening, the Mongolian commercial still registers high recall and affection for the brand.

The Mongolian music became so popular that music teachers used it as a classroom piece for students. In Singapore, CDs of the track were given away to Nippon Paint customers.

"

This case demonstrates how Asian consumers think in terms of brands and not in terms of individual paint products. Nippon Paint has built its sales in China largely with corporate branding, and of course, other marketing initiatives — a wonderful departure from expectations of building sales with product efficacy communications. It also demonstrates the power of television as it was the major communications vehicle to build the brand in China."

PATRICIA CHUI, Managing Director,
Bentley Porter Novelli Communications Singapore

The commercial opens in the classroom of a small, remote Mongolian village. Children are singing their *A-B-C*.

A cartload of Nippon Paint arrives in town and immediately becomes the centre of attention.

Soon the villagers are helping each other transform their drab village into a vibrant outpost of colour.

category   country   advertiser   agency

BRANDT GROUP ASIA/THOMSON WASHING MACHINES SAMSUNG TOSHIBA KELON GROUP/RONGSHENG REFRIGERATORS

SAMSUNG KELON GROUP/RONGSHENG REFRIGERATORS BRANDT GROUP ASIA/THOMSON WASHING MACHINES

TOSHIBA HOUSEHOLD EQUIPMENT AND APPLIANCES

DT GROUP ASIA/THOMSON WASHING MACHINES TOSHIBA KELON GROUP/RONGSHENG REFRIGERATORS

SAMSUNG KELON GROUP/RONGSHENG REFRIGERATORS SAMSUNG TOSHIBA

Household Equipment AndAppliances

WHITE goods brands targeting Asia-Pacific consumers have to come to terms with a different market — and a new mindset. Consumer expectations are redefining the ground rules. The language of the category has changed, too. Once advertising messages were based solely on the hardware. Naturally, individual product benefits are still important, but not necessarily in media communications. Brands need to convey a more holistic picture of themselves. Consumers appear to respond more to communications that surprise and reward them.

DOING THE WASHING IN PUBLIC
DOING THE WASHING IN PUBLIC   DOING THE WASHING IN PUBLIC

DOING THE WASHING IN PUBLIC

DOING THE WASHING IN PUBLIC
DOING THE WASHING IN PUBLIC   DOING THE WASHING IN PUBLIC
DOING THE WASHING IN PUBLIC   DOING THE WASHING IN PUBLIC

the problem Singaporeans buy 110,000 washing machines every year. Japanese washers dominate with 70% of the market; European drum-type washers hold the balance.

Thomson has been in Singapore for 24 years. It was the first brand to introduce top-load European drum-type washing machines that sell on average for US$480, twice the price of Japanese washers. Until 1994, Thomson remained the only brand to develop this new niche market.

Once the first signs of success were on the board, competition arrived. Over eight brands struggled for control of the top-load European drum-type category, including traditional rivals Whirlpool, Electrolux and Ariston. By 1997, Thomson's market share had shrunk from 100% to 34%.

the strategy Thomson set out to reclaim market leadership.

First, it changed its sales operation. For many years, Thomson dealers were not required to make monthly or yearly stock commitments. They could fax their orders as and when they made their sales. Thomson would then do the end delivery and installation, collect the cheque from the customer, and reimburse the retailer's margin on a monthly basis. The system had worked well in the past. Thomson could monitor selling prices, as well as build up a complete database of customers.

However, dealers were prone to temptation. Competitors offered quantity discounts if they committed to more units at one shot. As a result, dealers soon became tied down with competitive brands and were obliged to promote them in order to clear stocks and earn back their investment.

Thomson modified its system, retaining the benefits of the old (direct delivery and price monitoring) as well as introducing a new system of dealer commitment. Thomson also embarked on a very aggressive marketing strategy themed "innovation and quality", producing its own point-of-sale material, direct mailings to customers, and special loyalty programmes.

As Thomson clawed back its marketing leadership, it also claimed leadership in brand communications. It was the first advertiser in Singapore to use a 3D taxi top, and certainly the first in the world to demonstrate washing clothes from moving cabs.

The taxi top was structured with a three-dimensional aquarium-like tank, in which a pair of delicate "knickers" was gently washed as the taxi made its way through the streets of Singapore. The rhythm created by the moving vehicle replicated the washing action of the Thomson washer. Repeated tests were made to ensure that the quality of the taxi top lived up to the washer. Even the fabric for the floral "French knickers" had to be specially imported — from Germany, as it turned out. It was cut into a rectangle, secured with glue on two ends, with the middle of the fabric left lax.

The tops first appeared on 50 Comfort taxis in January 1999. Within six months another 50 were on the road, and more followed. The taxi top became the talk of the town and ran for two years.

the result Thomson's market share of top-load European drum-type washers reached 62% in 1999, due to the combination of taxi tops, a revamped sales system and intensive marketing measures.

With those results in hand, Thomson was able to focus on its sister brand, Brandt. Together, Thomson and Brandt have achieved 74% market share in their category.

DOING THE WASHING IN PUBLIC
DOING THE WASHING IN PUBLIC   DOING THE WASHING IN PUBLIC
DOING THE WASHING IN PUBLIC
DOING THE WASHING IN PUBLIC   DOING THE WASHING IN PUBLIC   DOING THE WASHING IN PUBLIC
              DOING THE WASHING IN PUBLIC   DOING THE WASHING IN PUBLIC

category
**HOUSEHOLD
EQUIPMENT
AND APPLIANCES**

countries
CHINA

advertiser
**KELON GROUP/
RONGSHENG
REFRIGERATORS**

agency
**McCANN-ERICKSON
GUANGMING LTD,
GUANGZHOU**

BRINGING MEMORIES TO LIFE

BRINGING MEMORIES TO LIFE
BRINGING MEMORIES TO LIFE

BRINGING MEMORIES TO LIFE

BRINGING MEMORIES TO LIFE   BRINGING MEMORIES TO LIFE   BRINGING MEMORIES TO LIFE
BRINGING MEMORIES TO LIFE

the problem The Kelon Group is China's largest refrigeration appliances manufacturer, with over 10,000 employees and assets of US$940 million. The 1998 merger with Huabao consolidated the group's market leadership. *Forbes* listed it as one of the top 300 companies in the world in 1999, while in the same year *Asian Money* cited Kelon as the Best Managed Company in China.

Since 1985 Kelon has promoted total quality control. ISO certification followed in 1997, along with the World Economic Forum award as East Asia's Largest Worldwide Economic Growth Corporation. In 1999, Kelon and Rongsheng were both awarded as "China Famous Brands", the Kelon Group becoming the first Chinese enterprise to possess two "China Famous Brands" at the same time.

Leveraging such success in consumer terms called for a fresh strategy. How could Kelon reposition Rongsheng not merely as a famous brand — but the brand most *preferred* by consumers?

the strategy The perception that Rongsheng refrigerators represented high quality was well established. The issue was how to communicate the quality proposition in a way with which Chinese consumers could relate.

The agency applied storytelling principles. One woman's life experience, seen through the eyes of her son, demonstrated the trusted role of Rongsheng in the lives of the people of China and provided an emotional connection with consumers.

the result The commercial contributed to the Kelon Group's market leadership — its turnover reached US$984 million in 1999, an increase of 24% over 1998.

It also established the brand's value in the market. Rongsheng is now rated as one of China's Top 10 most valuable brands. Its brand value was worth over US$620 million in 2000.

In recent studies by DRC (Development Research Centre of The State

Council), SIC (State Information Centre) and other related organisations, Rongsheng ranked number one in terms of unaided awareness, aided awareness, market penetration and intention to purchase within five years.

BRINGING MEMORIES TO LIFE
BRINGING MEMORIES TO LIFE   BRINGING MEMORIES TO LIFE

BRINGING MEMORIES TO LIFE

BRINGING MEMORIES TO LIFE   BRINGING MEMORIES TO LIFE   BRINGING MEMORIES TO LIFE

BRINGING MEMORIES TO LIFE

Open on a flashback: a young woman watches an early model Rongsheng refrigerator being hoisted up a stairwell on ropes.

A MAN'S VOICE NARRATES: *When the first refrigerator was bought, Mom was young.*

We see our narrator as a boy, placing a dish of water in the fridge and later pulling out ice which he holds up to the light.

VO: *I was fascinated by this cabinet which could make ice.*

Now he has grown up and he rides in a truck with his grey-haired Mom and the family's possessions. A modern skyline towers behind them.

VO: *Many years passed and our family moved many times. Mom became older. The refrigerator became our oldest possession. One day, I don't know when, I suddenly found that Mom was just like this old refrigerator that had given us so much.*

He visits the Rongsheng showroom, returning home to find his Mother picking up vegetables which had fallen out of the cramped old fridge.

VO: *I tried to persuade Mom to change to a new one but she refused.*

Then the son gets married.

VO: *The old one didn't leave us but the new one still came.*

His mother stares in wonderment at her new fridge. A note on it says, "Mom, this's for you!"

VO: *That moment, Mom seemed young again.*

ENDLINE: *Life changes, but the quality of Rongsheng remains the same.*

category	countries	advertiser	agency
HOUSEHOLD EQUIPMENT AND APPLIANCES	THAILAND	SAMSUNG	DENTSU YOUNG & RUBICAM, THAILAND

REBUILDING AN IMAGE
REBUILDING AN IMAGE   REBUILDING AN IMAGE

REBUILDING AN IMAGE

REBUILDING AN IMAGE   REBUILDING AN IMAGE   REBUILDING AN IMAGE
REBUILDING AN IMAGE

the problem As far as Thai homemakers were concerned, Korean appliance brands were perceived as "cheap" vis-à-vis their Japanese competitors. Samsung was no exception. The brand had no discernible personality.

In fact, with little to differentiate one brand from another, price and promotion strategies called the tune.

the strategy One group of Thai consumers appeared to offer fertile ground for Samsung brand building. The "aspirers", aged 23-35, were starting new families. They were smarter and more demanding than previous generations, had no apparent brand loyalties, and wanted to be seen as fashionable and stylish. However, despite their ambitions, they lacked confidence. How could Samsung revitalise its brand energy to win them over?

Samsung's new strategy defied the category conventions. Samsung would stake out premium status by shifting into a new brand territory — unusually exotic, even bizarre expressions of style with which younger homemakers could identify. But it was not without substantial risk.

For example, Samsung would demonstrate its clothes-washing efficacy through the medium of S&M — a water ballet, with two mistresses whipping the dirt out of a man with water.

Print executions conveyed a similar surreal imagery, challenging the market conventions.

the result Samsung's image improved substantially. Samsung became the number two brand in the market after Sony.

In *Whip*, S&M becomes a metaphor for removing stubborn dirt from clothes.

We see a man in shirt and tie floating and tossing in water, as the garments themselves might do in a washing machine, while two mistresses lash him with whips of water.

Judging by his responses, Samsung's efficacy is only harmful to dirt.

PRODUCT SHOT AND END SUPER: *Samsung. No mercy for dirt.*

category	countries	advertiser	agency
HOUSEHOLD EQUIPMENT AND APPLIANCES	TAIWAN	TOSHIBA	IDEOLOGY ADVERTISING AGENCY LTD, TAIPEI

SURREAL SELL

SURREAL SELL   SURREAL SELL

SURREAL SELL SURREAL SELL

SURREAL SELL   SURREAL SELL SURREAL SELL SURREAL SELL

the problem With a very limited budget vis-à-vis other Japanese appliance makers, Toshiba had to develop a brand identity appealing to Taiwan's trendy urban elite. But the advertising could not be too esoteric — Toshiba demanded measurable, cost-effective sales results and insisted that individual appliances were represented in the campaign.

The agency's task was to conceptualise to a budget, at the same time investing enough in executional values to separate the Toshiba brand and win the support of a highly critical, style savvy target audience.

the strategy Creatively, two decisions were taken: first, that the campaign should feature the potential life style Toshiba offered, but not sell product features per se. And secondly, that the commercials would executionally define Toshiba as a brand reflecting the tastes of the urban elite.

Ideas were kept simple. Each commercial's storyline was minimal. Cinematography, set design and music contributed unique brand language. Overall, the surreal tonality engaged the young homemaking audience and indulged their passion for the unconventional.

the result Toshiba achieved an image distinct from other Japanese appliance brands, enabling Toshiba to consistently promote its premium-priced, higher-margin appliances.

The setting is a surreal Oriental environment wherein a traditionally clad family dances and moves gracefully, fanning themselves and each other. A beautiful Chinese song accompanies their actions.

Their white fans have a special symbolism. Not only do they express coolness, but also the complete absence of any harsh, intrusive noise.

To reinforce this thought, when the fans flutter, streams of little feathers tumble softly out of thin air, much to everyone's amusement.

SUPER: *Patented cooler fan.*

The refreshing aura of coolness is one thing. The ambience of quietness is another.

VO AND SUPER: *Toshiba air conditioning. Reducing noise pollution in our world.*

Called *The Indifference*, this commercial opens in the changing rooms of a women's fashion department.

Elegant young urban women are trying on cool summer fashions.

SNIPPETS OF THEIR CONVERSATIONS:
I wish to buy 10 pairs of sandals.
I want to eat ice cream, it's so hot!

Much to everyone's surprise, a formidable young creature strides purposefully into a change room with a fur coat.

A WOMAN ASKS: *Why purchase a fur coat under these weather conditions? Do you live at the North Pole?*

Summer makes me chilly, she says. She buys it, carrying it home past briefly-clad people sweltering in the summer streets.

She enters her home and falls onto a couch next to her fur-clad companion. Above them we discover Toshiba air conditioning.

SUPER: *Toshiba air conditioning.*

NETEASE   FINATIQ.COM   ASIAONEMARKETS.COM   ADULTSHOP.COM   NETEASE

EPSON   CLP TELECOM/OXYGEN   CLP TELECOM/OXYGEN   CLP TELECOM/OXYGEN   FINATIQ.COM   ADULTSHOP.COM

PChome ONLINE   INFORMATION TECHNOLOGY AND DOT.COMS

ADULTSHOP.COM   ASIAONEMARKETS.COM   EPSON   ASIAONEMARKETS.COM   PChome ONLINE

ASIAONEMARKETS.COM   PChome ONLINE   ADULTSHOP.COM   NETEASE   FINATIQ.COM

Information Technology AndDot.Coms

TEN years ago the category barely existed. Then came the heady days when IT and dot.com brand communications were flavour-of-the-month. The bursting of the dot.com bubble undermined confidence and provided a much-needed reality check. Marketers now have to sharpen their focus on communicating substance. But while the old days of smoke and mirrors have gone, these case studies demonstrate that there is still room for imagination and profitable brand connections.

APPLYING A NEW DISCIPLINE
APPLYING A NEW DISCIPLINE   APPLYING A NEW DISCIPLINE

APPLYING A NEW DISCIPLINE

PPLYING A NEW DISCIPLINE
APPLYING A NEW DISCIPLINE   APPLYING A NEW DISCIPLINE
APPLYING A NEW DISCIPLINE

the problem Adultshop.com is an online retailer of adult products. Its mission was to be recognised as a global leader in adult product distribution. The challenge was to launch a completely new brand in a controversial category.

As the first publicly traded adult product company in Australia, Adultshop required investment support for its business model prior to international expansion. However, mainstream consumer, investor and media groups did not openly accept the category. The business was heavily biased towards males, the competition intense and cluttered, products were sold on price and promotion, and advertising was dominated by small space print ads.

the strategy The client's marketing strategy targeted current user groups, hoping to build market share by focusing on promotional offers in the key product area of videos. It was assumed that advertising would run in adult magazines using sexually provocative images typical of the category.

The agency recommended pursuing an untapped market opportunity. While most people felt uncomfortable walking into a sex shop, it argued, the anonymity of the Internet and a user-friendly site would break down the barriers and encourage a broader audience to purchase adult products. Women, in particular, had never been addressed by the category. In fact, Adultshop could create a new category by becoming the first adult company to directly target a mainstream audience and leverage the non-threatening online environment to create a brand with mainstream positioning. The adultshop.com website would become a totally acceptable place to shop, and appeal to both men and women.

The question was, could an adult shop become a successful, credible mainstream brand simply by acting like one?

The Adultshop proposition was developed to appeal to all adults 18–49. The company was restructured. Adultshop.com became the company's umbrella brand, a user-friendly, non-pornographic website, able to command price premiums, drive innovation and build investor support. An unbranded subsidiary business serviced the heavy user group.

Brand identity began with a custom-designed signature font and a 3D animated logo. Humour replaced sexually explicit images. Adultshop.com print ads splashed witty text messages on distinctive purple backgrounds that intrigued rather than intimidated. Media placements broke new ground, blanketing city streets with supersites, transit shelter posters and bus ads. The open, fun tonality dispelled the negatives surrounding adult product marketing. Adultshop.com became the first brand in the category to have its advertising accepted by mainstream media.

As a result of broad consumer acceptance, adultshop.com pioneered online shopping partnerships, site integration and content sharing. And while mainstream consumers embraced the campaign wit, a cult following carried the logo into tattoo shops. Brand building continued with nightclub sponsorships, event marketing, ambient media, radio, direct response ads and even in recruitment advertising.

the result Despite no pornographic content, adultshop.com has become the number one adult site in Australia and one of the top 10 e-tailing sites in the country. 30% of all customers are female, vis-à-vis the 5% norm for the category. Female products outsell male products 2 to 1.

Banner click-through rates of 12% are five times the industry average.

The site has registered consistent sales revenue growth; a sale campaign generated 120% sales increase.

Following its launch, adultshop.com became the best performing dot.com stock and is on target to turn a profit. International expansion is underway with live sites in the US and Germany.

APPLYING A NEW DISCIPLINE
APPLYING A NEW DISCIPLINE   APPLYING A NEW DISCIPLINE

APPLYING A NEW DISCIPLINE

APPLYING A NEW DISCIPLINE

APPLYING A NEW DISCIPLINE   APPLYING A NEW DISCIPLINE

APPLYING A NEW DISCIPLINE

Our customers always come first.

(Deluxe Vibrators from $59.95)

Shop at our secure website or call to order your free catalogue.
FreeCall **1800 609 000**

adult**shop**.com

Terrible dialogue, third rate acting, and crap story lines.

(Yep, we've got the hottest videos and DVDs)

Shop at our secure website or call to order your free catalogue.
FreeCall **1800 609 000**

adult**shop**.com

Moan, moan, moan. That's all we ever hear from our customers.

adult**shop**.com

category	countries	advertiser	agency
INFORMATION TECHNOLOGY AND DOT.COMS	SINGAPORE	ASIAONE MARKETS.COM	EURO RSCG PARTNERSHIP, SINGAPORE

CREATING A DOT.COM DIFFERENCE
CREATING A DOT.COM DIFFERENCE CREATING A DOT.COM DIFFERENCE

CREATING A DOT.COM DIFFERENCE

CREATING A DOT.COM DIFFERENCE CREATING A DOT.COM DIFFERENCE
CREATING A DOT.COM DIFFERENCE CREATING A DOT.COM DIFFERENCE

the problem When AsiaOneMarkets.com launched in Singapore, the market was congested with dot.com investment sites. Because many of the sites offered similar services, it was the advertising that had to create a difference.

the strategy The campaign was tasked to raise awareness of the new financial and investment website as well as the AsiaOne.com "mother" site, gain more visits and attract more users. Easier said than done.

The original brief was to sell AsiaOneMarkets.com as a source of real-time information from the Singapore, Kuala Lumpur and Hong Kong stock markets.

Somehow, the strategy did not stimulate advertising with a real point of difference. Other concept areas were explored — a stock market game and a campaign that showed how users could get "ridiculously" rich. Eventually, client and agency arrived at an entirely fresh proposition: credible investment information that enables smarter investment decisions. From that point, the creative breakthrough emerged.

The idea of avoiding harebrained investment schemes was simple, different, and highly campaignable. Inherent in the humour was a pertinent universal truth. The ads ran in colour print, supported by interactive media.

the result In the first month of the campaign, visits to the site doubled to over 2 million. As the campaign continued, visits peaked at 3.5 million. Within two and a half months, the site had secured 20,000 registered users.

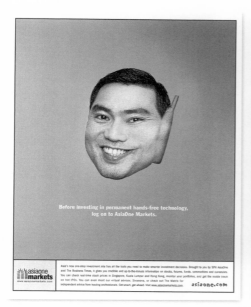

Before investing in permanent hands-free technology,
log on to AsiaOne Markets.

Before investing in the durian cosmetics industry,
log on to asiaonemarkets.com

Before investing in renewable rodent energy,
log on to asiaonemarkets.com

Before investing in angora frog farming,
log on to asiaonemarkets.com

category
INFORMATION
TECHNOLOGY
AND DOT.COMS

countries
HONG KONG

advertiser
CLP TELECOM/
OXYGEN

agency
SAATCHI &
SAATCHI,
HONG KONG

TARGETING PARENTS PAYS
TARGETING PARENTS PAYS
TARGETING PARENTS PAYS

TARGETING PARENTS PAYS

TARGETING PARENTS PAYS
TARGETING PARENTS PAYS   TARGETING PARENTS PAYS
TARGETING PARENTS PAYS

the problem Currently, only 20% of all Hong Kong Internet subscribers are on broadband. The rest are still using dial-up service. Oddly enough, they are aware of broadband's advantages — faster access, shorter download times, greater stability than narrowband, and better viewing of multimedia files. So why the inertia? Many adult subscribers have an inherent fear of technological change. They don't willingly embrace it; in fact, they resist it. The prospect of messy rewiring, disruption to fixed lines and poor customer service are also intimidating. It is easier to adopt a wait-and-see attitude.

Oxygen is the newest retail telecommunication brand in Hong Kong. It was launched by one of Hong Kong's great corporate institutions — China Light and Power (CLP) — a utility company that has been a familiar household name for over a century. As a new entrant to the telecom market, Oxygen has inherited a high level of consumer trust from its association with CLP. In a market dominated by complicated products, confusing service packages and fine print, Oxygen's value proposition is centred on "easy". Every aspect of the brand's service delivery is tailored to live up to this promise.

In the case of broadband, Oxygen is the first to employ ADSL G.lite technology. There is no need for rewiring. Customers are given a plug-and-play modem. They are literally connected to broadband within 10 minutes.

the strategy No matter how easily Oxygen could deliver the technology, customers first had to want it. As the agency strategised, the benefit to the user had to be made bigger than the technology itself.

The trouble was, adults by nature do not like change. They prefer the familiar. Children on the other hand have no fear when it comes to new technology. The strategic breakthrough came through with the insight that Hong Kong parents are competitive. They will do anything to help their children excel. If they thought connection to broadband would stop their children falling behind their friends, they would switch.

It was a case of shifting the goalposts. Suddenly, broadband was all about gaining faster and easier access to education. Parents were targeted with the idea that *Kids can learn faster than 56k*. The execution brought home the message tangibly and dramatically. A little boy in a classroom takes forever to access his "knowledge". A typical computer "Loading" display is located on his forehead. The bar barely moves. By the time he gets his answer, the rest of the school has gone home!

the result Oxygen's 2-month business target was exceeded within seven days of the campaign launch.

TARGETING PARENTS PAYS
TARGETING PARENTS PAYS
TARGETING PARENTS PAYS
TARGETING PARENTS PAYS
TARGETING PARENTS PAYS
TARGETING PARENTS PAYS
TARGETING PARENTS PAYS
TARGETING PARENTS PAYS

We are in a classroom where an unseen teacher is asking questions.

FEMALE TEACHER: *Who's the President of the United States?*

As one, all the kids put up their hands.

ALL: *George Bush.*

All the kids, that is, except one little boy in the front row. Going closer we see that he has a computer "Loading" display on his forehead. The bar is barely moving. He yawns as the teacher moves on to the next question.

TEACHER: *Then who is the President of China?*

ALL: *Jiang Zemin.*

The little boy yawns again, his knowledge still "loading".

TEACHER: *And who is the British Prime Minister?*

ALL: *Tony Blair.*

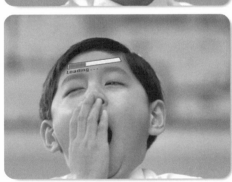

The bell rings and everyone leaves. The chairs are stacked on the desks, the cleaner is sweeping the floor. The little boy is still sitting there. Suddenly the "loading" bar is completed. His hand shoots up.

BOY: *George Bush!*

END SUPERS: *Kids can learn faster than 56K. It's easy with Oxygen Broadband.*

CHILD VO: *Thanks to Oxygen Broadband, it is fast and easy to install, and there's no rewiring. It has never been this easy.*

TEACHER: *Who is the President of Uzbekistan?*

POSITIONING WITH CLARITY
POSITIONING WITH CLARITY   POSITIONING WITH CLARITY
NING WITH CLARITY

POSITIONING WITH CLARITY
POSITIONING WITH CLARITY
POSITIONING WITH CLARITY   POSITIONING WITH CLARITY
POSITIONING WITH CLARITY

the problem Printers had become commodity products. Brands were indistinguishable. Consumers did not understand techno speak and saw little difference between products except price. While Epson had a genuinely superior inkjet printer, it had to communicate that fact to an indifferent, even cynical, audience.

the strategy Print clarity was the single most compelling product advantage. Creatively though, it was a well-worn path. Over the years many printers and colour copiers had demonstrated how their clarity delivered results more "real" than reality. Only a breakthrough demonstration would let Epson own clarity.

A new spin on the subject was needed. Ironically, the masters of "spin" — the CIA — were the answer. Epson was cast as the hero in a series of unconventional television commercials spoofing spy movies. Only Epson's true photographic quality allowed the CIA controllers to grasp the true picture of what their surveillance cameras were picking up.

Each commercial was so faithfully modelled on the genre in terms of scripting, casting and direction that viewers would have been forgiven for thinking they were watching scenes from an actual spy movie.

the result The campaign defined Epson's commanding difference and helped establish Epson as the leader in inkjet printers.

In *CIA I*, CIA controllers in a secret electronic surveillance centre are spying on a man writing.

Their conversation is typical of the genre.

AGENTS: *What's he doing? He's writing something. It looks like a list.*

The surveillance camera zooms in on the list. We can only make out one word, very blurred. It looks like *Hits*.

A CIA MAN, TRIUMPHANTLY: *Gentlemen, that's a hit list. This is going to save lives. If I could read it…*

The team leader smugly gives an order: *Print it…*

The spy camera image is printed on an Epson.

SUPER IN SPY MOVIE LETTERING: *Printing 720 x 720 dpi Hi-Definition.*

MALE VO: *Only an Epson Inkjet has true 720 x 720 dpi for true photographic quality prints.*

The print is taken from the Epson and handed to the team leader. Triumph turns to confusion. It is indeed a hit list — a list of the man's favourite Top 10 songs.

MALE VO: *With Epson Hi-Definition printing, you always get the true picture.*

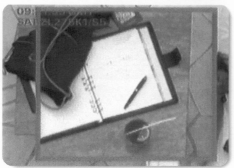

In *CIA II*, the same controllers in the same secret surveillance centre are monitoring one of their female agents. We see her, clad in a bikini, seducing an enemy agent poolside.

AGENT: *She's good. She is the best. I trained her. She's a real professional.*

The spy camera is trained on the table beside her.

AGENT: *There's a message. I can't make it out.*

JACK THE CHIEF CONTROLLER: *Print it.*

The spy camera image is printed on an Epson.

TYPICAL SPY MOVIE SUPER: *Printing 720 x 720 dpi Hi-Definition.*

MALE VO: *Only an Epson Inkjet has true 720 x 720 dpi for true photographic quality prints.*

The print comes out of the Epson and is handed to the chief controller. It is a message from his female agent.

IT SIMPLY SAYS: *Dear Jack, I quit.*

MALE VO: *With Epson Hi-Definition printing you always get the true picture.*

category
INFORMATION
TECHNOLOGY
AND DOT.COMS

countries
SINGAPORE

advertiser
FINATIQ.COM

agency
M&C SAATCHI,
SINGAPORE

LAUNCHING AN INTERNET BANK
LAUNCHING AN INTERNET BANK

LAUNCHING AN INTERNET BANK

LAUNCHING AN INTERNET BANK
LAUNCHING AN INTERNET BANK
LAUNCHING AN INTERNET BANK
LAUNCHING AN INTERNET BANK

the problem Singapore's OCBC Bank launched Asia's first virtual bank in April, 2000. The new stand alone e-bank was called finatiq.com, a derivative of the words "financial" and "IQ".

Targeted at English-educated male and female PMEBs, aged 25–45 years, finatiq.com offered the one site to research, compare and transact all financial matters online. On the surface, the psychographics were good: the target group looked to the Internet for information and entertainment, and had no qualms about transacting online. But while they were comfortable with self-guided help and liked to make informed decisions, they were more Internet savvy than investment savvy. They wanted to take control of their finances, but financial management seemed dull, boring and tedious.

There were other barriers to overcome, too. The business model was complex and the services were incomplete at the launch. The new bank had to be launched through unit trusts, a product still in its infancy in Singapore.

And then there was the name itself — difficult to read, spell, pronounce and remember.

the strategy Given the complexity of the offering and the ambitious launch targets, the campaign was structured in two phases.

The first concentrated single-mindedly on communicating the name and what it stood for, stimulating target customer curiosity to visit the website the day they were made aware of it. Finatiq would have a friendly, rather quirky personality to break the mould of typically straight-laced bricks and mortar banks. (In fact, finatiq's TV commercials made no reference to the OCBC parent.) Getting rich should be fun, so finatiq's name should be launched with an irreverent tonality. The idea was that the letters "f-i-n-a-t-i-q" would be spelt out with a phonetic alphabet, but instead of the usual Foxtrot-India-Norway, the words chosen would be more locally relevant, like Fishball-Is-Nice-And-Tofu-Is-Questionable. The multimedia launch combined television, newspapers and financial magazines, outdoor adshels, posters in strategic business and commercial districts, and Internet banners. The campaign culminated with a contest offering a free unit trust investment.

In phase two, print ads used deliberately large type with bold headlines communicating finatiq's proposition of demystifying finance. Finatiq was positioned as being on the side of the consumer, helping to choose the best deals at the lowest cost, thereby enabling consumers to get rich online. The complexity of messages was lightened through humour and a very approachable executional style. The visibly cleaner layout ensured better standout in newspapers.

the result Within the first two weeks of the launch, finatiq.com received many millions of hits. Positive media coverage was coupled with favourable response from site visitors, not to mention the thousands of people who called with their own versions of what "f–i–n–a–t–i–q" stands for.

Even though the unit trust prize was worth only $1,000, the contest garnered thousands of entries.

Phase two saw fixed deposit account holders increase by 190%. Total deposits surged by over 150%.

"**f**inancial **i**ntelligence **n**ow **a**vailable **t**hrough **i**nternet **q**uickly."

f i n a t i q . c o m

finatIQ

Remembering our name is the only difficult part. Because, believe it or not, we can make managing your finances easy. We'll gladly share our expertise to help you choose the best investments. And we promise to use plain English and common sense. Just don't forget us when you get rich, okay?
finatiq.com. get rich. click here.

famished **i**talians **n**ibble **a**pple **t**arts **i**n **q**uantity.

f i n a t i q . c o m

finatIQ

Remembering our name is the only difficult part. Because, believe it or not, we can make managing your finances easy. We'll gladly share our expertise to help you choose the best investments. And we promise to use plain English and common sense. Just don't forget us when you get rich, okay?
finatiq.com. get rich. click here.

for **i**nspiration **n**eed **a**lcohol **t**onight **i**n **q**uantity.

f i n a t i q . c o m

finatIQ

Remembering our name is the only difficult part. Because, believe it or not, we can make managing your finances easy. We'll gladly share our expertise to help you choose the best investments. And we promise to use plain English and common sense. Just don't forget us when you get rich, okay?
finatiq.com. get rich. click here.

friendship **i**s **n**ot **a** **t**hing **i**mmediately **q**uestioned.

f i n a t i q . c o m

finatIQ

Remembering our name is the only difficult part. Because, believe it or not, we can make managing your finances easy. We'll gladly share our expertise to help you choose the best investments. And we promise to use plain English and common sense. Just don't forget us when you get rich, okay?
finatiq.com. get rich. click here.

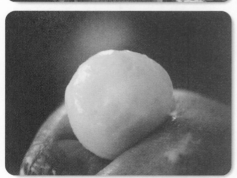

In a typical Singapore hawker centre, a fishball seller is trying to remember the name "finatiq". He recites his phonetic of the letters "f–i–n–a–t–i–q" over and over, much to the annoyance of his neighbour — the tofu man.

FISHBALL SELLER:
Fishball Is Nice And Tofu Is Questionable...

Fishball Is Nice And Tofu Is Questionable...

Fishball Is Nice And Tofu Is Questionable...

Cut to finatiq.com logo.

MALE VO: *Want to get rich online? Just remember our name... finatiq.com.*

END SUPER: *Get rich. Click here.*

category
INFORMATION
TECHNOLOGY
AND DOT.COMS

countries
CHINA

advertiser
NETEASE

agency
SAATCHI &
SAATCHI,
BEIJING

INSPIRING A NATION   INSPIRING A NATION   INSPIRING A NATION

INSPIRING A NATION

INSPIRING A NATION   INSPIRING A NATION   INSPIRING A NATION
INSPIRING A NATION   INSPIRING A NATION

the problem Netease is a Chinese Internet portal. Its ambition was to be seen as China's largest, most successful portal. By adopting a local position of leadership, it could combat the onslaught of international players like Yahoo and AOL.

Credibility was the hurdle. Research by NFO WorldGroup indicated that Chinese Internet users perceived Netease as being not quite up to speed with its bigger, global competitors. Owning leadership would require a more subtle form of communication.

the strategy The key insight emerged in the agency's discussions with the 29-year old founder of Netease, the "Bill Gates" of China. When asked if he was a techie his reply was, "Absolutely not. I am a humanitarian." His view was that there is no power in technology as such because it is constantly changing and adapting; the real power, he believed, came in how the technology was used. By empowering China's 1.2 billion people to use Internet technology properly, the entire country would benefit.

Instead of corporate chest thumping, the agency explored the idea that the power of the Internet is in the hands of the people who use it. How could that intangible notion become a compelling message for China?

Creatively, a series of "What if" scenarios took shape. The lone user of the Net was compared with a single individual attempting to build the Great Wall of China, stone by stone. How could one person play table tennis, or perform a lion dance, or operate a dragon boat? Each scenario had local relevance and brought home the message of empowering the Chinese people to work together.

Production values underscored the brand's leadership, with China's awesome landscapes providing the backdrop to the communication.

the result Prior to the launch of the campaign, Netease was seen as the number three portal in China. Post-advertising, it was ranked as China's leading Internet portal with the highest number of daily page views — averaging

50 million, up 8 million in just three months. Registered users went up by 57%. Brand awareness trebled. Within a month of airing the commercial, 70.3% of all home Internet users in China had visited the Netease site, a 39% increase over the previous month.

INSPIRING A NATION   INSPIRING A NATION   INSPIRING A NATION

INSPIRING A NATION

INSPIRING A NATION   INSPIRING A NATION   INSPIRING A NATION

INSPIRING A NATION   INSPIRING A NATION

要是节日只有一人庆祝？

任何庆祝，只有更多人参与，才能拥有更多的欢乐。网络时代每个人的欢乐都能变成大家的欢乐。因为互联网把所有人联在一起。当所有人同参与，共分享时，12亿人的力量谁可估量？网易致力于推动中国互联网发展。

率先开发出全中文搜索引擎、免费电子邮件系统、网上虚拟社区等先进技术、建造中国互联网的平台。然而若没有数百万人的共同参与，我们又如何创造日均页面浏览量2,400万登记用户590万，聊天室34,000人，同时共用的网人业绩？感谢大家的参与，期盼更多人参与进来，与我们一起共建中国互联网的美好未来。

网易新一代搜索引擎——网聚资讯的动力
这日网易推出新一代搜索引擎。为国内第一家采用开放式目录管理方式，鼓励各界专业人士参与目录编辑，确保搜全搜准。详情登录网易查询。

网聚人的力量

網易 **NETEASE**
www.163.com

• 本记录载止于2002年4月25日

要是面对挑战 都是孤军奋战？

任何挑战，唯有更多同伴支持，才能临危不惧、赢得胜利。网络时代你绝不会再孤军奋战。因为互联网把所有人联在一起。当所有人同参与，共分享时，12亿人的力量谁可估量？网易致力于推动中国互联网发展。率先开发出全中文搜索引擎、免费电子邮件系统、网上虚拟社区等先进技术、建造中国互联网的平台。然而若没有数百万人的共同参与，我们又如何创造日均页面浏览量2,400万登记用户590万，聊天室34,000人，同时共用的网人业绩？感谢大家的参与，期盼更多人参与进来，与我们一起共建中国互联网的美好未来。

网易奥运站点（http://aoyun.163.com）火速开通
网易事献真正互动：人人参与的奥运站点。与全国有线电视联播网携手悉尼，双重互动，有参与、才够high！详情登录网易查询。

网聚人的力量

網易 **NETEASE**
www.163.com

• 本记录载止于2000年6月30日

A lone figure, stooped beneath a heavy burden, climbs through snow-covered peaks. Going in closer, we see it is an old man.

Carefully he places a brick on a solitary tower he has constructed.

vo: *What if the Great Wall of China had been left to just one person?*

The Mongol hordes are drawn up to attack. A canon ball rolls towards them and comes to rest harmlessly at a horse's feet.

vo: *What if gunpowder had been kept a secret?*

A lone man is performing a Chinese lion dance. The empty lion wriggles like a giant worm in the heart of the deserted square.

vo: *What if people were left to celebrate alone?*

A lone girl is playing table tennis by herself in an empty stadium.

vo: *What if ping had no pong?*

A lone dragon boat racer sets down his oars so he can leap up and pound on the drum.

vo: *What if people had to face every challenge on their own?*

The dragon boat is going round in circles on a vast lake.

vo: *Only by helping each other can we be 1.2 billion times stronger. That's the power of the Internet. Netease. Power to the people.*

END WITH NETEASE LOGO AND LINE: *Power to the people.*

category
INFORMATION
TECHNOLOGY
AND DOT.COMS

countries
TAIWAN

advertiser
PChome
ONLINE

agency
IDEOLOGY
ADVERTISING
AGENCY LTD,
TAIPEI

SECURING SUBSCRIBERS   SECURING SUBSCRIBERS   SECURING SUBSCRIBERS

SECURING SUBSCRIBERS **SECURING SUBSCRIBERS** SECURING SUBSCRIBERS

SECURING SUBSCRIBERS   SECURING SUBSCRIBERS

SECURING SUBSCRIBERS

the problem At the time of the campaign, three portals dominated Taiwan — Kimo, Yam and PChome. The goal of PChome was to become the number one portal on all counts — subscribers, traffic and user satisfaction.

the strategy The campaign had to communicate that PChome delivered the richest, most spectacular Internet experience. It concentrated on PChome's most popular features — free e-mail accounts, free 10MB web hard-drive, on-line diary, SMS, and more. These features had garnered several "Top 1" titles for portal development in Taiwan.

the result During the campaign, PChome Online scored impressive growth, attracting several hundred thousand new subscribers, and sparking a controversial battle for number one portal.

Intriguingly titled *The High Intelligence Biological Entity,* this commercial was made for PChome Magazine under the PChome Group. Living in the information age, it reminds us, the learning process is never ending.

A band of teenage girls is searching for a middle-aged man — in this case the founder of PChome Group, H. J. Jang, widely recognised as one of the smartest men in Taiwan.

GIRL: *He might be an intelligent alien life form from another planet... he must be captured.*

After pursuing the wrong men through numerous real scenarios, and then the right man through numerous virtual scenarios, the girls eventually connect with Jang.

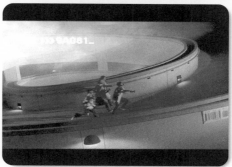

OS: *H. J. Jang, we want your brain.*

H. J. JANG: *Have you no brains?*

VO: *PChome Magazine expands your brainpower.*

SUPER: *The learning survives. PChome.*

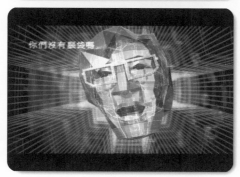

NATIONAL TOBACCO CAMPAIGN   NATIONAL TOBACCO CAMPAIGN   PEDESTRIAN COUNCIL OF AUSTRALIA

SINGAPORE PRISON SERVICE   UNICEF   SINGAPORE PRISON SERVICE   SINGAPORE PRISON SERVICE

NKA ARMY INSTITUTIONAL AND GOVERNMENT   UNICEF

LACK THAI/DRINK DRIVE CAMPAIGN   UNICEF   BLACK THAI/DRINK DRIVE CAMPAIGN   TRANSPORT ACCIDENT COMMISSION

PEDESTRIAN COUNCIL OF AUSTRALIA   TRANSPORT ACCIDENT COMMISSION   SRI LANKA ARMY

Institutional AndGovernment

CHANGING consumer attitudes is one thing; changing their behaviour is another game entirely. Behavioural change is the ultimate goal of all advertising, but in this category it is usually the immediate objective. The consumer-in-a-cage metaphor, propounded by Australian social researcher Hugh Mackay, is never more pertinent than here. In order to penetrate the bars of the consumer's cage, communications must be crafted with enormous skill to overcome consumer apathy and deeply entrenched habits. The successful case studies that follow are inspiring examples of how to avoid message rejection.

category
INSTITUTIONAL
AND
GOVERNMENT

countries
THAILAND

advertiser
BLACK THAI
WHISKY/
DRINK-DRIVE
CAMPAIGN

agency
BBDO BANGKOK
LIMITED

237

ANGING HABITS WITH HUMOUR   CHANGING HABITS WITH HUMOUR

CHANGING HABITS WITH HUMOUR

CHANGING HABITS WITH HUMOUR

CHANGING HABITS WITH HUMOUR   CHANGING HABITS WITH HUMOUR

CHANGING HABITS WITH HUMOUR

CHANGING HABITS WITH HUMOUR

the problem Thailand is like any other country — drink driving is a major cause of deaths on the road. As a corporate citizen, Black Thai Whisky sponsored a television campaign to help counteract the drink-drive habit.

the strategy Thai advertising has long displayed a preference for humour. Humorous commercials, even for serious issues like drink-driving and national energy-saving programmes, have proved more effective in influencing the public consciousness.

the result The television commercial attracted a popular response and generated public discussion, especially among the target audience — Thai drinkers.

We open on an all too familiar scene — a group of five men stumbling out of a bar. They have obviously been drinking heavily. As is the custom, they make straight for their car.

MALE VO: *Drinking alcohol impairs your driving ability. So don't drink and drive.*

What happens next is totally unexpected. They don't get in and drive. Instead, they pick up their car and carry it from the car park. One man reaches out to pay the parking attendant.

The five men carry the car past a poster for Black Thai Whisky.

MALE VO: *Sponsored by Black Thai Whisky.*

As the commercial concludes, the five men are still carrying the car through the traffic, running towards an expressway tollbooth. They are making car noises.

MALE VO: *Remember, when you drink don't drive.*

As they stop to pay their toll, one of them makes a braking noise.

END VO: *When you drink, don't drive.*

END SUPER AS CAR IS CARRIED THROUGH TOLLGATE: *Don't drink and drive.*

category	countries	advertiser	agency
INSTITUTIONAL AND GOVERNMENT	AUSTRALIA & GLOBAL	NATIONAL TOBACCO CAMPAIGN	BROWN MELHUISH FISHLOCK, SYDNEY

EVERY AD DOES TOBACCO DAMAGE   EVERY AD DOES TOBACCO DAMAGE

EVERY AD DOES TOBACCO DAMAGE

EVERY AD DOES TOBACCO DAMAGE   EVERY AD DOES TOBACCO DAMAGE   EVERY AD DOES TOBACCO DAMAGE

EVERY AD DOES TOBACCO DAMAGE   EVERY AD DOES TOBACCO DAMAGE

the problem By 1995, despite the best efforts of previous campaigns, the decline in smoking prevalence in Australia had stalled. In 1996, the Australian Federal Government convened an advisory group to develop the first national campaign in collaboration with States and Territories to reduce the incidence of smoking in Australia.

The brief had two behavioural objectives: to encourage current smokers aged 18-40 to quit, and to ensure those people who had quit stayed quit. Encouraging cessation support by family, friends, other smokers, recent quitters and GPs was the subtext.

Smokers were united in their attitudes to smoking, and were adamant that "there's nothing you can tell me about smoking that I don't already know". They knew that smoking was bad for them, and research suggested that around 80% of all smokers "intended" to quit. The problem was, quitting was not on "today's agenda".

the strategy The campaign had to ask for a fundamental and immediate change in behaviour. The target audience had to give up something it enjoyed, and was physically and mentally addicted to. Somehow the campaign would have to shatter the average smoker's "self-exemption" by presenting new information that could not be denied. The message had to demonstrate certainty not risk, and elicit the shock of personal recognition. The decision to quit had to be shifted from "one day" to "today". Critically, the campaign had to provide hope that quitting was achievable.

The agency team spent days in cancer wards talking with patients and surgeons. It even observed brain surgery and spent time in the mortuary watching autopsies. Quizzing the experts uncovered tangible negative health effects that happen at any time of life. This process was creatively invaluable, best exemplified by a cardiologist who likened a severe case of atherosclerotic damage to "squeezing Brie cheese from a toothpaste tube, except it's an artery".

In crafting the campaign, the emphasis was on certain rather than probable effects. The campaign line *Every cigarette is doing you damage* stressed the ongoing result of the habit — not some long-delayed, clinical outcome. Showing uncomfortable things smokers do to light up — like using the stove — highlighted personal relevance. Great care was taken crafting these "smoker moments" to engage smokers and convey empathy with their situation.

In every ad, a key visual was brought to life every time a smoker lit up. These visuals — like a sliced brain or the buildup within an artery — were also utilised in print ads, posters, on bus sides and supermarket trolleys, and other tactical media.

Each advertisement carried the Quitline telephone number. Smokers who were stimulated to quit had assistance available. Radio provided support — how to deal with cravings, how to avoid smoking triggers — and reassured smokers that quitting reversed the disease processes.

Television was the primary medium. Five commercials were made. A lower socio-economic bias governed media placement, reflecting the social class gradient of smoking in Australia. Programmes were selected that provided the best opportunities for shared viewing to stimulate the influence process. Non-English speakers were targeted in nine different languages using print and radio, multilingual brochures, posters, and workplace strategies.

the result International research had established benchmarks for success. A reduction in smoking prevalence of 1 percentage point would be an outstanding result. In California, a well-funded and sophisticated programme run over several years had just reached that target.

Every cigarette is doing you damage was launched in June 1997. The first six months of the campaign saw an estimated 190,000 smokers quit their habit — a decline in smoking prevalence of 1.4%. Within 18 months, the incidence of smoking had decreased by 1.8% points nationally. In that same period, the campaign is estimated to have saved around US$14 million in health-related costs.

The Roy Morgan Research Centre conducted benchmark research. Campaign advertising awareness rose from 13% to a peak of 83%, with validated recall of the campaign line peaking at 80% in week four. Advertising recognition peaked at 90% for the *Artery* commercial, 85% for *Lung* and 60% for *Tumour*. "Those more likely to quit" rose from 31% to almost 70% within the campaign. "Has the campaign caused discussion in the household" rose from 27%

to a peak of 63%. Over half the ex-smokers interviewed said the campaign had helped them stay quit.

Calls to the Quitline increased up to 500% during the launch phase. In the first year, 351,108 smokers called for help. By 2001, the Quitline had received 438,385 calls. On a national aggregate level, the Quitline call volume correlated closely with television TARP weights.

Approximately 1 in 25 Australian smokers called Quitline during the first year of advertising, and more than 25% of those who called had quit smoking one year later.

It is estimated that at least 250,000 Australians have now quit smoking since the campaign launched. Significantly, there was no substantial change in cigarette prices during the launch phase that might have reduced smoking prevalence.

From 1996 to 2000, Australian Federal Government expenditure on the campaign totalled US$9 million. As a direct result of this investment, new cases of lung cancer fell by 1.76%, strokes by 1.61%, and coronary heart disease, heart failure and cardiac dysrhythmias by 1.40%.

The campaign is widely hailed as one of the most successful anti-smoking campaigns in the world. It has now been used in more than 30 countries worldwide including the USA, the United Kingdom, Germany, Norway, Armenia, New Zealand and Singapore. The campaign formed the central theme for a worldwide convention on anti-smoking strategy in Chicago in 2000.

❝

It helped many smokers to quit for life — literally. It is a great result which shows that a well-targeted campaign...can make a genuine difference."

DR. MICHAEL WOOLDRIDGE,
Australian Federal Health Minister 1999

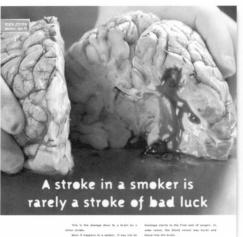

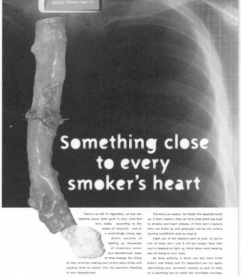

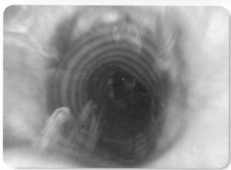

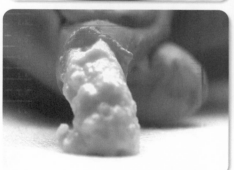

Unable to find matches, a young man lights his first cigarette of the day from the stove.

As he inhales, we follow the swirling smoke past his lips and down his trachea.

vo: *Every cigarette is doing you damage.*

Against a dark background, we see a section of human aorta on a kidney dish.

vo: *This is part of an aorta, the main artery from the heart.*

A doctor's hand picks it up and squeezes along its length. Yellow, cheesy "gunk" comes out like toothpaste.

vo: *Smoking makes artery walls sticky and collect dangerous fatty deposits.*

He finishes squeezing and lays the artery down.

vo: *This much was found stuck to the aorta wall of a smoker…aged thirty-two.*

As our smoker exhales, we reverse back up his throat to see him puff away, blissfully unaware.

vo: *Every cigarette is doing you damage.*

Super: *Every cigarette is doing you damage.*

Quit 131 848. The National Tobacco Campaign.

category INSTITUTIONAL AND GOVERNMENT

countries AUSTRALIA

advertiser PEDESTRIAN COUNCIL OF AUSTRALIA

agency SAATCHI & SAATCHI, SYDNEY

KILLERS ARE KILLERS KILLERS ARE KILLERS KILLERS ARE KILLERS

KILLERS ARE KILLERS KILLERS ARE KILLERS

KILLERS ARE KILLERS

KILLERS ARE KILLERS KILLERS ARE KILLERS

KILLERS ARE KILLERS

the problem The Council believed many drivers had become immune to drink drive warnings. It particularly wanted to focus attention on the dangers to pedestrians from drunk drivers and generate public debate.

Given a small budget and an apathetic audience, how could the Council provoke drivers to rethink their personal values and reassess their own positions?

the strategy The campaign reframed drink driving: it shifted the context of public discussion by asserting that a drunk driver killing a pedestrian was no different than any other deliberate killer.

In the first year of the campaign, print ads "positioned" drivers who killed innocent pedestrians as the same as any other killers of innocent victims — like Charles Manson and Jeffrey Dahmer. The line, *A killer is a killer*, carried with it an undeniable truth and the campaign's non-negotiable tonality provoked immediate public debate.

The second year brought a real killer into Australian lounge rooms, former hit man and convicted killer Mark "Chopper" Read. Read, wearing a colourful shirt and relaxing in his kitchen, argued that he was doing ads for something he knew a great deal about, which was killing. In one execution, he takes us for a tour of his body, showing off his prison scars — including his severed ears — and suggests that any viewers who kill a pedestrian while driving under the influence should pray they aren't sent to prison.

the result The budget was minuscule, but the campaign attracted the attention of the "free media", sparking wide debate on TV news and current affairs shows, talkback radio, in the daily press and through Internet chat.

Clothing worn by victim of Jeffrey Dahmer.

Clothing worn by victim of drunk driver.

A KILLER IS A KILLER. DON'T DRINK AND DRIVE.

Saatchi & Saatchi 3201

Charles Manson. Killer of innocent victims.

Robert Hardy. Killer of an innocent victim while driving under the influence of alcohol.

A KILLER IS A KILLER. DON'T DRINK AND DRIVE.

Saatchi's 3201

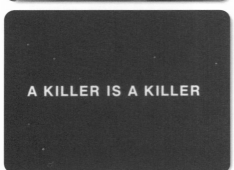

Brutal killer "Chopper" Read is a big, tough looking man with close-cropped hair and heavily tattooed arms. He is talking to us in his kitchen.

"CHOPPER" READ: *A lot of you people might be very upset that I'm doing this commercial, but I'm advertising something that I know a great deal about, and that's killing.*

REVERSE WHITE TITLE OVER SILENCE: *Mark "Chopper" Read.*

READ CONTINUES: *I've shot people, I've baseball batted them to death, I've iron barred them to death, I've stabbed them to death, I've set fire to them. If you get into a car and you've been drinking too much, and you kill somebody, then you're no different than me. That's all there is. You're a murdering maggot.*

END TITLES: *A killer is a killer. Don't drink and drive.*

LOGO: *Pedestrian Council of Australia.*

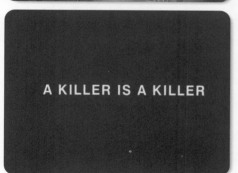

"Chopper" Read talks to us again in his kitchen. This time he shows us his gruesome injuries.

"CHOPPER" READ: *When I was in prison, I got slashed down the face... my ears cut off... I had a claw hammer put through my brain, just here...*

He then opens his shirt and points to more injuries on his tattooed body.

READ: *Cutthroat razors here, and here... an eight-and-a-half inch butcher's knife there... ice pick there... ice pick up the back there...*

REVERSE WHITE TITLE OVER SILENCE: *Mark "Chopper" Read.*

READ CONTINUES: *If you drink and you drive, and you are unfortunate enough to hit somebody, you want to pray to God you don't ever go to prison...*

END TITLES: *A killer is a killer. Don't drink and drive.*

LOGO: *Pedestrian Council of Australia.*

CORRECTING AN IMAGE

CORRECTING AN IMAGE
CORRECTING AN IMAGE

CORRECTING AN IMAGE CORRECTING AN IMAGE

CORRECTING AN IMAGE

CORRECTING AN IMAGE   CORRECTING AN IMAGE
CORRECTING AN IMAGE

the problem As far as the public is concerned, prisons are basically places where offenders are sent to serve their sentences, with prison officers their custodians. And, in comparison with other "Home Team" agencies like the Singapore Police Force and the Central Narcotics Bureau, the Singapore Prison Service (SPS) was generally viewed as a conservative organisation.

The SPS wanted to challenge these misconceptions, and give the public a clearer perspective of its role. The advertising had to communicate its new mission — ensuring the safe custody and rehabilitation of offenders through prevention and aftercare — and project SPS as a professional, "New Economy" organisation that is helping to shape a more positive, productive society.

the strategy The campaign theme — *Captains of Lives* — established the new corporate image as professional providers of correction with compassion.

The campaign addressed the different aspects of the prison service that were important in changing public perceptions. It showed inmates were treated in a humane way and given rehabilitation to help them change and reintegrate into society. Ex-convicts who had successfully undergone rehabilitation were seen contributing to society in a responsible way. Prison officers were identified as having a special ability to look beyond the flaws and see the good in people.

Tonally, the campaign employed both drama and humour. Television commercials unfolded with an unexpected twist. Witty headlines in print and bus ads engaged the public. Each communication concluded with the theme, *Captains of Lives*, and the three key words from SPS's mission: *Rehab, renew, restart*.

the result The campaign received positive feedback in terms of likeability and awareness of what the Singapore Prison Service is all about.

Campaign pre-test research confirmed the high overall appeal of commercials — 85% of respondents said it was a good way to advertise SPS, and 86% said it was clear and easy to understand. The overall opinion of SPS increased significantly after being exposed to the advertising — 87% agreed they had a good impression of SPS. Respondents particularly liked the aspect of giving ex-convicts a chance and not prejudging them, teaching them new skills, and helping to reform and rehabilitate offenders.

Changes in perception of SPS resulted in a very good overall opinion: +32%. Specific scores included "SPS is a progressive and forward looking organisation" +20%, "SPS is a place where offenders got a second chance" +25%, and "SPS's role is not only to lock away and punish offenders" +30%.

CORRECTING AN IMAGE
CORRECTING AN IMAGE
CORRECTING AN IMAGE
CORRECTING AN IMAGE
CORRECTING AN IMAGE CORRECTING AN IMAGE
CORRECTING AN IMAGE
CORRECTING AN IMAGE CORRECTING AN IMAGE
CORRECTING AN IMAGE

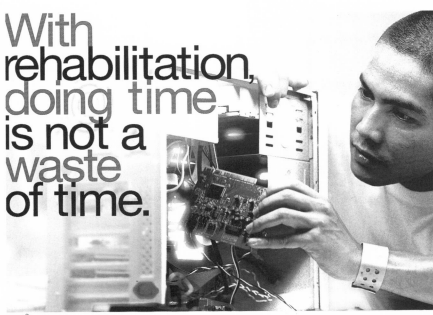

With rehabilitation, doing time is not a waste of time.

In Singapore Prisons, inmates are encouraged to spend their time wisely while serving their sentences. As part of our rehabilitation programme, we provide academic and IT courses, as well as vocational training. Inmates are also given social and religious counselling to help them manage their problems and relationships with their families and peers.
By providing these opportunities, we are preparing them to face life's challenges once they are released from prison. For more information on Singapore Prison Service or how you can be a part of it, log on to www.prisons.gov.sg or call our career hotline at 1800 5420000.

Singapore Prison Service

CAPTAINS OF LIVES
REHAB • RENEW • RESTART

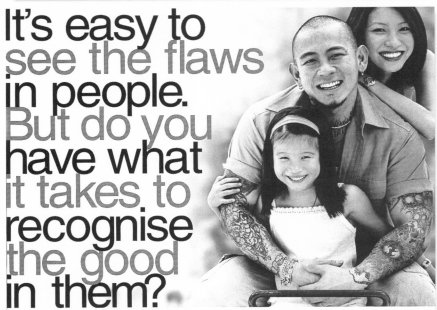

It's easy to see the flaws in people. But do you have what it takes to recognise the good in them?

In Singapore Prison Service, we aspire to be Captains in the lives of offenders committed to our charge. We are dedicated to helping these offenders renew and restart their lives as responsible citizens.
To achieve this aim, we need officers who can balance firmness with compassion, and at the same time, be disciplinarians and mentors. They are required to look beyond the flaws of the offenders and bring out the best in them. Only then will we be able to recommend the appropriate rehabilitation programmes to help them change for the better. For more information on Singapore Prison Service or how you can be a part of it, log on to www.prisons.gov.sg or call our career hotline at 1800 5420000.

Singapore Prison Service

CAPTAINS OF LIVES
REHAB • RENEW • RESTART

A sense of impending violence is quickly established. We intercut between shots of rich businessmen dining in a plush Chinese restaurant — and a tattooed man with a closely-shaved head who is selecting and testing knives.

When he finds the one he needs, his concentration becomes intense.

MALE VO: *Who says ex-convicts can't serve society with conviction?*

Only then do we realise that the man we had prejudged a criminal is in fact a successfully rehabilitated ex-convict. He now works in the restaurant kitchen where he is carving a melon.

He shoots a grin to camera.

END SUPERS: *Rehab, renew, restart. Captains of Lives.*

LOGO: *Singapore Prison Service*

For a few moments we believe we are watching a prison escape. Shots of forbidding walls, barbed wire, security cameras, guards watching monitors interplay with a young man's narrowed, watchful eyes.

He appears engrossed in some technical procedure.

Is he setting explosives or neutralising the alarms?

MALE VO: *We believe, with rehabilitation, doing time is not a waste of time.*

Only then is it revealed that the young man is developing his computer skills in the prison's workshop.

END SUPERS: *Rehab, renew, restart. Captains of Lives.*

LOGO: *Singapore Prison Service*

category	countries	advertiser	agency
INSTITUTIONAL AND GOVERNMENT	SRI LANKA	SRI LANKA ARMY	LEO BURNETT SOLUTIONS INC., SRI LANKA

BATTLING A NEGATIVE IMAGE BATTLING A NEGATIVE IMAGE BATTLING A NEGATIVE IMAGE

BATTLING A NEGATIVE IMAGE

BATTLING A NEGATIVE IMAGE BATTLING A NEGATIVE IMAGE BATTLING A NEGATIVE IMAGE
BATTLING A NEGATIVE IMAGE BATTLING A NEGATIVE IMAGE

the problem Sri Lanka had been torn by war for years. Separatist guerrillas in the north had even mounted lightning raids on the capital, Colombo. The morale of the army was at an all-time low. Recruitment had stalled and the country was facing disaster. And there was no indication of better times to come.

the strategy Unlike most recruitment campaigns, Sri Lanka's army could promise more than war games. There was every chance that new recruits would step into a real firing line and face the possibility of death or injury. The advertising had to acknowledge that reality.

The campaign was built on a series of human insights. Young Sinhalese males wanted to fight, were prepared to defend their nation, and were not afraid to die. The campaign's success would depend on how that challenge was portrayed. Camaraderie, masculinity and pride in the uniform were key triggers.

The creative breakthrough harked back to Sanskrit and tapped into a wellspring of national pride. *Singha* is the Sanskrit word for lion and, according to legend, the Sinhala (Sri Lankan) race is believed to have descended from lions.

The campaign theme, in Sinhalese, centred on the pride of the lion: *Singha patawuge paradisiya*. New recruits were portrayed as young lions, or lion cubs, who could take pride in their decision to enlist.

Phase 1 rebuilt the army's image in television and print. Phase 2 was the call to action in print.

the result Within the first month of the campaign 2,000 recruits had entered the army. A further 200 applications for officer cadetships were received. Better morale and pride in the army was evident in the regular companies.

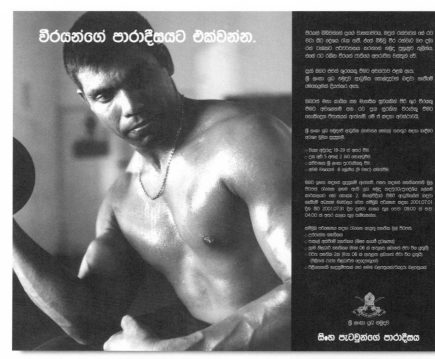

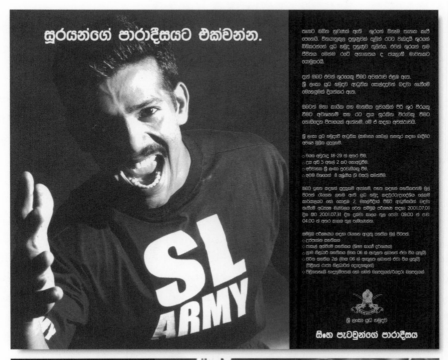

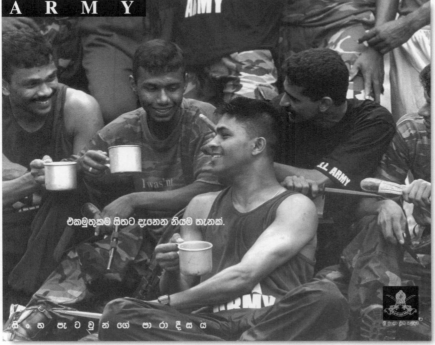

category	countries	advertiser	agency
INSTITUTIONAL AND GOVERNMENT	AUSTRALIA	TRANSPORT ACCIDENT COMMISSION	GREY WORLDWIDE, MELBOURNE

MARKETING ROAD SAFETY
MARKETING ROAD SAFETY
MARKETING ROAD SAFETY

MARKETING ROAD SAFETY

MARKETING ROAD SAFETY
MARKETING ROAD SAFETY
MARKETING ROAD SAFETY
MARKETING ROAD SAFETY

the problem In the period 1984 to 1989, despite public outrage and demands that "something" be done, the road toll in the Australian State of Victoria continued its upward climb. It peaked at 776 deaths in 1989, and if the graph continued was heading for disaster.

the strategy The Transport Accident Commission (TAC), a state-owned enterprise set up by the Victorian State Government, initiated its road safety campaign in 1989. TAC operates an insurance scheme funded by premiums levied through vehicle registration fees. All road users are automatically insured against injuries as the result of road accidents anywhere in the State, whether they are at fault or not. TAC's objective was to keep the incidence and therefore the cost of road accidents as low as possible.

The community was angry about the road toll, and initial research gave the advertising permission to shock, outrage and appal, to be emotional, and to establish a link between drink-driving, speeding and real accidents. However, research also warned against too much twisted metal, too many boring statistics, a lecturing tonality, authority figures in uniforms, and telling the public they couldn't have a drink. The huge clutter of road safety messages that already bombarded the public from various sources further complicated the task. TAC had to establish a new, single voice on road safety.

TAC and Grey Worldwide decided to market road safety as though it were a consumer product that had to survive in a tough, cynical market. The first task was to develop brand names: "Drink/drive" and "Speed". These brand names became themes in two campaigns: *If you drink, then drive, you're a bloody idiot* and *Don't fool yourself, speed kills.* The marketing proposition — finding yourself responsible for the death of another human being — struck deep at core emotions, personal fears and feelings of vulnerability. But, like any consumer product, the market had to believe the product was relevant to their needs, their values, and their lifestyle. With a proposition built on responsibility for death, credibility was critical. When people saw the ads, they had to spontaneously think: "That could be me, that could so easily be me." They had to believe that what they saw was real — real accidents, real emotions, real people suffering real pain and trauma.

The campaign was launched on the eve of the Christmas party season in 1989. After sixty executions its tonality has not changed. The campaign always applies the rules of documentary drama to advertising; the camera observes a person that could well be the viewer having a drink, doing something stupid, like not putting a seat belt on, or dropping off to sleep at the wheel. The audience has to feel that it is watching itself, rather than a piece of Hollywood, or a piece of slick advertising. The audience has to be emotionally involved, firstly with the kind of behaviour that leads to a particular kind of crash, and then with the aftermath — death or serious injury, leading to the awful emotional trauma.

Every commercial has to be utterly credible, and is subject to a reality check in post-testing. The minute the execution becomes unbelievable, viewers can find an emotional way out. Crashes, for example, can't be "too big", otherwise the commercial crosses the border from reality into entertainment.

Mostly the commercials let people work out the message for themselves. Voice-overs and other overt advertising techniques are rarely used. Sometimes, the commercials will deliberately give instructions. One famous example was the car hitting the man carrying a box of pizza. As the man's body flips up and smashes onto the car, a surgeon rationalises that had the car been travelling 10 kilometres an hour slower the man would have received nothing more than a severe shock.

The TAC campaign is generally regarded as the world's longest-running campaign funded by a public authority through the same advertising agency. Four or five new commercials are still made every year.

the result When the campaign started in 1989, the Victorian road toll was 776. In 1990, the TAC campaign had contributed to a 29% drop in road fatalities to 548; a reduction of 49% followed in 1992. By 1999, the State road toll stood at 383.

Over eleven years, the TAC campaign has contributed to the saving of 3,514 lives and financial savings of US$4 billion in claims and costs to the community. In tracking studies, the campaign enjoys around 90% unaided recall and 98% community support. Victoria now boasts one of the lowest road fatality rates in the world — 1.24 deaths per 10,000 vehicles registered. The annual media spend averages around US$6 million.

❞

Compared to other advocacy campaigns around the world, we make quite sure we don't have any *advertising* ideas in our commercials. We want them to show reality, to be believable and compelling; put an *advertising* idea in it, and it becomes an ad. It's a far more disciplined campaign than anything I've ever worked on. A kind of formula has evolved as a result of the tripartite relationship between Grey, TAC, and the researchers."

NIGEL DAWSON, Creative Director
Grey Worldwide Melbourne

MARKETING ROAD SAFETY
MARKETING ROAD SAFETY
MARKETING ROAD SAFETY **MARKETING ROAD SAFETY**
MARKETING ROAD SAFETY
MARKETING ROAD SAFETY
MARKETING ROAD SAFETY
MARKETING ROAD SAFETY

Some friends are sharing a beer after renovating a house. One of them is with his son.

When he receives a tip-off by phone that the police are conducting random breath tests nearby, he decides it's time to call it a day. He whistles his dog.

ONE OF HIS MATES GIVES HIM ANOTHER BEER: *Go on, one more's not going to kill you.*

THE YOUNG FATHER STOPS AND TAKES IT: *Hey, I'm still capable of driving...*

At last, he and his son drive off in their pick-up truck. He stops at the first intersection, but ignores the Stop sign at the next.

WE HEAR HIS SON SCREAM: *Dad!*

A huge tanker ploughs into the truck, crushing it into a mass of twisted metal.

Back at the work site, a mobile phone rings and one of his mates hears the news just as more beer arrives.

END SUPER: *If you drink, then drive, you're a bloody idiot.*

If you drink, then drive, you're a bloody idiot.

TAC

Dr Richard Gilhome.

10 kph less
will save lives.

TAC

A man carrying a pizza steps onto the road, into the path of a car. The impact is sickening. Witnesses scream in horror.

Cut to Dr Richard Gilhome who reconstructs the accident while the film replays in slow motion, so we can see every detail.

DR GILHOME: *I'm a trauma surgeon and I want to reconstruct what happens to the human body, in less than two-fifths of a second, when hit by a car braking from 70 kilometres per hour over a braking distance of 50 metres. Even in a car equipped with ABS, the first impact will occur at around 46 kilometres. The bumper hits the knee joints, tearing flesh and ligaments. The full weight of the skull smashes through the windscreen, the neck snaps, the skull shatters, and the pedestrian's brain is turned into pulp. In little more than a second, the pedestrian's body will hit the road with a 70% chance of being dead.*

We then see what happens when a car is driven at a slower speed...

DR GILHOME: *But had you been braking from 60 kilometres, not 70, there's a good chance you could have stopped in time and the pedestrian would have suffered nothing worse than a severe fright. Think about it.*

END SUPER: 10 kph less will save lives.

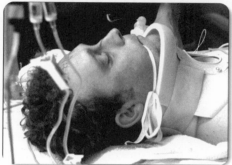

**If you
drink, then drive,
you're a
bloody idiot.**

TAC

The Twelve Days of Christmas used an episodic format. A young girl humming the famous song was an audio mnemonic.

On Monday, a father arrives home with a Christmas tree. His pregnant wife, son and daughter greet him.

Wednesday is the office party. Liquor flows. On the way home he grows impatient, loses control and a split second later has crashed into a tree.

On Thursday, the pregnant wife and her in-laws are convinced that her husband will regain consciousness at any time.

On Sunday the doctors announce that his brain has stopped working and that he should be taken off life support. The curtains are drawn shut. *See you later, son,* says his distressed father.

The funeral takes place on Christmas Eve. Tempers are frayed. A child asks if Daddy will be at the church.

Christmas Day. The two children climb into bed with their mother.

A LITTLE VOICE ASKS: *Mummy, is Santa going to find Daddy?*

SUPER: *If you drink, then drive, you're a bloody idiot.*

A car slams into the back of a semi-trailer. The events leading up to the crash, and its aftermath, are painstakingly woven together.

The blood-smeared young male driver is alive, breathing his girl friend's name: *Julie.* There is no reply.

We see her father's 53rd birthday cake. Flashback to the young couple at his party. Cut back to the rescue team trying to extricate them from the car. We flashback again as Julie wishes her father happy birthday.

HER FATHER'S VOICE: *I'll never see her again... I'll never hear her voice... hear her laugh...*

In another flashback, the father waves goodbye to his daughter and her boyfriend as they leave the party. *Take care of my baby girl,* he tells the young man. The boyfriend says he will.

THE FATHER'S VOICE CONTINUES: *I'll never see her get married... cuddle her children...*

Julie asks her boyfriend if he'd like her to drive. He says no, he's only had a few. Then the distraught father is at the accident scene, restrained by rescue workers, screaming her name, sinking to his knees.

HIS VOICE CONTINUES: *I'll never forget having to choose a coffin...For my beautiful baby...*

SUPER: *If you drink, then drive, you're a bloody idiot.*

SEEING CHILDREN IN A NEW PERSPECTIVE

SEEING CHILDREN IN A NEW PERSPECTIVE

SEEING CHILDREN IN A NEW PERSPECTIVE

SEEING CHILDREN IN A NEW PERSPECTIVE

SEEING CHILDREN IN A NEW PERSPECTIVE

SEEING CHILDREN IN A NEW PERSPECTIVE

SEEING CHILDREN IN A NEW PERSPECTIVE

SEEING CHILDREN IN A NEW PERSPECTIVE

the problem UNICEF, a familiar name around the world, was largely unknown in China. Most people could not even read its corporate logo.

UNICEF wanted a television commercial that would establish its brand among the masses and communicate its Chinese slogan: 儿童之友 (*Ér tóng zhī yǒu*, meaning children's friend). The commercial had to tell the people of China how UNICEF was helping the nation by caring for its neediest children.

the strategy The agency embarked on a unique planning mission. After six weeks travelling 15,000 km across China, interviewing families, helping mothers take care of their children, and even turning the agency van into a school bus for the day, it became clear that an awareness-driving commercial would have little impact on the masses.

People in China, like people everywhere, love and adore their own children, but that doesn't mean they care about other people's. On the other hand, it was a very acceptable Chinese idea that in everyday life everyone depends on the contributions made by other people. If it could be communicated in the Chinese context that other people were actually "other people's children", and that UNICEF was taking care of the neediest ones, then the Chinese people could feel positively towards the organisation.

The creative breakthrough was to reframe the concept of needy children by demonstrating how other people's children grew up to have a big impact on the viewer's life, and as a whole represented a better future for China.

the result Because of the emotional and executional values of the commercial, UNICEF gained significantly more free media space than expected — it was telecast more than 3,000 times on prime time television over 300 Chinese television stations free of charge, an all-time record. UNICEF reported a marked increase in the number of corporate and individual offers to help raise funds. The commercial also received coverage in print media, including the influential *Far Eastern Economic Review*.

Black-and-white images in slow motion flow to traditional Chinese music. There is no voice-over.

A woman slowly pulls a barrow piled high with vegetables through frame.
SUPER: *Someone else's child will supply food for your family.*

Dissolve to a road building crew at work.
SUPER: *Someone else's child will pave the road you walk on.*

Dissolve to a taxi driving along a Chinese street, trees reflected in its windscreen.
SUPER: *Someone else's child will take you to work every day.*

Dissolve to a policeman apprehending a thief in an alley.
SUPER: *Someone else's child will protect you from danger.*

Dissolve to an ambulance arriving at a hospital gate and nurses rushing to open its doors.
SUPER: *Someone else's child will save your life.*

Dissolve to soldiers riding in an army truck.
SUPER: *Someone else's child is even prepared to die for you.*

Dissolve to a teacher writing on a blackboard and her class putting up their hands.
SUPER: *All they need is a chance... to grow up like yours.*

DISSOLVE TO UNICEF LOGO WITH SLOGAN:
Eŕ tóng zhī yŏu. (children's friend.)

SINGAPORE CABLE VISION   CHINA TIMES

BEIJING EVENING POST   THE TIMES OF INDIA   CHINA TIMES

NG EVENING POST   MEDIA   THE ECONOMIST GROUP   SINGAPORE CABLE VISION

CHINA TIMES   THE TIMES OF INDIA   CHINA TIMES

SINGAPORE CABLE VISION

Media

GIVEN the proliferation of choices and growing audience sophistication, it is not surprising that media owners often find themselves under siege. Many newspapers and television channels have become distinctive brands. Others, in countries as diverse as China and India, have had to rebrand themselves. Their marketing communications are amongst the most visible in Asia-Pacific and offer many learnings.

| category
MEDIA | countries
CHINA | advertiser
BEIJING
EVENING
POST | agency
McCANN-
ERICKSON
GUANGMING LTD,
BEIJING |

NEGATIVE SELL, POSITIVE RESPONSE   NEGATIVE SELL, POSITIVE RESPONSE   NEGATIVE SELL, POSITIVE RESPONSE

NEGATIVE SELL, POSITIVE RESPONSE

NEGATIVE SELL, POSITIVE RESPONSE   NEGATIVE SELL, POSITIVE RESPONSE

NEGATIVE SELL, POSITIVE RESPONSE

the problem The *Beijing Evening Post* was seen as the government's official newspaper, authoritative but conservative. A campaign was needed to revitalise the newspaper's image and make the *Evening Post* a compelling daily purchase.

the strategy If newspaper readers needed a jolt, the agency argued for provocative ads. How provocative? The average reader in Beijing is not accustomed to seeing a headline that shouts, *Oppose the evening newspaper! Fǎn dùi wǎn bào*, 反对晚报.

In Chinese, the word for evening newspaper is *wǎn bào*. However, *wǎn* (晚) does not simply mean evening. Its other meaning is "late", which puts a new interpretation on the headline: *Don't put up with late news.*

The subcaption reads: *People have every right to read the news on the same day it happens.*

The launch announcement was immediately followed by a flight of ads delivering the "same day's news" proposition in the context of an unfolding news event — the Sydney Olympic Games. The *Evening Post* exploited its advantage of reporting the morning news from Sydney in its evening editions. Each ad featured the Olympic topic of the day. And whether China won or lost, the *Evening Post* kept its readers entertained and focused on its message.

the result According to conventional wisdom, negative headlines — so popular in the sophisticated West — do not work well in Asia. The *Beijing Evening Post* dispelled that myth. Circulation rose from a pre-campaign 800,000 to over 1,000,000 copies daily.

玫瑰,依旧鎗鎗!

晚报,不晚报

黑马,不晚报!

羽毛球决赛

晚报,不晚报

category	countries	advertiser	agency
MEDIA	TAIWAN	CHINA TIMES	IDEOLOGY ADVERTISING AGENCY LTD, TAIPEI

A YOUNGER READ   A YOUNGER READ

NEGATIVE SELL, POSITIVE RESPONSE

A YOUNGER READ A YOUNGER READ A YOUNGER READ

A YOUNGER READ   A YOUNGER READ

the problem The *China Times*, Taiwan's venerable newspaper, needed to strengthen its leadership status against its two main rivals. Part of the problem was that the paper had lost touch with the younger generation.

Advertising alone would not be enough. In order to rejuvenate its brand, The *China Times* had to overhaul editorial content and then present itself to the market with a new voice.

the strategy First, a new value proposition was developed: the *China Times* delivers the most profound reading experience.

Rationalising that an overload of information only serves to ignite anxiety, the *China Times* positioned itself as more user-friendly. For example, it strengthened its ability to distil and analyse the news for busy young readers. It recruited leading intellectuals as commentators. Their voices lent a fresh, more innovative tone to the product.

Television commercials portrayed the new image of the newspaper. In one, a young female executive reads the paper before her husband does. In another, a young man wanders through a vast crowd of clones seeking sanity in a bleak urban wilderness.

the result Younger readers have steadily increased since the campaign launched. In research, college students perceive the *China Times* as the quality newspaper.

The concept communicated is that a person's charm is not only determined by outward appearance, but also by knowledge and brainpower.

An elegant young woman is reading the *China Times.*

Her equally elegant husband waits on her hand and foot. Like a perfect valet, he offers her a choice of skirt. Dutifully he dresses her without disturbing her reading experience. He brushes her hair, serves her tea and even puts on her shoes for her.

FEMALE VO: *Why love me?*

MALE VO: *Because you read.*

Then it is her turn to wait on him while he savours his *China Times.*

SUPER: *Knowledge enhances your charm.*

In *The Information Maniac*, the actor and actress are well-known entertainment show hosts in Taiwan. They are thirsty for news and information. Happily, reading the *China Times* relieves them from the anxiety of craving up-to-the-minute information.

The commercial begins as they dispense newspapers for themselves and scan story after story in their insatiable search for truth and information.

Their conversation expresses how sensitive they are to news in their profession.

Their search becomes more and more frantic. The young woman even clips headlines in her chair at a hairdressing salon.

They can only relax after they discover that the *China Times* delivers precisely the news that they need.

CUTTING THE COST OF WINNING NEW READERS   CUTTING THE COST OF WINNING NEW READERS

CUTTING THE COST OF WINNING NEW READERS

CUTTING THE COST OF WINNING NEW READERS   CUTTING THE COST OF WINNING NEW READERS

CUTTING THE COST OF WINNING NEW READERS

CUTTING THE COST OF WINNING NEW READERS

the problem Founded in 1843, *The Economist* is a weekly international news and business publication written for an audience of senior business, political and financial decision-makers. Editorial independence is at its heart. Trustees who are independent of commercial, political and proprietorial influences appoint the Editor. Its stories have no bylines; its collective voice and personality matter more than the identities of individual journalists. It has achieved a continuity of tradition that few other publications can match.

In Asia, *The Economist* faces fierce competition. Awareness is aided by a world famous campaign employing witty, provocative lines of white type out of a red background that replicates the *Economist* masthead. Captions are location-specific: *Watch for indicators* and *Avoid crashes* on bus panels, *Rest your case* on airport luggage trolleys, *Never one sided* on round pillars.

Four regional mailings a year drive new readership subscriptions. The problem is, Asian response rates are notoriously low compared to those in Europe or North America.

Beginning in 1998, *The Economist* experienced diminishing response rates for their control mailing pack, falling as much as 53%. A new test pack was developed offering a free trial of four issues. The offer was appealing; it brought the average response rate back up by 67%. However the test pack required outbound telemarketing to recipients in order to win a subscription, adding to the cost of acquiring each new reader.

In April 1999, *The Economist* set new targets: the response rate had to achieve a new high of 23% above 1998 successes — and deliver a higher return on investment — despite a limited choice of over-worked mailing lists and limited brand awareness in Asian countries like Taiwan and Japan.

the strategy The marketing solution focused on local Asian market variations in the mail pack design, a creative back-to-basics approach, and test scenarios such as giving away a premium item vis-à-vis a discount on the cover price.

Economist regional mailings normally go out to 500,000 names in 12 countries — including the Asian Businessman Readership Survey markets of

Hong Kong, Indonesia, Malaysia, the Philippines, Singapore, South Korea, Taiwan and Thailand. One major barrier was that creative executions could not be localised due to the associated production costs. One pan-Asian pack had to appeal to all markets. In addition, the same pack needed to appeal to a wide audience, from those relatively well informed about *The Economist* to those only vaguely aware.

By revisiting the Brand Print, a back-to-basics strategy was adopted. The mailing would project the core components of *The Economist*: red and daring, provocative, opinionated, brutally honest and nonconformist. Creativity had to reaffirm those values for recipients who were familiar with the brand, and set up a value proposition for those who were not.

The strategy challenged the potential reader by posing and answering five negative questions. The questions were designed to eradicate the most fundamental misconceptions and barriers to subscribing: *The Economist* is only for economists; it offers coverage you can pick up elsewhere; you have to read *The Economist* from cover to cover to justify the expense; you are committed to a subscription for the length of the tenure chosen; and *The Economist* is easier to buy from a newsstand than from a subscription.

The mail pack was designed to be physically outstanding — an over-sized 175-sq. mm, that folded out to eight times its envelope size. The design and unusual folding construction not only highlighted the breadth of coverage; it also created a higher degree of reader interaction with the pack.

It was mailed to 350,000 names in eight countries — China, Hong Kong, Indonesia, Japan, Malaysia, Singapore, Taiwan and Thailand, plus a Rest-of-Region mailing. Recipients included subscribers to business weeklies, business dailies, frequent international travellers, MBA holders, top-performing countries, chambers of commerce members, Internet lists and book clubs.

A test matrix assessed the relative appeal of three different offers: *The Economist* Business Book as a premium giveaway, free additional copies of *The Economist* combined with the standard discount rate, and a higher than normal discount without any premium offer.

the result The new direct mail piece generated a weighted average 234% improvement over the previous regional mailing.

45% of the mailings offered a standard discount with a premium item and earned a response rate improvement of 244%. Another 45% of recipients were offered a standard discount with free extra issues, generating an improvement of 211%. The final 10% of names were offered a higher than normal discount with no premium, resulting in a response improvement of 156%. A coding system identified local response idiosyncrasies that will be reflected in future mailings; for example, unlike other Asians, Thai recipients preferred free extra issues, out-pulling the free book offer by 30%.

Localised response mechanisms in the local language proved effective in Japan, Taiwan and Thailand, with Japan's response rate soaring 400%.

The new regional pack managed to generate a positive return on investment and for the first time in Asia, *The Economist* acquired new subscribers profitably from the start date of their subscription.

❝

There is a fine line between discounting the product and devaluing the brand. Local market response rates can be improved with careful tailoring of a regional creative execution. Spending more on marketing can create higher revenue generation, where a higher cost per pack is offset by an even higher return on investment."

**CHRIS RILEY, Managing Director,
OgilvyOne Worldwide, Hong Kong**

CUTTING THE COST OF WINNING NEW READERS

CUTTING THE COST OF WINNING NEW READERS

CUTTING THE COST OF WINNING NEW READERS

CUTTING THE COST OF WINNING NEW READERS   CUTTING THE COST OF WINNING NEW READERS

CUTTING THE COST OF WINNING NEW READERS

CUTTING THE COST OF WINNING NEW READERS

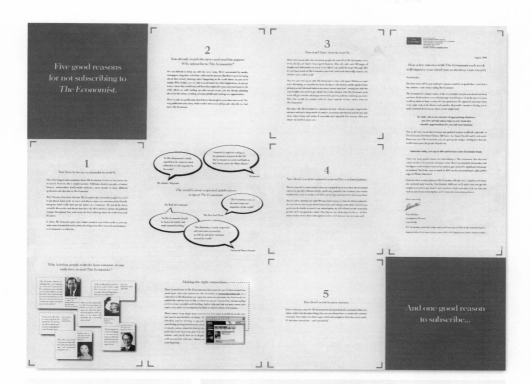

1

You have to be an economist to read it.

One of the biggest misconceptions about *The Economist*, is that you have to be an economist to read it. However, this is simply not true. Politicians, business people, scientists, lawyers, ambassadors, intellectuals, students... many people in many different professions all subscribe to *The Economist*.

Why? Because they know that only *The Economist* gives them the insight they need to get ahead. Each week, we cover such diverse topics as environmentally friendly transport, third world debt and the future of e-commerce. We unveil the latest scientific discoveries and discuss how they will affect our lives; debate the political changes throughout Asia, and review the latest offerings from the world of art and literature.

In short, *The Economist* gives you a more rounded view of the world, so you can make more informed decisions about the things that affect you and your business – be it economics or otherwise.

Why is it that people with the least amount of time make time to read *The Economist*?

2

You already watch the news and read the papers.
Why subscribe to *The Economist*?

It's not difficult to keep up with the news today. We're surrounded by media: newspapers, magazines, television, radio and the internet. But there's more to staying ahead than merely knowing what's happening in the world about us; you need *insight*. With insight, you are able to understand the wider implications of current issues, where they could lead, and how they might affect you and your business. So while others are still catching up with current events, you are already planning ahead for the future, avoiding potential pitfalls and creating new opportunities.

There is only one publication that delivers this insight to your door each week. The very publication that many of the world's most successful people subscribe to. And that's *The Economist*.

category	countries	advertiser	agency
MEDIA	INDIA	THE TIMES OF INDIA	ENTERPRISE NEXUS/ LOWE & PARTNERS WORLDWIDE, INDIA

MODERN TIMES   MODERN TIMES

MODERN TIMES **MODERN TIMES** MODERN TIMES

MODERN TIMES   MODERN TIMES

MODERN TIMES

the problem *The Times of India* was traditionally known as "The Old Lady of Boribunder", after the district which houses its main office. Its image was stuffy, serious, conservative, and "of the old school". It was losing its appeal and relevance to the new generation of Indian readers.

The Times of India had to be repositioned to appeal to the contemporary Indian professional — and timing was critical. New editions were going to be launched in other parts of India. A receptive audience was essential.

the strategy The modern Indian reader wanted unbiased reporting. The key insight was, "just tell me it as it is — it would be nice to be able to trust a source to give me a true picture of what's going on".

From this, the agency refined a proposition: You can trust *The Times of India* to give you the real story as it knows the real India.

Creatively, "the real India" provided fertile ground for a witty, intelligent campaign that satirised the hot issues in India at the time. Government bureaucracy, inefficiency and corruption were ripe for parody. So were over-commercialised sports stars who put money before everything. The cricket team bribes scandal, politicians full of empty rhetoric and a lazy police force were more grist for the campaign's mill. Significantly, the tonality was more than satirical; it was collaborative, inviting the viewer to participate in the newspaper's crusade against social and political ills.

What emerged was some of Asia's funniest and most pungent advertising.

the result *The Times of India* is now the fastest growing English daily newspaper, based on subscription figures audited by ABC. In addition, the majority of new editions launched since the campaign are now market leaders in their regions.

OPENING TITLE: *A day in the life of India.*

The film opens on an old man inquiring about submitting his pension file to a clerk at a typical government office — shabby, paper-littered desks, wheezing ceiling fans, long colonial-style corridors and stairwells.

Throughout the film the old man's pension documents are in camera frame as he is shunted from desk to desk in predictable bureaucratic form. No one is willing to pay heed to his inquiries.

The camera movements, edit pattern and running commentary take on the style of a fast-playing hockey match. The man is the ball, and the government officials the players. He is shuttled from desk to desk, up and down stairs and along corridors, "deflected" and "passed on". Throughout this hectic visual treatment, the running commentary of the match in progress is in perfect sync with the visual action.

Finally he reaches one officer, the "referee", who suggests he give a bribe — "a green card appeal" — and after making the payment, the documents are signed and sent for processing.

The final VO of a common man victoriously saying *What a game, India has won* sums it all up.

END TITLE: *The Times of India. The masthead of India.*

OPENING TITLE: *A day in the life of India.*

The film opens on a televised cricket match. The batsman at the wicket awaiting the first ball is a lookalike of popular young cricket star Sachin Tendulkar, a real life celebrity well known for endorsing all kinds of products for huge fees. The film highlights the idiosyncrasies of India when it comes to advertising and "star" credibility. The commentator's voice runs throughout: *The sky's perfectly clear, the stadium is filled to the brim, a wonderful day for the game of cricket.*

Suddenly the film cuts to the batsman in a toothpaste ad. His teeth are shining. SUPER: *25% more teeth.* The commentator wildly describes the cricket in terminology commonly used in toothpaste commercials.

The film cuts back to the batsman at the crease when he suddenly becomes the star of a soft drink commercial. We cut back to the match. He is about to bat when the film cuts to him relaxing in a chair beneath a fan. SUPER: *Free air with every fan.*

About to bat again, we cut to him advertising suits surrounded by adoring girls. Then he is holding up a tyre. Then he is demonstrating detergent. SUPER: *Removes spots from inside pockets.*

The batsman in the various commercials is shot in exaggerated fashion, in direct contrast to the real life televised cricket match, which suddenly comes to a halt when he pulls a muscle. A physiotherapist administers a pain relief spray to his back.

THE FINAL VO OF A COMMON MAN:
One poor guy does what all for the country.
Batting, bowling, brushing, washing…

END TITLE: *The Times of India. The masthead of India.*

category
MEDIA

countries
SINGAPORE

advertiser
SINGAPORE
CABLE VISION

agency
DENTSU YOUNG
& RUBICAM,
SINGAPORE

CHANNELLING AN OBSESSION CHANNELLING AN OBSESSION CHANNELLING AN OBSESSION
CHANNELLING AN OBSESSION # CHANNELLING AN OBSESSION CHANNELLING AN OBSESSION
CHANNELLING AN OBSESSION CHANNELLING AN OBSESSION CHANNELLING AN OBSESSION
CHANNELLING AN OBSESSION

the problem Successfully launch a new football channel for Singapore's cable television network.

the strategy Football fans are fanatically loyal to their teams, sometimes ridiculously so. That universal truth suggested a strategic proposition: SCV's new Football Channel is as *totally devoted* to football as you are.

The campaign ran on posters in bus shelters and showrooms. Each poster presented a visual example of someone's extreme devotion to his or her team, signed off with the channel logo and product promise, *Totally devoted*.

the result The subscription target was substantially exceeded.

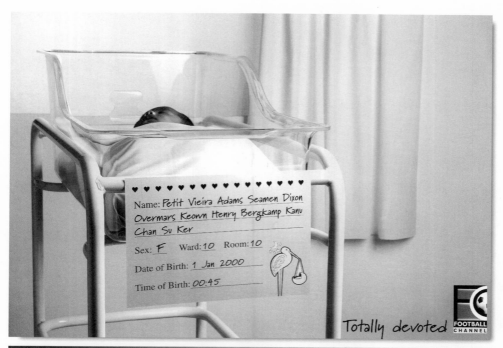

Name: *Petit Vieira Adams Seamen Dixon Overmars Keown Henry Bergkamp Kanu Chan Su Ker*

Sex: *F*   Ward: *10*   Room: *10*

Date of Birth: *1 Jan 2000*

Time of Birth: *00:45*

Totally devoted

Totally devoted

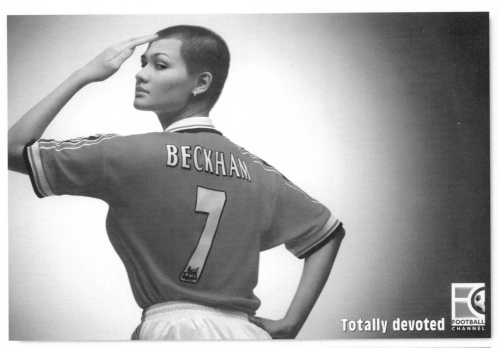

DOUBLE A PAPER
DOUBLE A PAPER   DOUBLE A PAPER   DOUBLE A PAPER   DOUBLE A PAPER

UBLE A PAPER   OFFICE EQUIPMENT AND SUPPLIES

DOUBLE A PAPER   DOUBLE A PAPER   DOUBLE A PAPER   DOUBLE A PAPER   DOUBLE A PAPER

DOUBLE A PAPER   DOUBLE A PAPER   DOUBLE A PAPER

OfficeEquipment AndSupplies

PRICE-SENSITIVE and overcrowded with me-too technology, this category demonstrates a lack of true brand building activity. Frequently, brand communications are in the hands of distributors not principals. Expediency has become the norm, reducing substantial brands to commodity products. However, when brand values and benefits are communicated with skill and single-mindedness, the results can be impressive.

WHEN A COMMODITY BECOMES A BRAND

WHEN A COMMODITY BECOMES A BRAND

WHEN A COMMODITY BECOMES A BRAND

A COMMODITY BECOMES A BRAND   WHEN A COMMODITY BECOMES A BRAND   WHEN A COMMODITY BECOMES A BRAND

WHEN A COMMODITY BECOMES A BRAND

WHEN A COMMODITY BECOMES A BRAND   WHEN A COMMODITY BECOMES A BRAND

the problem Advance Agro Public Co. Ltd. is Thailand's largest coated and uncoated wood-free paper manufacturer. The company has progressively launched its flagship product, Double A paper, using the JWT regional network. After a highly successful launch in Thailand, Advance Agro decided to enter the markets of Singapore, Hong Kong, Malaysia, Taiwan and Australia.

Photocopy paper was a low interest commodity. The common perception was that if a photocopier was stuck, it was because of some mechanical fault. The truth is, the real culprit is low quality photocopy paper. With fibres unevenly distributed on its surface, the paper absorbs moisture, warps and gets stuck in the copier. Not only were consumers unaware of this, engaging their attention long enough to change their perception was going to be a tough call.

the strategy The agency's research had revealed that super white Double A paper had the most evenly distributed fibres. This guaranteed it had the smoothest surface and least moisture absorption factor among competing brands of photocopy paper.

The agency decided to spare the consumer a lecture on the science of photocopy paper. Instead, it chose to highlight the single most compelling benefit: Double A paper would never get stuck in the photocopier, printer or fax machine — in other words, no jam.

Creatively, the attribute was communicated with a lateral twist. In the 30-second TV commercial, several sheets of paper emerge from a photocopier with nothing but the picture of a piece of toast on them. After a while the legend *No Jam* appears on the screen.

The *No Jam* idea was translated to other media. Print ads showed a plain slice of toast, an empty jam bottle, a lone dab of butter — in each case, *No Jam*. Posters shaped like huge slices of toast and empty jam jars sprouted at bus stops. Buses arrived with toast painted on them. At MRT stations, innovative posters scrolled out of dummy photocopiers — with no jam. Even the morning newspaper came wrapped in super white Double A sheets.

the result The launch was highly successful. Distributors reported high brand recall as consumers started to ask for Double A paper by name, rather than merely photocopy paper. Meanwhile, Double A redemption offers created long queues.

❝

It is not every day that you get a client who trusts you completely with the launch of his flagship brand in a new market. So we took it upon ourselves to create a campaign that would work for Double A in the long term. The copy and art team recognised the rare opportunity and made maximum use of it. (The jam bottle incidentally carries their names — Jacob and Benson.) The servicing and media folks also closed ranks and pulled out all plugs to make this campaign work. And of course the client stood by us every step of the way. In sum, it was work that we enjoyed thoroughly."

NORMAN TAN, Executive Creative Director,
J. Walter Thompson Singapore

WHEN A COMMODITY BECOMES A BRAND
WHEN A COMMODITY BECOMES A BRAND

WHEN A COMMODITY BECOMES A BRAND

WHEN A COMMODITY BECOMES A BRAND
WHEN A COMMODITY BECOMES A BRAND
WHEN A COMMODITY BECOMES A BRAND
WHEN A COMMODITY BECOMES A BRAND
WHEN A COMMODITY BECOMES A BRAND
WHEN A COMMODITY BECOMES A BRAND

No Jam

Double A paper, with evenly distributed fibres that make it the smoothest paper ever, is guaranteed to come out of your photocopier each time.

Double Quality Paper

No Jam

Double A paper, with evenly distributed fibres that make it the smoothest paper ever, is guaranteed to come out of your photocopier each time.

Double Quality Paper

No Jam

Double A paper, with evenly distributed fibres that make it the smoothest paper ever, is guaranteed to come out of your photocopier each time.

Double Quality Paper

A steady stream of paper is emerging from a photocopier. Each page carries the picture of a plain slice of toast.

After a while the legend *No Jam* appears on the screen.

MVO: *Double A paper is the smoothest paper to go into and come out of your photocopier.*

Pack shot appears on screen.

SUPER: *Double A. Double Quality Paper.*

UNCLE BEN'S OF AUSTRALIA/*SCHMACKOS*

UNCLE BEN'S OF AUSTRALIA/*SCHMACKOS*

UNCLE BEN'S OF AUSTRALIA/*SCHMACKOS*

PETFOOD AND ACCESSORIES

UNCLE BEN'S OF AUSTRALIA/*SCHMACKOS*

UNCLE BEN'S OF AUSTRALIA/*SCHMACKOS*

UNCLE BEN'S OF AUSTRALIA/*SCHMACKOS*

UNCLE BEN'S OF AUSTRALIA/*SCHMACKOS*

UNCLE BEN'S OF AUSTRALIA/*SCHMACKOS*

UNCLE BEN'S OF AUSTRALIA/*SCHMACKOS*

Petfood AndAccessories

NUTRITION and owner-pet relationships are at the heart of most brand communications in this category, which is only logical. However, logic can be eschewed in favour of something different, something more radical. The launch of a new brand that built a new market demonstrates how, with imagination and courage, fresh ideas can be developed for profitable results.

CREATING A MARKET CREATING A MARKET CREATING A MARKET
CREATING A MARKET # CREATING A MARKET CREATING A MARKET
CREATING A MARKET CREATING A MARKET
CREATING A MARKET

the problem The dog snack market was underdeveloped. Despite the bond that people have with their dogs, research showed that when it came to treats and rewards dog owners didn't think to buy them. Owners believed their pets enjoyed tidbits and table scraps as much as anything.

While they loved to reward their dogs, owners had low awareness of any product or brand in the market and traditional product claims of nutritional value did not appear relevant.

Until 1997, *Schmackos* was a "sleepy" sub-brand for Good O, an Uncle Ben's brand that is predominantly a main meal dog food.

The challenge was, could *Schmackos*, as a stand alone brand divorced from its well known mother brand Good O, be launched into what was virtually a non-existent market, dominate it, and then grow it?

the strategy The idea emerged: giving your dog a treat is great, but giving your dog a *Schmackos* will be appreciated much, much more, giving great enjoyment to both the dog and owner!

Humour and exaggeration became the order of the day. Fun drove the commercials, not logic and nutrition. The promise to dog owners was a catchy branding line, *Dogs go wacko for Schmackos*.

Claymation picked up the wackiness and charmingly captured the essence of the owner's relationship with the dog.

the result Within 18 months of its launch, *Schmackos* was the dominant brand leader with 35% market share. Importantly, the dog snack category also grew by 16% during the same period.

Schmackos continues to grow, reaching over 40% share in 2001 in a market which now exceeds US$37 million.

Uncle Ben's continues to expand the *Schmackos* product range and the brand is rolling out into selected global markets. Six commercials, based on the same theme, have been made to date.

The commercial uses charming claymation animation.

A housewife is waving a biscuit as she tries to cajole Roger the Dog into having his bath.

HOUSEWIFE: *Roger, bathtime!*

Roger is unimpressed. He cowers under the house.

MVO: *There's ordinary snacks...*

The housewife tries again to tempt him with the biscuit: *Bickie for Rogie...*

Roger retreats further.

HOUSEWIFE: *Bathtime, and I've got a biscuit for you...*

Roger's teeth chatter with fear.

MVO: *Or there's Schmackos, lip-schmacking snacks packed with real beef.*

Housewife re-emerges from the house holding *Schmackos*.

HOUSEWIFE: *Look what I've got for you... Schmackos!*

Faster than a speeding bullet, the dog zips up to the roof from where he executes a spectacular dive into his bath. He happily scrubs his back while his owner sighs adoringly.

JINGLE: *Dogs go wacko, dogs go wacko for Schmackos...*

IMODIUM
IMODIUM BLACKMORES BLACKMORES IMODIUM BLACKMORES BLACKMORES BLACKMORES IMODIUM
BLACKMORES PHARMACEUTICALS, HEALTH FOODS, VITAMINS
IMODIUM BLACKMORES IMODIUM BLACKMORES BLACKMORES BLACKMORES BLACKMORES
IMODIUM BLACKMORES IMODIUM BLACKMORES
IMODIUM

Pharmaceuticals, HealthFoods, Vitamins

RIDDLED with regulations, bedevilled by consumer resistance and scepticism, and mostly limited by smaller budgets, this category separates the men from the boys. All too often, medical advertising codes restrict what can be said in words. Descriptions of product efficacy become hopelessly watered down. The more successful marketers employ visual ideas to communicate product benefits and brand values. As will be shown, visuals can transcend a variety of marketing and communication problems and create impact beyond the category itself...in one case, all the way to the stock exchange.

RELIEVING AUSTRALIA'S STRESS

RELIEVING AUSTRALIA'S STRESS RELIEVING AUSTRALIA'S STRESS

NG AUSTRALIA'S STRESS

RELIEVING AUSTRALIA'S STRESS

RELIEVING AUSTRALIA'S STRESS RELIEVING AUSTRALIA'S STRESS

RELIEVING AUSTRALIA'S STRESS RELIEVING AUSTRALIA'S STRESS

RELIEVING AUSTRALIA'S STRESS

the problem Blackmores Executive B Stress Formula had been in the Blackmores range for several years, but had received no significant advertising support since its launch. However, in 1998/1999 an investment of about US$10,000 in the financial pages of national newspapers showed a promising return. Given an explosion of interest in the subject of stress in the workplace, Blackmores decided to invest around US$600,000 (including media and production) in advertising Executive B Stress Formula.

The campaign had two objectives. First, it had to deliver a 35% increase in ex-factory sales for the financial year 1999/2000. Second, it had to grow Blackmores' share of the stress category and achieve category dominance.

the strategy Superficially, the task appeared easy. But the target was as broad as "those who experience stress in their everyday life" — which was effectively everyone. Demographically though, it was skewed towards people aged 25-55 with a busy lifestyle.

Further communications barriers awaited. Most consumers were new to the supplements market. Beyond Vitamin C and multivitamins, their knowledge was zero. Nor did they see any difference between brands.

Finding a message that everyone could relate to was another challenge. For one thing, few people admitted to suffering from stress; to do so would have been an admission of weakness. Attempting to identify stress in specific terms was equally fraught with difficulties. How could a single stressful situation be dramatised in a commercial when a bus driver's stress was vastly different to a manager's stress — and to a mother's?

The insight came by identifying the core proposition: *living with stress every day*. Creatively the search began for the ultimate stress. The honours went to the charming albeit doleful metaphor of Larry, the last crayfish left in the tank at a Chinese seafood restaurant. Larry was totally stressed out; he could be popped into a boiling pot at any moment. His predicament allowed consumers to laugh at their own stress without embarrassment. And he busted the category. The crayfish metaphor was different from any competitive ads, stood out memorably, offered a universally appealing connection with a broad spectrum of consumers, and was creatively transferable to any medium: TV, print, radio, taxi backs, and point-of-sale.

Television provided initial mass exposure over the first three months. A week on/week off strategy built rapid reach within the target group. Rotating the 30-second version with a 15-second cutdown extended the campaign by additional weeks. Pre-Christmas, a key "stress occasion", received mid-week print support when jangling nerves were at their peak, while the January to February low stress holiday season saw a campaign hiatus.

the result Previously a niche product, Blackmores successfully aligned itself with a broad mass-market audience. The advertising generated a sustained 70% increase in product sales, twice the level of the pre-defined target (+35%).

According to Newspoll Data December 1999, the campaign helped Blackmores acquire 23% more new customers. Brand loyalty as measured by "Only/Preferred Brand" shot up from 22% to 37%.

Aztec Sales Data 1999/2000 reported the launch of 70 new vitamin supplements while 195 products advertised within the category. Over one year, this equates to a new vitamin option every second day. Despite all this activity, the total category registered less than 1% growth — while Blackmores Executive B Stress Formula grew by 8%.

In the Millward Brown Link Test, the Larry commercial achieved an Awareness Index score of 6.0, which was above the average for all Australian commercials and indicated the concept's potential to stand out in a cluttered break. 72% of people reported they would enjoy watching Larry each time he ran. 96% said the ad was easy to follow, with 92% taking out the main message as "relief of stress".

Over the campaign period Blackmores' share price increased ahead of sales and profit growth, exceeding the All Ordinaries Index.

❝

The 'Larry' Blackmores Executive B Stress Formula campaign is an excellent example of how an integrated strategic campaign with a unique creative execution and a simple uncluttered message can have a powerful effect on sales, despite a small budget."

JOSEFA FERNANDEZ, Marketing Director,
Blackmores

RELIEVING AUSTRALIA'S STRESS
RELIEVING AUSTRALIA'S STRESS   RELIEVING AUSTRALIA'S STRESS
RELIEVING AUSTRALIA'S STRESS   RELIEVING AUSTRALIA'S STRESS
RELIEVING AUSTRALIA'S STRESS   RELIEVING AUSTRALIA'S STRESS
RELIEVING AUSTRALIA'S STRESS
RELIEVING AUSTRALIA'S STRESS

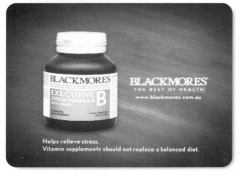

Being "Larry", the last crayfish in the tank of a Chinese seafood restaurant, is about as stressful as it gets.

As the commercial unfolds, the crayfish darts behind a rock whenever a Chinese employee emerges from the kitchen or passes the tank. We hear the Chinese restaurant ambience as Larry might hear it — an alien, threatening hubbub beyond the glass. Larry's agitated underwater scuttling noises add to the tension.

Just when Larry finally retreats behind a rock, a super establishes the subject matter: *Living with stress?*

Cut to the product and end super.

FEMALE VO: *Executive B Stress Formula with Herbs from Blackmores. The best of health.*

category	countries	advertiser	agency
PHARMACEUTICALS, HEALTH FOODS, VITAMINS	AUSTRALIA	JANSSEN-CILAG/ IMODIUM	THE CAMPAIGN PALACE, SYDNEY

FLUSHED WITH SUCCESS

FLUSHED WITH SUCCESS

FLUSHED WITH SUCCESS

FLUSHED WITH SUCCESS FLUSHED WITH SUCCESS

FLUSHED WITH SUCCESS FLUSHED WITH SUCCESS

FLUSHED WITH SUCCESS

FLUSHED WITH SUCCESS

the problem Up to 18% of the Australian population suffers from diarrhoea every year, but only 3 out of 10 sufferers actually treat the problem.

Until 1997, diarrhoea products were available through pharmacies and doctors only; no products were marketed directly to consumers. That year, the anti-diarrhoeal drug Imodium (Loperomide Hydrochloride) was rescheduled as an over-the-counter product. The opportunity then existed to create and market the first consumer brand in the category.

However, market growth for anti-diarrhoeal products was relatively slow in the five years prior to the launch. And in terms of brand building, mass communications barriers abounded. According to Chris Adams Research 1998, diarrhoea ranked second only to cold sores in terms of embarrassment. Because diarrhoea created a feeling of insecurity and anxiety, it would be difficult to address through advertising. The lack of consumer knowledge about diarrhoea and the high levels of confusion were such that many sufferers were not even aware that convenient dose format treatment was available.

In fact, the market was divided into two broad segments: those who treated diarrhoea (28% of the population) and those who didn't (72%). Many people believed diarrhoea was the body's natural way of flushing out a bug; others perceived diarrhoea was caused by everyday dietary factors. Consequently, immediate treatment was less of an issue.

Another hurdle that advertising would have to overcome was the product's image. While Imodium's prescription heritage underscored its efficacy and credibility, it also alienated consumers by creating the perception that Imodium was for serious sufferers only. The name, too, perpetuated this "serious sufferers" image.

The objective was to launch Imodium as a brand leader with premium price positioning. But it could only be sold through pharmacies where competitors Lomotil and Gastrolyte were well entrenched. Another rival, Gastrostop, retailed in some shops for 40% less than Imodium.

Could advertising effectively build a brand in such a low interest, low involvement category dominated by lack of consumer knowledge, apathy and embarrassment?

the strategy Advertising was tasked with creating a memorable and appealing brand that would become synonymous with anti-diarrhoeal treatment. "Treaters" had to be encouraged to use Imodium instead of other brands, while "non-treaters" had to be persuaded to treat their problem instead of just putting up with it.

Strategically the advertising was focused on sufferers ("treaters" and "non-treaters" alike). The agency saw a need to normalise the treatment of diarrhoea, even if it meant growing the entire category. The brand would be approachable, especially on an emotional level, by addressing loss of confidence, anxiety, embarrassment, loss of control and social discomfort.

Creatively, humour offered an empathetic and appealing means to communicate the two key consumer benefits — speed and confidence. An icon was sought for the brand that would create a unique creative mnemonic and unify communications across the board from television to point-of-sale, brochures and promotional material.

The icon was already in place, on toilet doors everywhere. The well-known silhouette of a man, affectionately dubbed "Dunny Boy", would become the brand property. The logic was clearly that every time anyone saw the character on a toilet door, they would think of Imodium.

Television was the selected medium. Somehow, on a budget of just US$750,000 for the year, media planning had to take into account that diarrhoea strikes at any time and anywhere. The initial four-week launch was followed by a strategy of continuity, buying a small amount of audience increments in key programming areas. By not trying to chase the high awareness created in the first four weeks, the budget was eventually stretched over six months.

Ambient media opportunities also existed to reach the audience while potentially in the "need" state. *Don't just sit there*, said posters on the back of toilet doors at Australian international airports; buy Imodium at the airport pharmacy before you leave home.

the result Within eight months of its launch, while maintaining a premium price position, Imodium grew its market share by 35.7%. Ex-warehouse sales were up 59% in 12 months. The campaign increased top-of-mind awareness by 500% in a low interest category, and increased brand consideration by 250%, taking substantial share from each of its competitors.

Imodium single-handedly grew the anti-diarrhoeal market by 20.8% in 1998. Ongoing tracking indicates that people's attitude towards treatment has changed. The number of people who consider that diarrhoea should be treated right away increased 69.3% in 12 months. Successfully growing the number of "treaters" achieved a behavioural change that many in the industry had thought impossible. The number of "treaters" rose from 5% of all adults to 7% in 12 months, a remarkable success considering that it took 11 years of consistent advertising to grow 7 percentage points in the category in the US.

Meanwhile, further successes were recorded at airports. January-to-July airport pharmacy sales increased 219% in volume and 237% in revenue dollars.

After the initial launch burst, every dollar spent on advertising returned 2.3 times in retail sales. Even including the initial launch, the advertising paid for itself in the first nine months.

❝❝

You don't get a dramatic increase like that unless you do something amazing. There is no question, it was the advertising that achieved this."

JASON CARROLL, Marketing Manager,
Janssen-Cilag

FLUSHED WITH SUCCESS
FLUSHED WITH SUCCESS   FLUSHED WITH SUCCESS
FLUSHED WITH SUCCESS FLUSHED WITH SUCCESS
FLUSHED WITH SUCCESS   FLUSHED WITH SUCCESS
FLUSHED WITH SUCCESS
FLUSHED WITH SUCCESS

Track in towards the familiar male symbol on a toilet door.

Suddenly the silhouette clenches its stomach, groans, and runs off the edge of the sign.

MALE VO: *Diarrhoea can be a real inconvenience.*

Relieved, the symbol walks back into place and resumes its familiar position. Pretty soon it has to race off again, before returning once more to the classic position.

MALE VO: *When it happens, it stops you being where you need to be.*

The silhouette reaches into its pocket and pulls out of pack of Imodium. Go in to tight shot of pack as he tips two caplets into his hand and takes them.

MALE VO: *But now there's Imodium. Just one dose of Imodium can control diarrhoea fast.*

A female toilet sign joins the male sign. After a happy embrace, they walk out of frame together.

MALE VO: *So you can get on with your life with confidence.*

End pack shot.

MALE VO: *Imodium. Controls diarrhoea fast.*

Only available from pharmacies. Use only as directed.
If symptoms persist, seek medical advice. Always read the label.

IKEA
TANGS   HALLENSTEINS
IKEA   SUNRISE DEPARTMENT STORE
SUNRISE DEPARTMENT STORE
ALLENSTEINS   RETAIL   SUNRISE DEPARTMENT STORE
IKEA   IKEA
TANGS
HALLENSTEINS
SUNRISE DEPARTMENT STORE   IKEA
TANGS   HALLENSTEINS
TANGS

Retail

WHEN it comes to developing strategic brand communications in the retail sector, it could well be a case of damned-if-you-do and damned-if-you-don't. Driven by merchandise and prices, and obsessed with immediate turnover, few retail campaigns have ever contributed lasting brand images to their paymasters. Yet there is absolutely no reason why more great retail brands can't be built. The selected case histories will show what happens when brand communications are conveyed in tandem with tactical activity.

FUTURE-PROOFING A BRAND
IN FIFTEEN SECONDS

FUTURE-PROOFING A BRAND
IN FIFTEEN SECONDS

FUTURE-PROOFING A BRAND
IN FIFTEEN SECONDS

FUTURE-PROOFING A BRAND
IN FIFTEEN SECONDS

FUTURE-PROOFING A BRAND
IN FIFTEEN SECONDS

FUTURE-PROOFING A BRAND
IN FIFTEEN SECONDS

FUTURE-PROOFING A BRAND
IN FIFTEEN SECONDS

FUTURE-PROOFING A BRAND
IN FIFTEEN SECONDS

the problem Hallensteins is a publicly-listed men's wear retailer that started out in the 1880s on New Zealand's South Island making and selling men's clothing through mail order. The first commercial stores opened in the 1920s and grew into today's nationwide chain of 40 outlets. While Hallensteins does not manufacture clothing these days it offers its own branded merchandise, frequently sourced from independent New Zealand manufacturers.

Originally, Hallensteins was an aging brand catering to an aging population. The brand had to become younger, even for basic clothing products. The core target audience was redefined — males 18 to 39. But in truth, even "subversive" brands like Mambo are worn by the 30s-plus. Age, it seems, is in the eye of the beholder.

Hallensteins dynamically reinvented itself. Every six weeks merchandising teams visit the world's cutting edge fashion centres, and their designs reflect the latest global trends. But the group still has to compete in a very tough retail arena, and when it comes to advertising its US$500,000 budget has to cover both brand building and retailing.

the strategy Brand positioning comes from the product itself, because the clothing in the store is very much the brand. Hallensteins has become synonymous with masculinity, an environment created for men.

However, as a rule of thumb, New Zealand men don't buy fashion — they buy clothes. So while the core target males are 18 to 39, women 18 to 39 were identified as the key influencers. Media is bought against both groups, ensuring the influencers are aware of the offers. The advertising itself is unashamedly male. Hallensteins advertising projects an attitude, behaviour and personality that comfortably fits the New Zealand male psyche. On one hand, Hallensteins is a brand that a man would like to sit down and have a beer with, while on the other it is a brand that women feel very attracted to because of its strong masculinity.

Hallensteins does not overtly sell fashionability but functionality. Each new product offering is presented creatively against two criteria: what is the most important selling point of the merchandise, and how does the merchandise demonstrate what is being said about the brand?

Television is the main medium. Every commercial is offer-driven, but must contribute to the future-proofing of the brand against its competitors. The commercials are always 15-seconders, turned around in a three-week time frame. They are made on a shoestring. Concepts are simple and single-minded, and as a result their effect is more enduring. Creativity follows no formulae. Each new commercial is fresh and surprising. Very often the opening scene is the entire commercial, the action unfolding in just one shot. The ads always demonstrate something about the brand and its relationship with masculinity. Irreverence resonates for Hallensteins: witness the commercial where the featured garment was stuffed into a car's petrol tank to replace the missing cap.

Each new commercial breaks on a Sunday night when viewership peaks, and runs until Thursday night. The effect is to push the market at the beginning of the week and pull sales throughout the week.

the result Nielsen Omnibus tracking registered a 71% "Total spontaneous awareness" of Hallensteins amongst all people, 15 and over, naming "Top of mind men's clothing store brands". The next-mentioned "Highest awareness" score was 59%.

66% of all Hallensteins customers were in the 15–44 age group, with 41% of those in the core 15–34 core group.

The performance of each new commercial was tracked through sales and measured against historical data. As one example, the station wagon commercial increased sales volume of the product on offer by 605% over the previous week.

The Hallensteins-Glassons group is acknowledged as one of the most successful retail operations in Australasia. Recently, Hallensteins opened its first store in Melbourne, Australia and is outperforming against long-entrenched local competitors.

A man wearing shorts sits cross-legged in a chair in an interrogation room.

Then, like the famous scene with Sharon Stone in *Basic Instinct*, he slowly and deliberately crosses his masculine-looking legs in the opposite direction.

SUPER: *Basic Shorts any 2 for $35*

END LOGO: *Hallensteins*

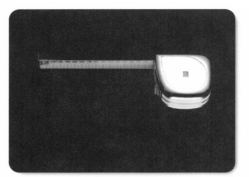

A metal tape measure slowly retracts against a black background.

SUPER: *Cold?*

Cut to a man standing in Carpenter Pants in a cold, desolate landscape. He gives his crotch a reassuring pat.

SUPER: *Heavyweight Carpenter Pants*

END LOGO: *Hallensteins Technical Equipment*

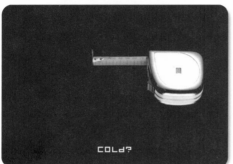

The camera is locked-off on a shot of a men's washroom. A man in a suit comes out of a cubicle, zips his fly and walks out of frame.

The shot is held. A second man exits from another cubicle and zips the leg of his pants just above the knee.

SUPER: *$10 off zip-leg pants now $39.95*

END LOGO: *Hallensteins*

Two young men are travelling in a yellow station wagon that has seen better days. The windscreen is missing and the cold air blows straight in. Both men are wearing polar sweats and goggles.

SUPER: *Polar sweats $49.95*

Cut to a T-shirt stuffed into the petrol tank to replace the missing cap.

SUPER: *With free t-shirt*

END LOGO: *Hallensteins*

A thief in a Richard Nixon mask is fleeing the police. He ducks into an alleyway for a quick change.

He pulls off his long-sleeved T-shirt, revealing he is wearing a second T-shirt of a different colour beneath.

SUPER: *Long sleeve T's 2 for $25*

Stuffing the incriminating T-shirt into his bag, but still wearing his Nixon mask, he walks back out to the street.

The police ignore him and run past into the alley.

END LOGO: *Hallensteins*

category	countries	advertiser	agency
RETAIL	SINGAPORE	IKEA	DENTSU YOUNG & RUBICAM, SINGAPORE

CONNECTING WITH A SMILE   CONNECTING WITH A SMILE   CONNECTING WITH A SMILE

CONNECTING WITH A SMILE CONNECTING WITH A SMILE

CONNECTING WITH A SMILE   CONNECTING WITH A SMILE
            CONNECTING WITH A SMILE   CONNECTING WITH A SMILE

the problem IKEA has successfully broadened its appeal in Singapore against a plethora of aggressive competitors. It is not shy of taking on local, topical issues and its market leadership strategy is to sell furniture with a twinkle in the eye.

the strategy IKEA has consistently pursued a clean, upscale, Scandinavian look in its advertising. The brand has eschewed typical black-and-white retail pages in favour of less frequent, more expensive colour pages. Merchandise is carefully themed so that only related items appear in the same ad. Classy art direction successfully packs a lot of product-price detail into each ad, designed so that one or two larger items catch the eye first. Witty headlines occasionally defy non-English educated Singaporeans, deliberately underscoring IKEA's aspirational brand values.

Beyond its regular advertising, IKEA seized a topical opportunity during a recent Singapore election. Singaporeans enjoy poking good-natured fun at politics so IKEA spoofed political jargon on a series of bus ads. Interestingly, the buses were those on routes passing through the Prime Minister's electorate.

the result IKEA's bus ads registered a significant increase in store traffic during the advertising period plus strong recall of their messages.

Free oxygen with every purchase

YOU DON'T HAVE TO BE RICH TO BE CLEVER
IKEA

There's more than one way to hang your mother-in-law

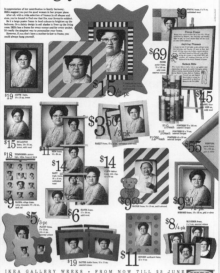

IKEA GALLERY WEEKS • FROM NOW TILL 23 JUNE
IKEA

CABINET RESHUFFLE PUTS HOUSE IN ORDER.

CUSTOM-MADE CABINETS
IKEA

PUT HIM BEHIND BARS TILL HE TALKS.

CHILDREN'S FURNITURE AND BABY COTS
IKEA

category	countries	advertiser	agency
RETAIL	TAIWAN	SUNRISE DEPARTMENT STORE	IDEOLOGY ADVERTISING AGENCY LTD, TAIPEI

RETHINKING RETAILING

RETHINKING RETAILING   RETHINKING RETAILING

RETHINKING RETAILING RETHINKING RETAILING

RETHINKING RETAILING   RETHINKING RETAILING   RETHINKING RETAILING

RETHINKING RETAILING

the problem Taipei's young elite are uncompromising. They are smart, sophisticated, worldly. They live on the cutting edge of style, drawing inspiration from Japan and the West. When they shop, they have high expectations.

Given that its audience had "seen everything", how could the Sunrise department store bond with them? What kind of advertising would build its image as a fashion magnet for some of Asia's most discriminating yet fickle young adults?

the strategy Sunrise repositioned itself from a department store to a boutique. The campaign was lateral in concept and execution. Subjects from the domains of culture, politics, philosophy — even psychoanalysis — were translated into the language of fashion. The nihilistic coexisted with the flamboyant.

Radical imagery and startling propositions like *Living well is the best revenge* were communicated through television and print, challenging the young elite to change their shopping habits.

the result The Sunrise campaign was hailed as one of the most successful retail campaigns in Taiwan. Sunrise became a fashion venue and was able to improve space utilisation within the store. Target customers reportedly looked forward to each new execution in the series.

Its impact and influence extended far beyond the category. The campaign became arguably the most talked about advertising in Taiwan, redefining the aesthetics and executional values of television creativity.

After a missile test was conducted in the vicinity of Taiwan, consumers quickly felt the political tension. The pressure greatly influenced the demand for luxury products, and inspired this commercial called *The Slapping*.

A man in curious medieval garb and a woman wearing a feathered headdress slap each other throughout the commercial. In the background, girls in elegant long dresses parade with umbrellas. Strange rhythmic chanting intensifies as the man and woman strike each other with increasing violence.

ENGLISH GRAPHICS APPEAR: *Love, hope and shopping.*

The slapping continues until they both collapse in a cloud of feathers.

VO AND SUPER: *People have the freedom to enjoy shopping.*

An eerie Zulu-style war cry pays tribute to the two vanquished warriors.

A new meaning has been given to shopping at a fashion boutique and browsing through a bookstore. Unlike conventional thinking, their roles have been swapped...

Fashion models wearing open books on their heads sashay through a bookstore. A panel of erudite judges applauds them.

A WOMAN IS SINGING: *Do not hesitate, What are you thinking...?*

Pages of text are intercut with hip young people reading books on cushions and an elegant model with an umbrella.

VO: *What do you need after you have acquired breasts? A brain.*

Female pallbearers draped in black carry an open coffin filled with books.

An old scholar with a quill pen observes the proceedings.

VO: *To cultivate disposition at a fashion boutique, exhibit fashion at a bookstore.*

Creative rationale: in the present era, we have endured much change and destruction. People are desperate and without hope, and find it difficult to have faith in anything. Fashion, at least, offers some relief...

We are in a surreal workhouse environment.

Beautiful robotic models shake out dustsheets and clean the surfaces of long workshop benches.

vo: *To care for your clothes is as important as buying them.*

Then they carry in the clothes that have to be very carefully folded.

Clones bend to their task, folding each garment with painstaking precision, watched by female overseers armed with canes.

vo and super: *Clothes are the last appealing condition of this era.*

category
RETAIL

countries
SINGAPORE

advertiser
TANGS

agency
WORK,
SINGAPORE

BUYING INTO CHANGE
BUYING INTO CHANGE
BUYING INTO CHANGE
BUYING INTO CHANGE
BUYING INTO CHANGE BUYING INTO CHANGE
BUYING INTO CHANGE BUYING INTO CHANGE
BUYING INTO CHANGE
BUYING INTO CHANGE

the problem C. K. Tang stepped off a junk from China with nothing but ambition and a tin trunk full of cloth. He peddled his wares door-to-door to the housewives of Singapore, steadily building a reputation for honesty and value. When he opened his own store in 1932, he specialised in linen, housewares, and all kinds of inexpensive knick-knacks.

Then came the watershed period of the early 1980s. A new, younger chairman became the catalyst for change, introducing fashion and cosmetics to his father's traditional merchandise. He catered for a new type of Singaporean, the young working couples called Yuppies. He hired new visual merchandisers with fashion backgrounds. Then came Tangs Studio in 1988, the cutting edge of fashion with a new, American-designed store ambience.

By 1998, after further refinements, Tangs had a new positioning to communicate, and they looked for advertising that would deliver it with freshness and style.

the strategy Tangs had decided to target two groups: contemporary adult Singaporeans and the tourists attracted by their location at the junction of Orchard and Scotts Roads. Both are worldly, affluent and sophisticated shoppers. Tangs were conscious that they had to benchmark themselves against the best in the world. Their new advertising voice had to be interesting, intriguing, and more intellectually engaging.

Tangs bit the bullet. They knew they could not be all things to all men. If their new type of advertising alienated some older core customers, so be it. Branding and positioning had to become more aspirational.

The advertising broke fresh ground in Singapore's mainstream retail category. In fact, Tangs have been accused of being too daring, too ahead of their time. For their part, Tangs keep a wary eye on credibility. The smartness and intelligence of the advertising must be reflected in the presentation of merchandise and the shopping experience. The advertising must not overpromise nor underdeliver.

Significantly, Tangs strive for a balance between strategic and tactical communication in each campaign. And while most retailers fear that people won't "get" something clever or different, Tangs pursues freshness at every opportunity — sales events, Christmas, and Chinese New Year. The advertising agency is charged with providing imaginative, witty executions that not only get the message through, but also create a longer lasting impression in the market. For example, a full page Anniversary Sale ad presented readers with an application for urgent leave set in a sea of expensive white space. Another full page, full colour ad, worth around US$13,000, featured a well-known local female impersonator and the intriguing proposition, *Dumped? Shop!* Anecdotal evidence cites people who "got" the ad explaining it to people who didn't, which Tangs consider bonus mileage for any advertiser. Maintaining freshness led to a Tangs Studio campaign where girls were illustrated with incredibly stretched necks; by employing cutting edge creative executions, the campaign signalled that Tangs Studio — like its customers — knew what was "out there".

the result The new advertising, in tandem with new store visual merchandising, has brought back younger working adults and trendy families who had given up shopping at Tangs thinking it was "my mother's store", or "my auntie only shops there".

According to Tangs, cleaner, uncluttered ads worked because people could better appreciate the simplicity of the ideas. The new advertising represented accurately what the store was offering.

Tangs attribute other successes to their advertising. In world terms, for example, Tangs describe themselves as a "small retailer", but when they present their advertising to manufacturers abroad, it never fails to impress those with whom they are negotiating. The greatest tribute to their new branding came in 2001. Tangs was recognised as one of the top 5 housewares retailers in the world. They received the GIA Global Innovator Award, bestowed by the International Housewares Association based in Chicago.

❝❝

The biggest customer we really have to convince is not the external customer but the internal customer. We have to challenge ourselves, and you get a little scared every day, but you have to try. The realisation of your goals is not over just one campaign, it's over time before it sinks in. The worst thing is to underestimate your customers, both intellectually and in their sense of aesthetics. When you get shaky and you feel this time round it didn't work, and you drop everything, you could actually be doing yourself a great disservice."

GERRY REZEL, Vice-President Group Marketing & Communications, C.K. Tang Limited

❝❝

We are more like a creative department to Tangs. We do not have to carry the burden that they are the typical client and we are doing chores for them. That eradicates a lot of psychological barriers so we are free to discuss work."

THESEUS CHAN, Creative Director, WORK, Singapore

BUYING INTO CHANGE
BUYING INTO CHANGE
BUYING INTO CHANGE
BUYING INTO CHANGE **BUYING INTO CHANGE** BUYING INTO CHANGE
BUYING INTO CHANGE BUYING INTO CHANGE
BUYING INTO CHANGE
BUYING INTO CHANGE

*style

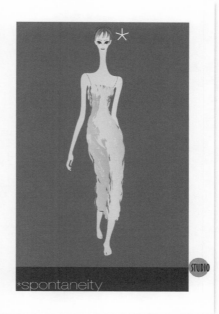

*spontaneity

*substance

*sublime

The Tangs
Anniversary Sale
starts today

✂----------------------------------

APPLICATION
FOR URGENT LEAVE

SUBMITTED BY

DEPARTMENT

NO. OF DAY(S) APPLIED

FROM   TO

LEAVE BALANCE

SIGNATURE   DATE

APPROVED / NOT APPROVED

DEPARTMENT HEAD   DATE

HR DEPARTMENT   DATE

REMARKS

NO FRILLS FUNERALS   NRMA
NO FRILLS FUNERALS   SERVICES   NO FRILLS FUNERALS
NRMA   NRMA
NO FRILLS FUNERALS   NRMA

Services

BUILDING brands in the service category requires a special discipline. Many services are intangible, and the risk is that service brands can easily become generic. Too many campaigns in this category show stereotypical scenarios in which any number of brands could reside. While "protection" and "care" can be demonstrated, the brand must be fundamental to the message. And when one brand spans different types of services the task becomes correspondingly harder. Highly original strategic thinking is the category cornerstone.

NO LAUGHING MATTER?

NO LAUGHING MATTER?   NO LAUGHING MATTER?   NO LAUGHING MATTER?

LAUGHING MATTER? **NO LAUGHING MATTER?**

NO LAUGHING MATTER?   NO LAUGHING MATTER?

NO LAUGHING MATTER?   NO LAUGHING MATTER?

NO LAUGHING MATTER?

the problem Anticipating a funerals and cremations boom in 2016 when Baby Boomers begin turning 70, American funeral operators moved into the Australian market. And with them came sophisticated marketing methods.

For example, the company that owns No Frills believes in segmentation. It operates many different funeral parlour brands, including upscale and middle class brands and two different "no frills" brands.

The brand name No Frills Funerals certainly communicated a clear, quick promise, was instantly memorable, and conveyed a likeable, no-nonsense, back-to-basics attitude. But how should the brand be marketed, given the sensitivities of bereaved families and the rather brutal simplicity of the name?

the strategy The agency believed a "category buster" campaign was called for, something that would force consumers to both reassess and reposition all the brands they knew in the category. However, every category has its own set of unwritten advertising rules, which few brand owners and agencies are ever prepared to break.

For No Frills Funerals, the communications opportunity was clear: oppose the sentimentalist norms of funeral marketing. Instead, the agency concentrated on the proposition from the point of view of the deceased.

The campaign line, *When you're gone, you're gone*, is simple and disarmingly true. Despite its irreverence, the agency believed no one could reasonably take offence with the statement. But how much credit could the public be given? Could people laugh at themselves — in the context of death — and appreciate stark, blunt humour?

The back-to-basics direction necessitated "no frills" production. The first commercial used a black screen, a couple of supers and some library music. Following commercials used a neat little pile of ashes on a plate (for those seeking a no frills cremation) and a shot looking down at some lawn (for those seeking a no frills burial). The fourth commercial used "talent": a real gravedigger, shot by a fixed camera so the viewer's attention was focused on the maudlin man of the moment.

The campaign tonality was tightly controlled, the brand identity consistent from one execution to the next. The deliberately economical look was an integral part of the irony. The intelligence of the message gave the brand dignity, while its pragmatic honesty struck a chord with today's cynical, anti-commercial audience. In early cinema tests of the commercials, nobody took offence. In fact, they enjoyed the dark humour.

Carefully targeted media included TV, suburban cinema (well attended by retirees), selected radio, press and direct mail.

the result A 50% increase in telephone inquiries was recorded when the advertising ran. The campaign was also a big hit with the news media. A scoop by the Sydney *Sun-Herald* was followed by stories on Australian television, on the Net by the London *Times*, and as far away as Thailand, Greece and the USA.

❝

The campaign Saatchi & Saatchi developed perfectly captures the way our No Frills customers think. We're not out to talk people out of having fancy funerals. We have other brands that meet that need. By advertising No Frills, we want people already leaning to the simple route to feel OK about it and to know there is a brand out there that thinks the way they do. For obvious reasons it's difficult to measure the success of an advertising campaign for a funeral business in terms of sales uplift. Instead, we prefer to measure increased awareness of our brand in the community by the number of calls to our offices during the period of the campaign."

CHRIS TIMMINS, **Marketing Director**

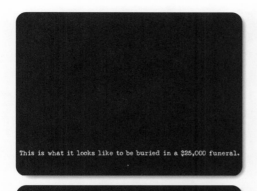

This is what it looks like to be buried in a $25,000 funeral.

This is what it looks like to be buried in a $5,000 funeral.

No Frills
FUNERALS & CREMATIONS

When you're gone, you're gone.

Black screen and classical music throughout. No voice-over.

FIRST SUPER: *This is what it looks like to be buried in a $25,000 funeral.*

NEXT SUPER: *This is what it looks like to be buried in a $5,000 funeral.*

LOGO: *No Frills Funerals & Cremations. Call 9247 6895.*

FINAL SUPER: *When you're gone, you're gone.*

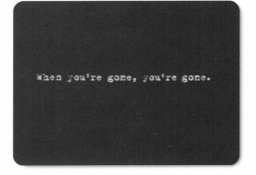

The camera is locked-off on a gravedigger, a rather bizarre figure standing in the midst of a cemetery.

Nothing moves. Nobody speaks. Just the same classical music is again heard throughout.

FIRST SUPER: *This is who buries you in a $25,000 funeral.*

NEXT SUPER: *This is who buries you in a $5,000 funeral.*

LOGO: *No Frills Funerals & Cremations. Call 9247 6895.*

FINAL SUPER: *When you're gone, you're gone.*

STRETCHING BRAND VALUES

STRETCHING BRAND VALUES

STRETCHING BRAND VALUES

STRETCHING BRAND VALUES

STRETCHING BRAND VALUES   STRETCHING BRAND VALUES   STRETCHING BRAND VALUES

STRETCHING BRAND VALUES   STRETCHING BRAND VALUES

the problem The National Roads and Motorists Association, better known as the NRMA, started up in 1920 as a road service organisation like the AA and the RAC for motorists in distress. Originally operating only in the Australian State of New South Wales, these days the NRMA is also Australia's largest general insurer.

In 1994, the NRMA's brief was to take the goodwill that the public felt towards the road service part of the brand and extend it to the commercial side of the organisation. "Trust" was the key word in that brief.

the strategy The agency took a different view. It believed the NRMA should think of itself strategically as a "help" organisation, a guardian angel, whether it was your car that had broken down or your house that had been broken into. "Help" was the single most powerful element of the brand's heritage, they argued. It could be leveraged across a wide range of product and service applications.

Creatively, the idea was to link the two words — *NRMA* and *HELP* — so they became synonymous. And, because the *NRMA* name itself has to be spelt out letter by letter to be pronounced, the promise of *HELP* was to be spelt out exactly the same way — *NRMA for H.E.L.P.* The result was a simple branding mnemonic that became the scaffold on which to build the brand.

The line delivered a bonus. It provided an internal vision for the organisation and a mission for its staff. Every employee, no matter in which part of the NRMA they worked, went to work with a clear focus on what had to be done that day: they had to *H.E.L.P.* As three quarters of all NRMA's sales take place through their branches, *H.E.L.P.* drove the company culture at every level.

Over the years the campaign has stretched heart-warming brand values and allowed the NRMA to launch into new categories and new markets. For example, the *Ladybird* commercial — for NRMA Insurance — was a powerful analogy for all the disasters that can befall a community. Inspired by the French film *Microcosmos*, it showed life and death drama on a miniature scale.

A rainstorm hurled water, leaves, and monstrous raindrops at tiny creatures in a field. The sense of reality was achieved by 3D animation. The sound effects were huge, the music pure Hollywood. Interestingly, when the ad was researched, it was shown up until the *Need help?* super was shown. The respondents were asked whose ad it was and unanimously said NRMA.

The *NRMA for H.E.L.P.* device worked across the core services of the organisation, too. A story of a young man seeking a job at the NRMA reaffirmed the public perception of NRMA roadside service. He was late for his interview because he stopped on the way to help a stranded motorist.

The theme line also sat nicely with all the NRMA's community work, from assistance for street kids to bushfire awareness campaigns.

It worked beyond traditional media. Lift doors re-enacted car smashes for NRMA Car Insurance. Specially painted crooked pedestrian crossings near pubs warned oncoming motorists to be wary of drunken pedestrians.

the result When the NRMA launched into the State of Victoria the campaign was so successful it had to stop running ads until more sales staff could be hired and trained. The recent introduction of NRMA Health Insurance resulted in over 20,000 policies written — 85% over target — which equates to revenue of around US$20 million. In addition, over double the amount of enquiries were generated. From a standing start in January 2000, prompted awareness for NRMA Health Insurance reached 37% in just two months.

❝❝

Saatchi & Saatchi's NRMA campaign is a good example of advertising that shows how a product or service can make our dreams come true, solve our problems, relieve our anxieties. It strongly enforces the NRMA position in consumers' minds as a 'guardian angel'."

HUGH MACKAY, Mackay Research Sydney

"

We judge the merits of a brand property on how readily it adapts itself not to one or two media, but to any media — *H.E.L.P.* has proved itself to be resilient in doing this over the years, sitting as comfortably on a postcard or a poster or a press ad."

ADRIAN LEPPARD, Group Account Director,
Saatchi & Saatchi Sydney

STRETCHING BRAND VALUES

STRETCHING BRAND VALUES

STRETCHING BRAND VALUES

STRETCHING BRAND VALUES

STRETCHING BRAND VALUES

STRETCHING BRAND VALUES

STRETCHING BRAND VALUES

STRETCHING BRAND VALUES

STRETCHING BRAND VALUES

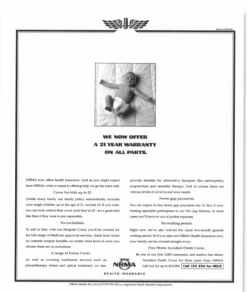

Leveraging the organisation's motoring heritage, the NRMA Health Insurance campaign achieved results 85% over target.

NRMA Car Insurance turned lift doors into moving posters.

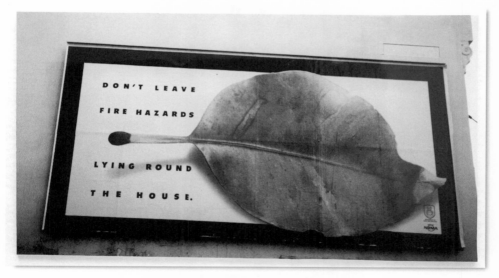

The NRMA helps prevent bushfires.

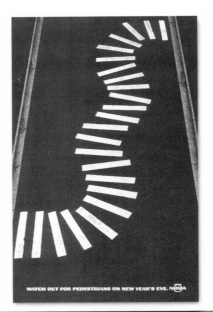

The NRMA helps warn drivers to watch out for drunken pedestrians.

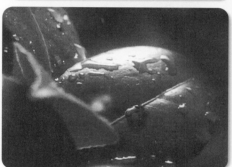

In the style of the film *Microcosmos*, we see the effects of a storm on the tiny inhabitants of a small field. 3D animation creates believable "reality".

Blades of grass sway in the wind like huge tree trunks. Leaves crash to the ground like heavy sheets of metal.

Ants flee into a hole. Little insects shelter under rocks, away from the tidal wave of an overfull puddle. The sounds of the storm are magnified to become awesome and more threatening. The music is cinematic.

We follow the plight of a ladybird. As it tries to run across a branch, it is pelted by gigantic raindrops.

One heavy drop knocks it onto its back.

SUPER: *Need help?*

Cut to the NRMA logo. The letters dissolve into the word *HELP*.

A child's hand delicately picks up the ladybird and puts it back on its feet.

MVO: *Every day, we help more Australians with the big things in life, their cars, their homes, than any other company. NRMA for H.E.L.P.*

A young man is rushing out the front door for a job interview. His mother offers last minute encouragement.

MOTHER: *I've got a good feeling about this one, darling. Take lots of deep breaths…*

He practises as he runs to his car. Just as he drives off a heavy rainstorm begins.

When he sees a woman and her two kids in a stalled car, he can't ignore their plight. He runs back through the rain to help, and pushes her car to the side of the road. Opening the hood he works on her engine. By the time it kicks into life, he is a total wreck, his suit saturated, spattered with oil.

At last he dashes into a big gleaming office building. People stare at him oddly. He leaps into a lift and takes a couple of quick deep breaths. But the interview section is full of immaculately dressed young men as he approaches the receptionist.

YOUNG MAN: *Sorry I'm late. Is there any chance that…*

By sunset, his mother anxiously awaits news by the front gate. An NRMA van drives up, lights flashing like a Christmas tree.

Her son leaps out, proudly showing off his uniform.

MALE VO: *NRMA, always have been, and always will be, dedicated to helping people on the roads.*

The NRMA logo dissolves into *HELP*.

category country advertiser agency

FAR EASTONE TELECOM CO. SMARTONE MOBILE COMMUNICATIONS/SMARTGUIDE HONG KONG POST/SPEEDPOST SINGTEL

SMARTONE MOBILE COMMUNICATIONS/SMARTGUIDE M1 SMARTONE MOBILE COMMUNICATIONS/INTERNATIONAL ROAMING

SINGTEL TELECOMMUNICATIONS AND POSTAL SERVICES

ASTONE TELECOM CO. FAR EASTONE TELECOM CO. SINGTEL SINGTEL

M1 HONG KONG POST/SPEEDPOST SMARTONE MOBILE COMMUNICATIONS/INTERNATIONAL ROAMING

HONG KONG POST/SPEEDPOST

TelecommunicationsAndPostalServices

PHENOMENAL growth in telecommunications has fuelled a new set of marketing and advertising conventions. Sadly, however, technology seems to dazzle marketers more than it does consumers. Technology, of course, is transient whereas brand building is still the name of the game. Brand communications should always employ simplicity and reach out to consumers with relevant, single-minded propositions. The most successful brand owners in the category have proved the truth of this, in many cases communicating complex new technology not with technospeak, but with irresistible humour and charm.

category	countries	advertiser	agency
TELE-COMMUNICATIONS AND POSTAL SERVICES	TAIWAN	FAR EASTONE TELECOM CO.	SAATCHI & SAATCHI, TAIWAN

TECHNOLOGY WITH A HUMAN TOUCH
TECHNOLOGY WITH A HUMAN TOUCH
TECHNOLOGY WITH A HUMAN TOUCH

TECHNOLOGY WITH A HUMAN TOUCH

TECHNOLOGY WITH A HUMAN TOUCH
TECHNOLOGY WITH A HUMAN TOUCH
TECHNOLOGY WITH A HUMAN TOUCH
TECHNOLOGY WITH A HUMAN TOUCH

the problem By May 2000, mobile phone penetration in Taiwan had reached 65%, and the revenue stream was poised to switch from voice to enhanced value-added services. In fact, market analysts were predicting revenues in mobile data would begin to exceed that of voice communication within three to five years in mature markets worldwide. Not surprisingly, all Taiwanese operators tried to own the value-added services category. Value-added WAP services were launched with celebrity endorsements and heavy media investment.

Far Eastone Telecom (FET) is Taiwan's second largest private telecom operator. While consumers perceived FET as a premium quality telecom company, it had maintained a very low profile in promoting its value-added offerings. As a result, few of its customers were able to recognise or appreciate them.

Against competitive pressure, FET planned to launch its new *147# mobile e-coupon service. However, its technology promised to be a double-edged sword. On one hand, 85% of the total FET customer base had handsets equipped with Chinese display and would be able to access the new service. But on the other, e-coupon was not deliverable via the most advanced technology such as WAP, which its competitors were heavily promoting.

the strategy While FET customers knew a mobile e-era was coming, many felt the new value-added services were irrelevant to them. Manufacturer jargon had confused the market, too. Misconceptions abounded. People were uncertain whether they needed to upgrade their current handsets to a WAP phone. Would they need to remember lots of new codes and protocols to harness all the dazzling new features? And above all, would their air time bills skyrocket in the process?

Strategically, FET opted to communicate tangible benefits over abstract technospeak. Its *147# service was positioned as a virtual shopping mall that offered discounts on all kinds of merchandise. The "shopping mall" already existed in current handsets, waiting to be accessed. Smart users could earn discounts through smarter shopping, a subject of universal interest in Taiwan.

The campaign creatively played on the fact that the shopping at *147#

is so good that everyone wants to find "the place". All kinds of amusing miscommunications built the intrigue. Old folks read the * and # keys as the Chinese words for rice and a well. One well-meaning chap even directs two little old ladies out to a rice paddy. Everyone is running around looking for *147# when all they have to do is dial *147# and they're there.

the result The campaign chalked up a 160% increase in SMS calls. Peak usage soared to 98,402 a day during the campaign — all up, *147# was accessed 5 million times while the advertising ran.

In terms of customer loyalty, research showed the indicator of "High quality communication" increased to 31% in August 2000, an 8% increase within 4 months. Measuring innovative brand image, the indicator of "Providing many useful services" increased by 13%, from 22% in April to 35% in August 2000. "Good company reputation" scored a 5% increase to 40% in August 2000, up from 35% in April.

TECHNOLOGY WITH A HUMAN TOUCH
TECHNOLOGY WITH A HUMAN TOUCH   TECHNOLOGY WITH A HUMAN TOUCH

TECHNOLOGY WITH A HUMAN TOUCH

TECHNOLOGY WITH A HUMAN TOUCH   TECHNOLOGY WITH A HUMAN TOUCH

TECHNOLOGY WITH A HUMAN TOUCH

TECHNOLOGY WITH A HUMAN TOUCH

A young woman gets onto a bus and eagerly asks the driver: *Does this bus go to *147#?*

The driver hasn't a clue what she is talking about: *What?*

The young woman tries to explain: **147#... It's a place where you can buy books and computers and we get a discount!*

By this time the other passengers have pricked up their ears.

The bus driver asks them: *Does anybody know where *147# is?*

One old lady (mistaking the * key for the Chinese word 米 *mǐ*, meaning rice) says it must be the rice shop.

An old man gets up and tells the bus: *There is a well in my home town...*

Everybody laughs at him — he has mistaken the pound key # for the Chinese word 井 *jǐng*, meaning a well.

Eventually the bus driver tells her: *I suggest you ask the next bus driver.*

Which she does without luck, bus after bus, until late into the night.

Cut to five mobile phone keys: **147#*

MALE VO: *Just dial *147# and you are there.*

END LOGO AND SLOGAN: *Only FarEasTone, closing the distance.*

Two rather bizarre twins on a motor bike pull up beside a young woman in a city street. They babble at her in non-stop twinspeak.

THE TWINS: *Excuse me, Miss, do you know where *147# is? We are going there to buy a mobile phone and clothes and a motor bike. It always offers a discount at any time.*

THE YOUNG WOMAN: *Maybe you should… go further in that direction…*

Which they do, only to return a few moments later.

TWINS: *Miss, you gave us the wrong directions.*

THE YOUNG WOMAN: *It should be the second street when you go further in that direction.*

The twins travel so far that their bike runs out of fuel.

One twin urges the other to push harder: *If you don't help me to push the bike, I will tell mum. Are we there yet?*

Again they meet the girl and ask sarcastically: *Where exactly is *147#?*

The five mobile phone keys appear: *147#

MALE VO: *Just dial *147# and you are there.*

END LOGO AND SLOGAN: *Only FarEasTone, closing the distance.*

category	countries	advertiser	agency
TELE-COMMUNICATIONS AND POSTAL SERVICES	HONG KONG	HONGKONG POST/ SPEEDPOST	OGILVYONE WORLDWIDE, HONG KONG

DELIVERING A NEW BRAND
DELIVERING A NEW BRAND
LIVERING A NEW BRAND

DELIVERING A NEW BRAND

DELIVERING A NEW BRAND
DELIVERING A NEW BRAND DELIVERING A NEW BRAND DELIVERING A NEW BRAND
DELIVERING A NEW BRAND

the problem With the change from a vote-funded government department to a trading fund department in late 1995, Hong Kong Post Office gained greater operational flexibility and financial autonomy. Then, with the return of Hong Kong to the People's Republic of China in 1997, the postal services were renamed Hongkong Post. In that same year, Hongkong Post decided to relaunch its Speedpost international courier service. Easier said than done.

Speedpost had been in operation since 1973. It had received little marketing or advertising support. As a result, market misconceptions had to be corrected and market share regained. At the very least, a new identity was needed. Beyond that, a massive business opportunity awaited Speedpost, provided that the brand could be successfully created and crafted from scratch.

the strategy Two target groups were identified: business users were mainly the office managers of small-to-medium sized local Hong Kong companies, particularly those in manufacturing which sent merchandise overseas; and general users, mainly expatriates, domestic helpers and Hong Kong Chinese with family members located overseas.

Speedpost's international competitors — UPS, FedEx and DHL — offered "reassuring reliability". None, however, showed the brand playing an active role in the user's life. Could this territory — giving the user a sense of being in control — provide a fresh point of differentiation for Speedpost?

The new Brand Print for Speedpost was James Bond, when the whole of the world is about to be destroyed and there is only 3 seconds left on the clock. In other words, time is in short supply — but it can be *stretched*! The Brand World was defined as a world where you don't have to battle with time, where you know you are always fully in control, where you never panic nor lose your sense of equilibrium.

The Speedpost brand idea became *"We put time on your side"*. Work began with a new brand identity. A stylised swift, a bird famous for its speed and stamina, became the corporate logo symbolising Speedpost's commitment to customers. New look courier boxes were introduced. Image advertising used analogies to demonstrate how the new Speedpost removed obstacles to speed. Sales messages were layered throughout the campaign: a service network offered 125 acceptance counters in Hong Kong; speedy deliveries were made to major cities worldwide and over 1,900 cities in China alone; urgent deliveries came with a money back guarantee. Customer acquisition, usage and retention programmes were introduced.

the result Within the first 6 months of the campaign, brand awareness increased from 11% to 30% among general users, and from 36% to 50% among account customers.

    Speedpost's account base increased by 100% in 9 months, resulting in greater usage of the service.

DELIVERING A NEW BRAND
DELIVERING A NEW BRAND
DELIVERING A NEW BRAND DELIVERING A NEW BRAND DELIVERING A NEW BRAND
DELIVERING A NEW BRAND DELIVERING A NEW BRAND
DELIVERING A NEW BRAND DELIVERING A NEW BRAND DELIVERING A NEW BRAND
DELIVERING A NEW BRAND

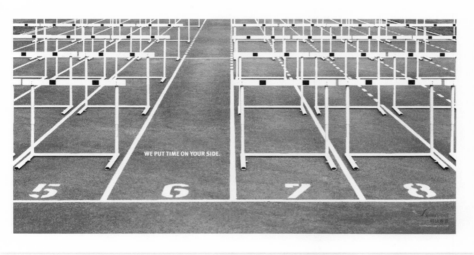

Print ads and outdoor posters used analogies to demonstrate how Speedpost removed obstacles to speed and put time on the customer's side.

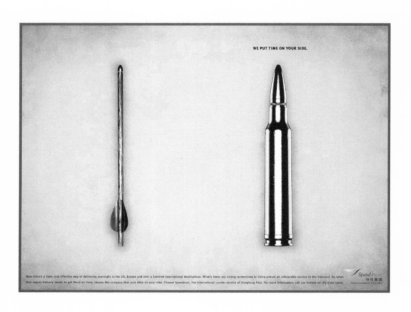

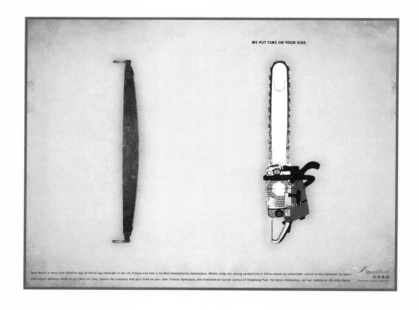

THE POWER OF AN ICON
THE POWER OF AN ICON

THE POWER OF AN ICON

THE POWER OF AN ICON   THE POWER OF AN ICON
THE POWER OF AN ICON   THE POWER OF AN ICON
THE POWER OF AN ICON
THE POWER OF AN ICON   THE POWER OF AN ICON

the problem MobileOne launched in April 1997, a venture owned by two local giants, Singapore Press Holdings and the Keppel Corporation, in partnership with Cable & Wireless. It was Singapore's first independent mobile telecom operator competing against the incumbent SingTel Mobile, which outspent it by three to one on advertising.

the strategy The new brand capitalised on the fact that it marked the end of a monopoly. It was launched as "the refreshing alternative", and offered three different subscription plans. Its name was shortened to an acronym — M1 — a shrewd move in a country where literally everything has an acronym. Its circular orange and blue logo was in stark contrast to SingTel's red and white. M1 built high awareness in the market. Within the first six months, 100,000 customers had signed up. Interestingly, most were new customers to mobile.

However, SingTel Mobile had spent years developing a network of base stations while M1 had put its together in less than nine months. So, in line with other markets where incumbents have had to face a challenger brand, SingTel Mobile promoted superior coverage. Its advertising icon was a big, SingTel corporate red umbrella. In one execution, a man holding a big red umbrella dwarfed a man holding a much smaller orange umbrella. The strapline was unequivocal: *No one covers more of Singapore than SingTel Mobile. Absolutely no one.* As a result, SingTel Mobile owned "coverage" and a lot of Singaporeans felt the incumbent was a safer bet.

When DDB Worldwide acquired the M1 account, it set out to convert high brand awareness into a brand personality. M1's advertising reflected an understated, approachable company. Its theme promised *A little more*, be it a little more friendly, a little more helpful, a little more innovative.

The breakthrough came in 1998 when M1 launched a direct response to SingTel Mobile's big red umbrella. Creatively, the agency wanted to "reposition" the umbrella as a negative icon. A commercial went to air with a man using a mobile phone standing in the rain beneath a red umbrella. As the camera panned to the left, the rain stopped and beyond was a girl in an orange bikini lying by a sundrenched pool talking on a mobile phone. The man under the umbrella kept looking at her enviously, but whenever he edged closer to her the rain followed him. The line, *Everywhere under the sun*, made a statement about M1 coverage. A child-like drawing of the sun became the brand icon.

A second commercial in 1999 featured people holding up the sun icon on placards and promised *M1 covers 99.98% of Singapore*. The song, *Walking on Sunshine* became the musical signature for the brand. The following year, *Rise and Shine* delivered an empowerment message using well-known local celebrities.

With the advent of a third independent player, StarHub, on April 1 2000, M1 developed what the agency calls "stractical" advertising — strategic brand-building combined with tactical promotions — in the belief that the massive volume of retail work must enhance the personification of the brand. A push-pull effect was employed; the strategic element built brand preference, while the retail message offered immediate opportunities to experience the brand.

For 2001, M1 demonstrated even more exuberance in its strategic campaign. A new theme saw the numeral "1" replace the letter "I" in the word "SMILE": *SM1LE! You're on M1* became the proposition conveyed with an energetic treatment of the song *Walking on Sunshine*.

the result In 40 months, M1 climbed from 10% market share to 36%, achieving more than 700% growth in its customer base.

Its customer base soared from 100,000 in 1997 to 800,000 in 2001. For example, in 1998 M1 had 28% of the available mobile market in Singapore — 300,000 subscribers. By 1999, it had attracted 450,000 subscribers, representing 34% of the available market. By 2001, with the entry of StarHub and Virgin Mobile, it held its market share at 36%.

By early 2000 M1 was connecting 55% of all new mobile customers in Singapore, exceeding the 40% target that it had set for itself.

M1 was voted in the Top 50 Brands in Asia by Asia Market Intelligence, alongside Singapore Airlines. In 1999, *Media & Marketing* magazine named M1 its Advertiser of the Year while the London *Financial Times* recognised M1 as having the world's most effective telecom marketing campaign.

❝❝

Everywhere under the sun, with its colours, its icons and its messages has, in my view, communicated the M1 brand positioning in a very powerful and effective way, and continues to convey the very essence of our brand. That it has remained relevant for some years now shows that it also possesses an enduring theme that has withstood the test of time."

NEIL MONTEFIORE, Chief Executive Officer, M1

❝❝

As a case study, it's an incredible example of how one icon can basically kill another, purely because one is seen as warm and friendly and nice. The sun icon has become the personality of M1."

TIM EVILL, President & Executive Creative Director, DDB Worldwide Singapore

❝❝

Don't let that warm and endearing branding fool you. The M1 brand is utterly competitive. Its mindset is about repositioning the competition, so it carries a persuasive appeal."

DAVID TANG, Managing Director & Brand Strategist, DDB Worldwide Singapore

THE POWER OF AN ICON
THE POWER OF AN ICON
THE POWER OF AN ICON
THE POWER OF AN ICON THE POWER OF AN ICON
THE POWER OF AN ICON
THE POWER OF AN ICON THE POWER OF AN ICON THE POWER OF AN ICON
THE POWER OF AN ICON
THE POWER OF AN ICON
THE POWER OF AN ICON

a little more innovative

In 1998, M1 directly challenged SingTel Mobile's leadership in coverage…

A man under a red umbrella in pouring rain is seen talking on a mobile phone. We pan left and discover a girl in an orange bikini also using a mobile phone, except that she is lying beside a sundrenched swimming pool. When the man with the umbrella enviously edges towards her, the rain follows him.

VOCALS: *You are my sunshine, My only sunshine…*

MALE VO: *With unbeatable GSM coverage of Singapore, we are with you everywhere under the sun.*

CUT TO A CHILD-LIKE DRAWING OF THE SUN AND THE LINE: *Everywhere under the sun. M1.*

MALE VO: *M1…*

The sun icon turns into the M1 logo.

SUPER: *A little more innovative.*

In 1999, M1 further developed its theme *Everywhere under the sun...*

The brand signature song, *Walking on Sunshine*, is heard throughout.

Singaporeans hold up placards of the M1 sun icon in one situation after another — in a coffee shop, in a cab, in a swimming pool, even while boxing.

A SUPER ACCOMPANIES THE FINAL ICON: *M1 covers 99.98% of Singapore.*

Cut to M1 logo.

SUPER: *Everywhere under the sun.*

In 2000, M1 launched an empowerment message using local celebrities...

Inspirational classical music is heard throughout as a dozen Singaporeans deliver their part of one continuous sentence...

CORPORATE BANKER SEOW BOON ANN: *Look at me, I have the power to reach out to anyone, anywhere, and with this power...*

ACTRESS BEATRICE CHIA: *I can make people laugh and cry...*

NATIONAL RUGBY CAPTAIN TERENCE KHOO: *I can tackle the world...*

ARTIST JACKI SOO: *I can hear voices of inspiration...*

A LITTLE BOY IN A MASK, RYAN LIM SUPERHERO: *Everywhere under the sun...*

SUPER: *Rise and Shine with one mobile communications company...*

M1 LOGO AND SUPER: *Everywhere under the sun.*

In 2001, the theme of sunshine was given another twist… *SM1LE! You're on M1…*

Exuberant shots of Singaporeans communicating with each other are cut to a big, energetic version of the brand's signature song *Walking on Sunshine*.

The sunny, smiling images keep building throughout.

The M1 logo appears and becomes part of the word *SM1LE!*

SUPER: *You're on M1.*

The sun icon dissolves into the M1 logo.

END SUPER: *Everywhere under the sun.*

category	countries	advertiser	agency
TELE-COMMUNICATIONS AND POSTAL SERVICES	SINGAPORE	SINGTEL	DENTSU YOUNG & RUBICAM, SINGAPORE

SELLING THE REAL SINGTEL SELLING THE REAL SINGTEL
SELLING THE REAL SINGTEL

SELLING THE REAL SINGTEL

SELLING THE REAL SINGTEL
SELLING THE REAL SINGTEL SELLING THE REAL SINGTEL SELLING THE REAL SINGTEL
SELLING THE REAL SINGTEL SELLING THE REAL SINGTEL

the problem SingTel, formerly Singapore Telecoms, could trace its origins back 120 years. Given Singapore's newly liberalised telecommunications market and the arrival of new brands, celebrating a 120th anniversary was an opportunity to reinforce SingTel's long-term commitment to Singaporeans.

The downside was that the anniversary might well rekindle memories of the "old" SingTel, the government-owned monopoly. Its former bureaucratic image would impact negatively when SingTel faced aggressive competition and was no longer the default option.

the strategy It was clear to the agency that consumers had taken SingTel's services for granted over time. SingTel had become so much part of daily life it was just "there".

If the 120th anniversary was going to be a celebration all Singaporeans could share, it was time to project the "unseen" SingTel. The campaign had to dig into the local culture and demonstrate how SingTel is interwoven into the essence of Singapore.

But to communicate that special relationship, the campaign had to defy the conventional rules of corporate celebrations. The theme line set the tone: *It's still about you.* Instead of high tech imagery and messages about growth, the ten commercials focused on ordinary people in familiar local surroundings. Each execution had almost the flavour of a home video — nothing slick, nothing extravagant or wasteful.

Slices of Life was the first campaign by a major Singapore corporation to run in all four of Singapore's official languages — English, Mandarin, Malay and Tamil.

the result A benchmark study established the parameters in the two months prior to the campaign. The actual tracking continued for five months.

Over the period of the campaign, significant improvements in the perceptions of SingTel brand imageries and core positioning strengths were achieved, cementing consumer preferences for the brand. Key shifts included increases of up to 10 points on SingTel positioning attributes such as "Allows me to keep in touch with family/friends", "Communicates a stylish image", and "Responsive to customers' needs". The critical attribute, "Listens to my needs", witnessed the biggest single increase — 12 points.

The campaign also attracted an unprecedented level of editorial coverage.

    ❝❝

Slices of Life tells, in a uniquely Singaporean way, stories to which our customers can relate. It is also about trust and relationships we have built with our customers over the years, and our way of demonstrating to them our continued commitment and dedication to serving them better in the next 120 years and beyond."

SingTel Spokesman

    ❝❝

This is not the usual corporate anniversary campaign which parades company milestones in a self-important way. Our advertising is a series of very personal glimpses. The commercials talk to real Singaporeans, and look at how the telephone has touched their lives and how telephony is changing."

**PATRICK LOW, Executive Creative Director,
Dentsu Young & Rubicam Singapore**

SELLING THE REAL SINGTEL
SELLING THE REAL SINGTEL   SELLING THE REAL SINGTEL

SELLING THE REAL SINGTEL <small>SELLING THE REAL SINGTEL</small>

SELLING THE REAL SINGTEL   SELLING THE REAL SINGTEL   SELLING THE REAL SINGTEL
SELLING THE REAL SINGTEL
SELLING THE REAL SINGTEL

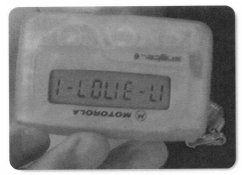

A young girl in a library is leaning forward, confiding in the camera.

GIRL: *This number keeps appearing on my pager. I know it's not a phone number, so what can it be?*

She holds the pager to camera so we can see the number.

GIRL: *17-31707-1. When I ask my friends, they tell me it's a code.*

She turns the pager upside down. Now the number can be read like a text message.

GIRL: *It says, I love you. So horrible, right? When I told my mother she said, Young lady, you're too young to have a secret admirer.*

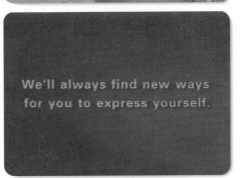

MUSIC AND GRAPHICS: *We'll always find new ways for you to express yourself.*

SINGTEL AND 120 YEARS LOGOS.

TAGLINE: *It's still about you.*

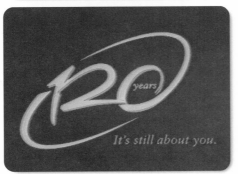

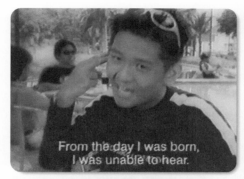

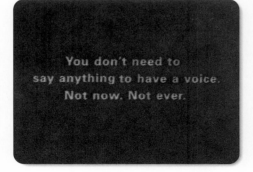

A young man by a pool is communicating with us through sign language. The soundtrack is totally silent. A series of supers convey his conversation.

SUPERS: *From the day I was born, I was unable to hear. The doctors told my family that it would be difficult for me to learn how to speak. Communication would have to be done face-to-face.*

The shot widens and we see he has a laptop computer. The screen flashes a *"You've got mail"* message.

The young man grins.

SUPER: *Well, they were wrong.*

MUSIC AND GRAPHICS: *You don't need to say anything to have a voice. Not now. Not ever.*

SINGTEL AND 120 YEARS LOGOS.

TAGLINE: *It's still about you.*

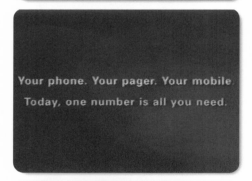

An old man tells us how his first phone number inspired him to try his luck with the 4D lottery.

OLD MAN: *231680 was my first phone number. Back then there were only four numbers. The last four numbers were 1680. Every week I bought $2 big, $2 small. One day I finally won. Not the first prize, but a starter.*

MUSIC AND GRAPHICS: *Your phone. Your pager. Your mobile. Today, one number is all you need.*

SINGTEL AND 120 YEARS LOGOS.

TAGLINE: *It's still about you.*

EXPANDING IN A SATURATED MARKET

EXPANDING IN A SATURATED MARKET

EXPANDING IN A SATURATED MARKET EXPANDING IN A SATURATED MARKET EXPANDING IN A SATURATED MARKET EXPANDING IN A SATURATED MARKET EXPANDING IN A SATURATED MARKET

the problem Hong Kong is one of the world's most competitive mobile communications markets. Mobile phone penetration is beyond 60%, and six network providers offer eleven different service brands. However, given the increasingly saturated market and the rising costs of each new consumer acquisition, growth could no longer rely on subscriptions. Improving existing subscriber satisfaction through new, value-added services emerged as the key to consumer loyalty and improving the revenue contribution per subscriber.

At SmarTone, one key revenue driver was the international roaming service. It contributed around 17% of total annual income. It was also rated one of the most important value-added services the brand provided. Because international roaming drove brand preference so directly, SmarTone saw a major marketing opportunity with the launch of the Motorola L2000 — a tri-band handset that provided greater convenience to roaming users. If SmarTone capitalised on the Motorola L2000, it could reinforce its position as Hong Kong's leading international roaming operator as well as stimulate purchase and usage of the phone itself.

the strategy Based on research, business is the primary use for international roaming. Main users are executives working in multinational corporations, or entrepreneurs trading with overseas partners. Career-minded and opportunistic, they can't afford to lose touch with their world of business, no matter where they are or what they're doing. For them, a mobile phone is much more than just a phone; it is a vital business tool to which they are deeply attached.

The agency's insight came from exploring this subscriber-phone relationship. Staying connected is so important that their phones must always be switched on. But staying on means they need coverage, wherever they are in the world. The proposition addressed this need directly: *With SmarTone international roaming, you are always on!*

The creative platform truthfully portrayed an executive's life today. The theme reflected the fact that no matter how unwillingly, his phone will still be turned on even when he is taking a break from things far away: *You can't get away with SmarTone roaming coverage.*

the result According to reaction monitoring research conducted by Market Behaviour (Hong Kong) Ltd, the campaign achieved excellent scores in advertising recall and brand awareness, and delivered a significant increase in preference towards SmarTone.

EXPANDING IN A SATURATED MARKET   EXPANDING IN A SATURATED MARKET

EXPANDING IN A SATURATED MARKET

EXPANDING IN A SATURATED MARKET   EXPANDING IN A SATURATED MARKET   EXPANDING IN A SATURATED MARKET

EXPANDING IN A SATURATED MARKET   EXPANDING IN A SATURATED MARKET

The camera tracks across a beautiful, virtually deserted beach. Two surfers stroll by with their boards. Kids are building a sandcastle, with a US flag planted on its ramparts.

FEMALE VO: *With SmarTone, you can now be reached just about anywhere in the world.*

A Chinese executive is relaxing in a deck chair, about as far from home as he can get. Suddenly he reaches for his ringing mobile phone.

OPERATOR: *Mr. Chan? Urgent call from your Hong Kong office.*

He scowls.

EXECUTIVE: *I hate SmarTone...*

A little girl walks by with her plastic beach bucket.

He puts his phone in the bucket without her knowing, then settles back to rest.

FEMALE VO: *SmarTone International Roaming. One phone, one number, the world.*

End on SmarTone logo.

category
TELE-
COMMUNICATIONS
& POSTAL
SERVICES

countries
HONG KONG

advertiser
SMARTONE
MOBILE
COMMUNICATIONS/
SMARTGUIDE

agency
LEO BURNETT,
HONG KONG

ANSWERING HUMAN NEEDS
ANSWERING HUMAN NEEDS
ANSWERING HUMAN NEEDS

ANSWERING HUMAN NEEDS ANSWERING HUMAN NEEDS

ANSWERING HUMAN NEEDS ANSWERING HUMAN NEEDS
ANSWERING HUMAN NEEDS
ANSWERING HUMAN NEEDS

the problem As one of the most developed mobile communications markets in the world, Hong Kong is widely expected to become the main hub for mobile technology advancement in the next decade. But despite headlines about GPRS and 3G appearing in the press almost daily, consumer research revealed a different story. Fancy technology was one thing. Consumers, however, still preferred practical innovations that solved their daily needs.

Rated by Market Behaviour (Hong Kong) Ltd in 2000 as having the most preferred mobile network, Leo1, SmarTone evolved a new brand essence to address these consumer demands. All product development strategy and subscriber services had to relate directly to consumer needs. The company's belief was that the power of innovative mobile technology depends on its relevance, and it will only be relevant if it simplifies people's daily lives.

To bring this new brand essence to life, SmarTone developed and launched a new location-based technology called SmartGuide — a "navigation" service for subscribers.

the strategy SmartGuide was ingenious. It made comprehensive location information available easily, anytime, anywhere, through a mobile phone.

It simplified how consumers navigated their way through their daily lives: where was the closest ATM, where was the nearest car park, where was a new restaurant to surprise a colleague. The timesaving answers to these and dozens of life's worries could all be accessed through SmartGuide.

The technology was a breakthrough in the category, and clearly the advertising had to be the same. Television commercials had to be faithful to the brand essence, and create a new way of projecting technological leadership without overtly claiming it. For example, the *Restaurant* commercial communicated simply, translating the power of mobile technology into a relevant, easy-to-understand message.

the result Post-launch, SmarTone achieved the highest score in spontaneous brand awareness — 76%. Perceptions of SmarTone in other relevant scales increased by as much as 40%.

ANSWERING HUMAN NEEDS
ANSWERING HUMAN NEEDS
ANSWERING HUMAN NEEDS
ANSWERING HUMAN NEEDS
ANSWERING HUMAN NEEDS
ANSWERING HUMAN NEEDS
ANSWERING HUMAN NEEDS
ANSWERING HUMAN NEEDS
ANSWERING HUMAN NEEDS

Two female attendants in red cheongsams stand outside a typical Chinese restaurant. A man and a woman approach.

MAN: *Let's have Chinese food.*

FEMALE: *I feel like having Thai food.*

MAN: *But is there one around here?*

Suddenly the two attendants spring into action. One shifts a Chinese column by the doorway to reveal a Thai sculpture. The other steps out of her cheongsam to reveal her Thai costume. She gives a graceful Thai greeting.

ATTENDENT: *Sa wa dee ka...*

The man and woman are stunned.

CUT TO TITLE: *In a perfect world...*

Cut back to the man and woman, still stunned.

CUT TO NEXT TITLE: *You wouldn't need our new "Dining Locations" technology.*

ADD LOGO: *SmarTone.*

A man walks up to stranger.

MAN: *Excuse me, is there an ATM around here?*

STRANGER: *Dunno. Need some cash? How much do you need?*

MAN: *Er... a few thousand.*

The stranger reaches into his coat and pulls out a wad of notes.

STRANGER: *Here, take it!*

CUT TO TITLE: *In a perfect world...*

Cut back to the man still staring at the stranger and his money.

CUT TO NEXT TITLE: *You wouldn't need our new "Cash Machine Locations" technology.*

ADD LOGO: *SmarTone.*

A young motorist in a bright yellow sports car talks to the traffic cop on a motor bike beside him.

MOTORIST: *Officer, is there a car park around here?*

The cop just stares at him and waves.

COP: *Just park right here.*

CUT TO TITLE: *In a perfect world...*

Cut back to a wider shot as the traffic cop rides off, revealing that their conversation has taken place in the middle of a busy street. The young sports car driver is still staring after him, bewildered.

CUT TO NEXT TITLE: *You wouldn't need our new "Car Park Locations" technology.*

ADD LOGO: *SmarTone.*

category country advertiser agency

SINGAPORE TOURISM BOARD
BRITISH AIRWAYS BRITISH AIRWAYS
SARAWAK TOURISM AUTHORITY TOURISM AUTHORITY OF THAILAND
S HOTEL, SINGAPORE TRAVEL AND TOURISM SINGAPORE TOURISM BOARD
SINGAPORE AIRLINES
SINGAPORE AIRLINES KOSCIUSKO THREDBO LIMITED KOSCIUSKO THREDBO LIMITED
SINGAPORE TOURISM BOARD RAFFLES HOTEL, SINGAPORE

Travel And Tourism

CONVENTION dictates most advertising in this category. The brands that pioneer fresh ground are generally the big winners. (Easier said than done, of course, in an age of recessions and uncertainty.) The case studies offered in this book reaffirm that the most respected brands have been built with courage and clarity. In each example, the brand builder has taken the high ground, frequently defying conventional wisdom. Irreverence emerges as an unexpected factor in success; category-busting executional techniques are another.

WHEN PICTURES BECOME HEADLINES

WHEN PICTURES BECOME HEADLINES

WHEN PICTURES BECOME HEADLINES

WHEN PICTURES BECOME HEADLINES

WHEN PICTURES BECOME HEADLINES WHEN PICTURES BECOME HEADLINES

WHEN PICTURES BECOME HEADLINES

WHEN PICTURES BECOME HEADLINES

the problem British Airways had a variety of messages to communicate in Asian regional print media, including sleeper beds in First Class, inflight entertainment, and snacks available at any time during the flight.

In the case of the sleeper bed, the market had been saturated with literal executions — endless shots of people sleeping in nice wide seats. Neither the brand owner nor the agency wanted to show the sleeper bed itself. However, in the case of pan-Asian campaigns, advertising must transcend language, culture and sophistication. Was there another visual way to communicate a good night's sleep, without first putting the reader to sleep?

the strategy The first execution had to target overnight travellers from Singapore to London. The key benefit was defined as being able to sleep all the way.

The creative leap was the visual of an eyelid. By adding the words "London" and "Singapore" at either end of the eyelid, the visual communicated a good night's rest without any explanatory headline or supporting body copy.

The ad layout followed a global print template originated by the agency's London office.

the result While the ad sold an attribute, it actually built the brand. It was more strategic than tactical, and its impact was difficult to measure purely in revenue terms. What was significant is that the ad travelled the world. It was adapted for Argentina, Australia, Brazil, Canada, Hong Kong, Malaysia, Mexico, Slovenia and Thailand, with the destinations changed and translated as required.

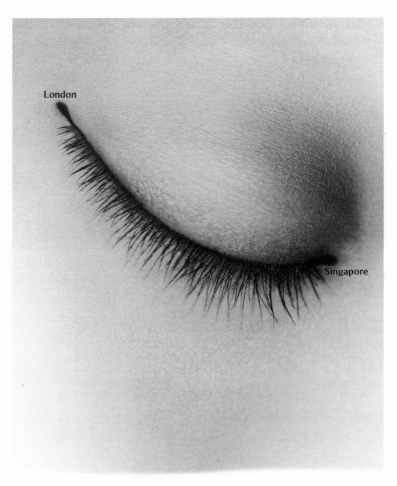

A BRAND BACK FROM THE BRINK
A BRAND BACK FROM THE BRINK
A BRAND BACK FROM THE BRINK
A BRAND BACK FROM THE BRINK

A BRAND BACK FROM THE BRINK

A BRAND BACK FROM THE BRINK
A BRAND BACK FROM THE BRINK
A BRAND BACK FROM THE BRINK
A BRAND BACK FROM THE BRINK

the problem Until 31 July 1997, Thredbo was widely regarded as Australia's premier ski resort. Located high in the Snowy Mountains of southern New South Wales, it could accommodate 4,000 visitors a night. Sophisticated yet unpretentious, Thredbo had a reputation for great skiing and a lively nightlife. Irreverent advertising had built Thredbo into one of the few destination brands in Australia.

Then, just before midnight, a section of the Alpine Way highway collapsed, demolishing two lodges and claiming the lives of 18 people, all but one of whom were Thredbo staff or residents including senior management. The rescue mission unfolded "live" on national television for the next ten days. Australia held its breath as the rubble was combed for survivors. Sydney TV news programmes actually increased their audiences by up to 28.6%. One newspaper's circulation rose by 25,000 copies a day in the week after the disaster. The tragedy had struck at the heart of Thredbo's close-knit community.

Kosciusko Thredbo Limited (KT) is wholly owned by publicly listed Amalgamated Holdings. KT's obligations were to protect the brand, the shareholder investment, and the 625 small business operators and property owners within the village itself. Around 90% of the resort's turnover is done in the short, 10-week ski season. KT is a fixed cost business. Virtually no adjustments can be made to overhead or operating costs. The impact of a reduction in skiers would be disastrous. (A 10% reduction in skier days equates to a 40% reduction in profit before interest and tax, while a 10% increase equates to a 40% increase in profit.) But if KT were unable to guarantee the safety of its visitors, Thredbo would not be a viable business. And there was no textbook to tell them what to do.

Prior to the landslide, Thredbo was seen as a class act that didn't take itself too seriously. Its positioning was defined as "sophisticated, upmarket, challenging, European and friendly". Its brand personality was "humorous, different, clever, unexpected, memorable, exhilarating and addictive".

After the disaster, all advertising was cancelled. A crisis management team was put in place to deal with the media. The village responded as a community, as a village family, speaking in one voice. An Open Letter of thanks was published, expressing gratitude to everyone that had helped in the rescue work or lent their support.

The tragedy had struck at the peak of the 1997 ski season. Skier days dropped by 46% the week following the landslide. Newspoll was contracted for a quantitative tracking study. The first wave revealed that skiers and the public felt Thredbo was unsafe, with 51.7% of female respondents feeling uncomfortable about visiting Thredbo during the season. In the third wave, 57.9% of women believed a landslide could happen again.

The embattled resort community asked themselves if they could salvage the rest of the season, and how they could rebuild their brand for the future.

the strategy The immediate need was to communicate that Thredbo was safe. Also, visitors had to be reassured that they should not feel guilty about having fun at Thredbo; the landslide victims themselves had loved Thredbo and would want it to go on. A second Open Letter, *A Message from Thredbo*, was published to deliver those messages.

By summer 1997/98, Thredbo was out of the news. Qualitative research indicated that people didn't connect Thredbo in summer to the tragedy; the landslide belonged to the ski season. It was a communications opportunity to signal that Thredbo was alive and active. Three spots epitomising Thredbo's irreverent personality ran on Sydney television. They positioned Thredbo as a fun alternative to the beach. Chair lift and bobsled rides, golf, tennis, and the Alpine Training Centre were popular summer attractions.

By early 1998, the landslide and who was to blame still received media coverage. The scars of the landslide were visual reminders of the tragedy. Major reconstruction of the Alpine Way only began in February 1998. Safety issues concerned skiers as winter approached. But qualitative research warned against any mention of safety in any context; if advertising told consumers that Thredbo was safe, the take-out would be that it was unsafe.

What advertising could do was communicate that Thredbo was still Thredbo. And with the Nagano Winter Olympics being held in February 1998, the Thredbo brand could indulge in some of its old irreverence. The Campaign Palace despatched a writer, art director and film director to Nagano with a Handycam to shoot a very lateral, tongue-in-cheek campaign. The idea was that even Japanese skiers would rather be in Thredbo than Nagano. Nine 15-second commercials were produced on a production budget of US$17,000.

But as the 1998 ski season approached, media interest heightened again. The anniversary of the landslide was shaping up as a major news event. The Coroner's report had still not been issued, which generated even more uncertainty. Pre-season bookings were down by 43%. At least 25% of Thredbo skiers still considered it unsafe for a holiday and negative media stories did nothing to quell their anxiety. Once again, advertising was charged with portraying a positive view of the resort.

Thredbo's irreverence was pushed even further. The rationale was if advertising could make skiers laugh, they were more likely to start thinking about a ski holiday. The campaign idea was that skiers would rather be in Thredbo. The commercials depicted loyal skiers dreaming about Thredbo while absentmindedly doing something else — like urinating. Meanwhile, a major activity programme was put in place on the mountain, including night skiing, a world record flare run and fireworks. But it was going to be an uphill battle. Competitive advertising increased. While Thredbo worked with reduced funds, its largest competitor Perisher Blue upped its budget by 64% and changed strategy with a campaign that mirrored Thredbo's tonality. New Zealand and Victorian ski fields became far more aggressive, wooing New South Wales skiers with a rumoured US$285,000 expenditure.

the result Helped by a couple of reasonable snowfalls after the 1997 landslide and the pleas for support in the second Open Letter, many skiers started to return. Skier days picked up after the last rescue workers had left. By end-August, they were back to almost pre-landslide level.

Summer revenue in 1998/1999 was up by 4% over the previous year, with chair lift rides up by 3%, while after the Nagano campaign Newspoll tracking showed a remarkable decrease in safety concerns.

The decline predicted for winter 1998 did not happen. Thredbo actually managed to grow its business on a reduced advertising budget. Despite the poorest snowfalls in over 15 years, Thredbo grew its market share by one point while Perisher Blue's remained constant. The Alpine Hotel occupancy level recovered from 48% in 1997 to 56% in 1998. Skier days grew by 1% over 1997, with the third week of July 1998 recording the highest numbers of skiers in eight years and the third highest in Thredbo's history.

The final Newspoll tracking was conducted in March 1999. By then, only 6% of Thredbo skiers had any safety concerns. Significantly perhaps, the poll was conducted the week after media coverage of avalanches in several Austrian ski resorts.

A BRAND BACK FROM THE BRINK

A BRAND BACK FROM THE BRINK

A BRAND BACK FROM THE BRINK

A BRAND BACK FROM THE BRINK

A BRAND BACK FROM THE BRINK

A BRAND BACK FROM THE BRINK

A BRAND BACK FROM THE BRINK

A BRAND BACK FROM THE BRINK

Thredbo's 1997/98 summer campaign marked a return to irreverence after the disastrous landslide…

A mother and daughter are seen at the beach.

vo: *There's something all Australians should be aware of before venturing into the water this summer…*

Menacing *Jaws*-style music is heard…

vo: *The average toddler urinates 5 times a day…*

Cut to the alternative — footage of Thredbo summer activities.

Cut back to toddler at the beach. We hear the sounds of "peeing".

SUPER OVER THE SATISFIED TODDLER'S FACE: *Thredbo, you'll like it. Call 1800 020 589.*

Early in 1998, the Nagano campaign gave Thredbo an opportunity for some more lateral irreverence…

Open on young Japanese ski enthusiast at Nagano. A microphone is thrust at him.

INTERVIEWER OFF CAMERA: *Excuse me, which do you prefer… The skiing in Nagano or in Thredbo?*

JAPANESE MAN: *Um… I like Nagano better.*

There's a "thud" and the man bends over, as though he has been kneed in the groin.

JAPANESE MAN: *Thredbo… I like it, I like it…*

CUT TO END TITLE WITH ORIENTAL-STYLE LETTERING ON RED BACKGROUND: *Ski Thredbo. You'll like it. 1800 020 589.*

We see a Japanese woman eating Japanese food.

INTERVIEWER OFF CAMERA: *How's the sushi here in Nagano?*

The woman is holding a piece of paper in her hand. She reads out loud what is written on the card.

JAPANESE WOMAN: *If they had sushi in Thredbo, it would be much better than this.*

INTERVIEWER OFF CAMERA: *Thanks!*

CUT TO END TITLE WITH ORIENTAL-STYLE LETTERING ON RED BACKGROUND: *Ski Thredbo. You'll like it. 1800 020 589.*

Open on the mountainside at Nagano, Japan. Two women are standing on the slope.

INTERVIEWER OFF CAMERA: *Excuse me, which do you prefer...the snowball from Nagano...*

At that, a snowball hits one of the women.

INTERVIEWER OFF CAMERA: *...Or the one we brought from Thredbo?*

At that, another snowball hits the woman.

BOTH WOMEN: *Thredbo.*

INTERVIEWER OFF CAMERA: *Thanks!*

CUT TO END TITLE WITH ORIENTAL-STYLE LETTERING ON RED BACKGROUND: *Ski Thredbo. You'll like it. 1800 020 589.*

The 1998 winter campaign featured skiers daydreaming about Thredbo while they are doing something else...

Beautiful ski footage accompanied by a Viennese waltz.

Dissolve to young man daydreaming that he is back at Thredbo on his skis...

His body sways to the music...

Suddenly we see he is standing at a urinal, so transported that he forgets what he is doing. He accidentally urinates on the legs of the men beside him who jump out of the way.

END TITLE: *Ski Thredbo. You'll like it.*

Beautiful ski footage accompanied by a Viennese waltz...

We cut to a female beautician who daydreams about Thredbo while waxing a woman's bikini-line.

Suddenly we hear a woman's painful cry and the stunned beautician is holding up a strip of wax covered in a perfectly-shaped patch of pubic hair.

END TITLE: *Ski Thredbo. You'll like it.*

category TRAVEL AND TOURISM	**countries** SINGAPORE AND GLOBAL	**advertiser** RAFFLES HOTEL, SINGAPORE	**agency** BATEY GROUP, SINGAPORE

RELAUNCHING A LEGEND
RELAUNCHING A LEGEND   RELAUNCHING A LEGEND
RELAUNCHING A LEGEND

RELAUNCHING A LEGEND

RELAUNCHING A LEGEND   RELAUNCHING A LEGEND
RELAUNCHING A LEGEND   RELAUNCHING A LEGEND

the problem Singapore's world famous Raffles Hotel closed on March 15, 1989. It was a pale shadow of its former self, and there had even been talk of demolition. Nevertheless, Raffles remained a prime tourist attraction. After extensive restoration, it reopened on September 16, 1991.

The relaunch had to build a brand identity for a completely renovated property. The new Raffles Hotel offered the most up-to-date facilities and amenities, while retaining the character and heritage that separated the "Grand Old Lady of the East" from merely modern luxury hotels. The values of history and tradition had to be appropriately projected without any impression of crass commercialism; on the other hand, the media communications could not become a history lesson.

And despite the modest budget, it was imperative to reach out to a select international target audience.

the strategy The new hotel was a celebration of the senses and its proud heritage could best be communicated visually. Distinctively "old-fashioned" graphics were consistently deployed across stationery, signage, menu cards, marketing support collaterals, and media advertising.

The strong visual style was coupled with witty, readable copy. Eclectic, small space reader-style ads appeared in upscale media. Local advertising for bar and food outlets maintained a similar sense of the quaint and quirky.

The public relations programme invited famous newspaper columnists and travel writers to experience the new hotel and share their impressions with readers.

More headlines followed when it was announced that an unpublished manuscript written by Somerset Maugham — a frequent guest in years gone by, who supposedly wrote *The Moon and Sixpence* at the Long Bar — had been found in an old trunk. The significance of the discovery being made on March 31 escaped the global media's attention — until the next morning.

the result Raffles Hotel continues to enjoy the highest occupancy rates and the highest average room rates in Singapore.

According to Singapore Tourism Board research, Raffles Hotel is the single most popular tourism attraction in Singapore. It enjoys a high volume of transient, non-resident custom from locals and tourists alike.

In the first year after reopening, Raffles Hotel secured worldwide editorial coverage valued at over US$5 million.

RELAUNCHING A LEGEND
RELAUNCHING A LEGEND   RELAUNCHING A LEGEND
RELAUNCHING A LEGEND RELAUNCHING A LEGEND
RELAUNCHING A LEGEND   RELAUNCHING A LEGEND
RELAUNCHING A LEGEND RELAUNCHING A LEGEND

THE HEAD WAITER
WATCHED WITH MOUNTING DESPAIR

as the magnificent Gieves & Hawkes tie slid like a sword into the Sauce Bearnaise. Mr Carruthers, who had just returned to his seat, was unaware of the disaster. The waiter glided silently forward and announced his presence with a tiny 'ahem'. Perhaps, he suggested with the tact of Jeeves, Mr Carruthers would be more comfortable if he took off his tie? The gentleman duly obliged and the pride of Savile Row was silently borne away to be subjected to the secret alchemies of the laundry manager. Less than an hour later it was returned to the bemused Mr Carruthers, cleaned, pressed and just in time for coffee. So impressed was the hotel guest, in fact, that he delighted his table companions with a piece of uncharacteristic jocularity. He would, he quipped, be returning the following week with a suit to be cleaned. The waiter merely observed that in that case he would ensure that an extra large dish of Sauce Bearnaise was on hand to receive it.

A RAFFLES INTERNATIONAL HOTEL

Raffles Hotel, 1 Beach Road, Singapore 189673, Tel: (65) 337-1886. Fax: (65) 339-7650. Internet: raffles@pacific.net.sg

SHE WAS, HE SAID,
AN ARISTOCRATIC EIGHTY YEAR OLD

French lady and he loved her with a passion that bordered on the physical. The young receptionist reached for her pen. The caller went on to explain that he would be coming to Singapore during the first week in March. And his travelling companion would be arriving a few days earlier. Could arrangements be made to look after the old lady in his absence? Despite her impeccable French pedigree, he said, she was liable on account of her great age to be a touch cantankerous. The receptionist explained that the hotel was always delighted to look after elderly ladies, cantankerous or otherwise. Let's hope so, the caller added. She was the one true love of his life and had survived all three of his marriages. Somewhat taken aback by this demonstration of gallic candour, the girl inquired if the gentleman had any particular suite in mind? Just put her in the garage he said. When she finally arrived, the gleaming 1908 Peugeot quietly excelled all expectations in the Singapore to Malaysia vintage car rally.

A RAFFLES INTERNATIONAL HOTEL

Raffles Hotel, 1 Beach Road, Singapore 189673, Tel: (65) 337-1886. Fax: (65) 339-7650. Internet: raffles@pacific.net.sg

category	countries	advertiser	agency
TRAVEL AND TOURISM	GLOBAL	SARAWAK TOURISM AUTHORITY	BATEY GROUP, SINGAPORE

MAKING THE RAINFOREST FRIENDLY
MAKING THE RAINFOREST FRIENDLY MAKING THE RAINFOREST FRIENDLY MAKING THE RAINFOREST FRIENDLY

MAKING THE RAINFOREST FRIENDLY

MAKING THE RAINFOREST FRIENDLY
MAKING THE RAINFOREST FRIENDLY
MAKING THE RAINFOREST FRIENDLY

the problem The island of Borneo is divided between two Malaysian States — Sarawak and Sabah — and the Sultanate of Brunei in the north, and Indonesia's Kelantan province in the south. Previously, the promotion of Sarawak as a tourist destination had been in the larger context of Malaysia.

Sarawak tourism was caught in a vicious circle. Tourism marketing funds were limited, and planning budgets were constrained by weak tourism receipts. Promotional efforts by tour operators were modest. Not surprisingly, the awareness of Sarawak was low. Few had heard of it. Even fewer knew where it was and what it offered.

Worse, Sarawak was not a destination suited to everyone. Sarawak needed a strong, clearly branded identity that would give target prospects a compelling reason to visit. But with traditional tourism media — television and glossy colour magazines — crowded by competitors and beyond the State's budget, Sarawak had to find a highly strategic formula and affordable creativity.

the strategy Borneo conjures up all kinds of images — tribes of headhunters who live in longhouses and still hunt with blowpipes and poison darts, untamed rainforests, wild rivers and vast caves. Sarawak, once ruled by a family of White Rajahs, boasts large concentrations of *orang utan*, literally "the jungle man", still living in the wild.

Sarawak itself sent mixed signals: how dangerous was it? Was it suitable for family holidays?

It was decided to focus on Sarawak's exotic flora and fauna, while exploiting the mystique and romance of Borneo. Sarawak was positioned as the last great wilderness adventure. The campaign theme: *Sarawak, the hidden paradise of Borneo.*

Another key decision in branding Sarawak's communications was to use illustration rather than photography, the category convention in tourism advertising. Illustration would deliver softer, friendlier images, and be infinitely more controllable. It was also more affordable. Sarawak could visually compete with its richer Asian competitors on its own terms.

Two very distinctive styles were chosen. The classic Rousseau-style illustrations, detailed and authoritative, were balanced with colourful scenes inspired by pulp fiction book covers of the 1950s.

All materials were fully integrated, from logo, stationery, posters, collaterals, advertising, promotions and press releases.

Print ads were tightly targeted at prime potential visitors, such as expatriate executives living in Singapore and neighbouring Asian countries.

the result Arrivals rose sharply, from 0.8 million in 1996 to 3.3 million in 1999.

The modest public relations budget generated editorial valued at over US$2.5 million.

Destination collaterals were distributed worldwide by travel agents, airline offices (MAS, SIA and Royal Brunei), the Malaysia Tourism Promotion Board, and the Singapore Tourism Board.

A competition conducted in *Asia Magazine* attracted over 100,000 entries.

MAKING THE RAINFOREST FRIENDLY
MAKING THE RAINFOREST FRIENDLY MAKING THE RAINFOREST FRIENDLY MAKING THE RAINFOREST FRIENDLY

MAKING THE RAINFOREST FRIENDLY

MAKING THE RAINFOREST FRIENDLY

MAKING THE RAINFOREST FRIENDLY

MAKING THE RAINFOREST FRIENDLY

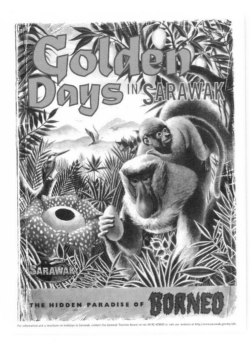

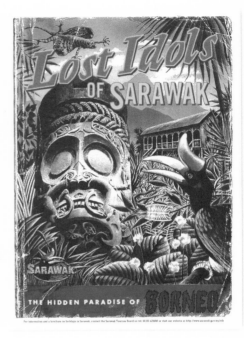

THE IBAN MAIDENS WERE TOTALLY MERCILESS. "NO PHOTOS,"
THEY LAUGHED, "UNLESS YOU DANCE THE NGAJAT!"

DRUM BEATS thudded out into the hot tropical night. Tribal gongs clanged. And the Iban girls, silver coins jingling on their tribal dresses, stepped forward with smiles of delight. For the honeymoon couple, there was now no possibility of escape. They were going to have to dance the *ngajat*.

But then no one comes to Sarawak just to sunbathe (even though the soft white sands, criss-crossed with turtle footprints, are ideal for this pastime). Instead, the wise traveller casts his fate into a boat and follows the call of the mighty Rajang River.

Over the years the river and its latticework of tributaries has borne countless generations of adventure-seekers – from traders and headhunters, to pirates and the odd novelist – deep into the ancient jungle. Through a botanic wonderland where proboscis monkeys squeal from the trees and lizards and frogs glide down from the skies. And where today you may stare into the eyes of an orang-utan and be forever haunted by the feeling of how human he seems. Just as he, too, will be perplexed at how much like an orang-utan you are.

Yes, a visit to this enchanted land on the northwestern edge of Borneo is proof that it is still possible to find adventure in this increasingly sanitised world. It no longer takes a week's sailing from Singapore by schooner, you can

get here in little over an hour. But the essential feeling of entering a different world is still the same. Especially at dusk when you break your journey upriver and sample

the legendary hospitality of the longhouses – the ancestral homes of the tribes which are strung out along the river like beads on a string. Here you may find, hidden away in the cobwebbed corners, the accumulated baggage of Sarawak's fascinating past: ancient Chinese jars; an antique brass cannon; a faded picture of Queen Victoria; and, occasionally hanging from the rafters, a dusty chandelier of skulls.

The rule of the longhouse is simple and it hasn't changed since the days when Joseph Conrad and Somerset Maugham wrote their stories here by the flickering light of the fire-flies. Guests, it is felt, should always make a little contribution to the entertainment. So when the gongs strike up, push aside the remains of your chicken-in-bamboo supper, take one last sip from the heady *tuak* rice wine, and dance the *ngajat* for all you're worth.

For more information and a brochure about holidays in Sarawak, please contact the Sarawak Tourism Board in one of the following ways: tel: 60 82 423600 or fax: 60 82 416700 or visit our website at http://www.sarawak.gov.my/stb

ARE THERE REALLY PLANTS OUT THERE IN THE RAINFOREST WHICH EAT ANIMALS?

THE IDEA had seemed just too far-fetched when Asun the guide first mentioned it to the young honeymoon couple. Then when he added that he would also be taking them to look for squirrels which flew and macaques which dived for crabs, they knew he had to be pulling their legs. (This was before he had even mentioned pigs sporting beards.)

But he was serious. Flying frogs and squirrels are actually some of the saner things you could encounter on a visit to Sarawak. Perched on the northwestern edge of Borneo just over an hour from Singapore, and covered with an expanse of primeval rainforest bigger than Austria, it's one of the last great lands of adventure left in this world.

Day begins here not with the common-place crowing of the cockerel, but the haunting sound of gibbons in the treetops, singing their hymn to the dawn. Among the foliage, you may see tiny deer the size of cats. Or hear, if you listen very carefully, the microscopic too-wit too-woo of an owl smaller than a butterfly. And nearby, find butterflies so big, that a Victorian naturalist – in one of his less sober moments – shot a specimen with his rifle.

The same Victorian naturalist complained that his sense of wonder almost died from overwork during his stay in Sarawak. You, too, may begin to doubt the evidence of your senses as you wander through caves bigger than cathedrals and trek across some of the oldest rainforest in the world. Or even encounter the famous carnivorous pitcher plants which trap flies in their saxophone shaped leaves and then digest them in a reservoir of corrosive fluid. Some varieties in Borneo grow so big that even drowned rats have been reported dissolving in the enzyme soup.

Day ends just as magically as it begins. Armies of fire-flies begin to flicker, phosphorescent mushrooms glow, and from the mouth of the great Deer Cave in Mulu National Park a river of bats emerges. Not just hundreds of bats. Nor even thousands. But a never-ending spiral of millions that will momentarily eclipse the Sarawak moon and consume three tons of insects before dawn.

Throughout the hot night they forage, over the dark canopy of the rainforest, over the gibbons sleeping in the trees, and over those strange pitcher plants with which they share the same taste in insects.

For more information and a brochure about holidays in Sarawak, please contact the Sarawak Tourism Board in one of the following ways: tel: 60 82 423600 or fax: 60 82 416700 or visit our website at http://www.sarawak.gov.my/stb

FOR 40,000 YEARS THEY'VE BEEN COMING HERE TO GET AWAY FROM IT ALL.

ARCHAEOLOGISTS tell us that the first humans to arrive in Southeast Asia chose to live in Sarawak. No one can say with any certainty why these early stone-age wanderers made for this particular corner of the region. But as you stroll through the spectacular caves of Sarawak, some so huge you could fit a handful of cathedrals in them, you can't help but wonder. Was this perhaps the first emergence 40,000 years ago of that essentially human characteristic, the desire for a more grandiose home?

Of course, we shall never know. But whatever their reasons, they certainly started something of a trend. Over the years, this charmed land on the northwestern edge of Borneo has been the essential port of call for generations of enterprising travellers. In the 6th century, the Chinese came in search of the finest edible bird's nest. In the 8th century, Arabian princes sent their emissaries to collect the world's best camphor.

And in the 16th century, the bedraggled remnants of Magellan's crew arrived. After two years at sea, during which hunger had forced them to eat the leather off the masts, they finally put Borneo on the European map. Not long after that, a host of would-be Indiana Joneses set sail to make their fortune. For some – like Rajah Brooke who established the dynasty of the White Rajahs – the dream came true. But others simply found themselves enslaved by pirates, and sold off in the classified ads section of the Java Courant.

Access to Sarawak has improved a lot since the days of sailing ships and pirates. It now takes just over an hour from Singapore. Nonetheless, for the traveller looking for something more rewarding than a simple beach holiday, Sarawak still possesses riches beyond measure. Not gold and diamonds – although there are plentiful deposits – but the sort of riches which screech and squawk. The gibbons which sing in the trees every dawn, for example. Or the bearded pigs which stand on their hind legs to reach the fruit up in the cocoa trees.

Trek, or climb or just simply wander in this country-sized botanic garden and you can discover a fresh wonder at every turn. A new variety of orchid, perhaps. Or you might even catch a glimpse of something more elusive still. The ancient Penan nomads – some of the world's last hunter-gatherers – slipping silently through the trees with their blowpipes and poison-tipped darts.

For more information and a brochure about holidays in Sarawak, please contact the Sarawak Tourism Board on tel: 60 82 423600 or fax: 60 82 416700 or visit our website at http://www.sarawak.gov.my/stb

category
TRAVEL AND
TOURISM

countries
GLOBAL

advertiser
SINGAPORE
AIRLINES

agency
BATEY ADS,
SINGAPORE

A GREAT WAY TO BUILD A BRAND
A GREAT WAY TO BUILD A BRAND A GREAT WAY TO BUILD A BRAND

A GREAT WAY TO BUILD A BRAND A GREAT WAY TO BUILD A BRAND

A GREAT WAY TO BUILD A BRAND A GREAT WAY TO BUILD A BRAND
A GREAT WAY TO BUILD A BRAND
A GREAT WAY TO BUILD A BRAND

the problem In 1972, Singapore and Malaysia agreed to restructure Malaysia Singapore Airlines. MSA split into two separate entities — Malaysian Airline System (MAS) and Singapore International Airlines (SIA).

SIA was launched with a small network and a fleet of aging aircraft inherited from MSA. It was virtually unknown outside Southeast Asia. Its objective was to break into a highly competitive arena in which the major airlines of the US, the UK, Europe and Australia reigned supreme — and if that weren't daunting enough, the airline's ambition was quite specific: to become one of the world's leading international airlines within ten years.

the strategy In the early 1970s, conventional wisdom in the airline industry called for advertising that promoted fleet size, network capability, frequency of flights and experienced pilots.

Realising it could not compete on those terms, SIA made its legendary decision: it would go to market with an inflight service proposition. The stewardess in her *sarong kebaya* would become the icon delivering the kind of inflight service "even other airlines talk about".

Against all advice to the contrary, the agency and airline stuck to their guns and chose television as the main advertising medium. Not only that, freshness was more important than frequency; a higher-than-average percentage of the advertising budget was invested in a stable of new commercials each year. Production values had to be nothing less than world-class. The intention was to communicate a travel experience so unique that it was worth paying a little more to enjoy.

Interestingly, no professional models were used. Only actual Singapore Airlines stewardesses have ever appeared on camera.

Over the years, the brand proposition has been supported by rational arguments — the world's most modern fleet, the best inflight entertainment. But with each new development, the soul of the brand has never changed.

the result Since 1973, independent traveller studies have consistently ranked Singapore Airlines among the top three airlines in the world, and first for inflight service and advertising.

The Singapore Girl is the instantly recognisable symbol of Singapore Airlines. She has become one of the world's best-known and most respected advertising icons and virtually the same campaign has run for 30 years.

Singapore Airlines continues to be the world's most profitable airline, and still totally committed to service delivery.

A GREAT WAY TO BUILD A BRAND

A GREAT WAY TO BUILD A BRAND

A GREAT WAY TO BUILD A BRAND

A GREAT WAY TO BUILD A BRAND

A GREAT WAY TO BUILD A BRAND

A GREAT WAY TO BUILD A BRAND

A GREAT WAY TO BUILD A BRAND

A GREAT WAY TO BUILD A BRAND

A GREAT WAY TO BUILD A BRAND

The ad that launched the icon. The phrase Singapore Girl *came later,*
making its first appearance in the lyrics of the song. The brand proposition has been
delivered consistently for 30 years.

Singapore Girl.
Gentle hostess in her sarong kebaya.
Let her take you across half the world and more.
She'll care for you as only she knows how.

The airline with the most modern fleet in the world, still believes in the romance of travel.

A FEW HOURS GRACE BEFORE THE MADNESS STARTS ALL OVER AGAIN.

The airline with the most modern fleet in the world, still believes in the romance of travel.

category	countries	advertiser	agency
TRAVEL AND TOURISM	GLOBAL	SINGAPORE TOURISM BOARD	BATEY ADS, SINGAPORE

A BREAK WITH CONVENTION A BREAK WITH CONVENTION A BREAK WITH CONVENTION REAK WITH CONVENTION

A BREAK WITH CONVENTION

A BREAK WITH CONVENTION A BREAK WITH CONVENTION A BREAK WITH CONVENTION A BREAK WITH CONVENTION A BREAK WITH CONVENTION A BREAK WITH CONVENTION

the problem In 1979, the tourism authority commissioned the agency to develop an international positioning for Singapore as a holiday destination. A consistent, fully integrated campaign was required for key markets in Europe, the UK, the US, Australia and Japan.

At that time, international tourism focused on UK/Europe and the US. Asia was not a primary destination — especially Singapore, which had few traditional tourism appeals: Singapore's beaches were few and paled in comparison with Bali's or Thailand's: there were no scenic attractions, no world-class entertainment, and certainly no nightlife worth talking about.

The nature of the target audience made matters even more complicated. Not only was it geographically and culturally diverse, it was ill-informed about Singapore. If it were to work, the new global campaign had to provide long-haul travellers with compelling reasons to visit Singapore — reasons that would be relevant and appealing to all of them.

the strategy Singapore decided to fight diversity with even more diversity. Singapore was positioned as a vibrant, exotic and culturally unique holiday destination. The advertising focused on the diverse experiences and encounters that tourists could expect. The proposition was that the whole was greater than the sum of its parts: *The most surprising tropical island on earth.*

The campaign broke with travel advertising conventions. Usually, destination advertising features a variety of photographs to convey the holiday experience — especially when the destination is unknown — and tries to shoehorn as much information as possible into its ads. Instead, the original *Surprising Singapore* print campaign used only one colour photograph in each ad, and no more than a few dozen words of text.

And when a variety of images did appear in the ads, they were presented in ways that again challenged travel advertising conventions.

Later, the media buy broke the rules as well. The campaign switched from colour magazines to full pages in black-and-white newspapers. A single bizarre picture was surrounded by long copy in which every second letter of every single word was typeset in italics.

The *Surprising Singapore* campaign ran from 1979 to 1996.

the result By the conclusion of the *Surprising Singapore* campaign, total visitor arrivals had risen from 2,247,091 in 1979 to 7,292,366 in 1996.

The *New Asia Singapore* campaign, also produced by Batey Ads, positioned Singapore in a 21st century context.

After a sharp falloff in the 1998 Asian recession, visitor arrivals quickly rebounded to a new record figure in 2000 — more than 7.7 million — and tourism was worth US$6 billion to Singapore.

A BREAK WITH CONVENTION   A BREAK WITH CONVENTION   A BREAK WITH CONVENTION

A BREAK WITH CONVENTION   **A BREAK WITH CONVENTION** A BREAK WITH CONVENTION

A BREAK WITH CONVENTION   A BREAK WITH CONVENTION

A BREAK WITH CONVENTION

WHERE WOULD YOU EXPECT
TO ENJOY THE TRANQUILITY OF A
DESERTED ISLAND FROM THE SHADE
OF A COCONUT PALM?

AND EXPLORE THE SIGHTS OF A
BUSTLING CITY FROM UNDER A
TRISHAW CANOPY?

TO SEE CLOTH DRAGONS
FLUTTER IN THE FRENZY OF A
CHINESE PROCESSION?

AND AN ENDLESS PARADE
OF EXOTIC GEMS AT DUTY-FREE
PRICES?

Singapore

THE MOST SURPRISING
TROPICAL ISLAND ON EARTH

WHERE WOULD YOU EXPECT
TO SEE BEJEWELLED INDIAN GIRLS
BEGUILE YOU WITH SPARKLING
EYES?

AND SAMPLE MARINATED
MALAY SATAY UNDER A STAR-
STUDDED SKY?

TO FIND ANTIQUE CHINESE
BUMBOATS STILL PLYING
THEIR TRADE?

AND BUY FUTURISTIC
TIMEPIECES AT PRICES FROM
A BYGONE AGE?

Singapore

THE MOST SURPRISING
TROPICAL ISLAND ON EARTH

Three bogies, one birdie,
two eagles and a rather nasty
python on the last hole.

It's not a UFO.

It's a Murtabak
from Zam Zam.

Looks like your dinner's
in the drink again.

category
TRAVEL AND
TOURISM

countries
GLOBAL

advertiser
TOURISM
AUTHORITY OF
THAILAND

agency
LEO BURNETT,
BANGKOK

BUILDING ON SUCCESS
BUILDING ON SUCCESS   BUILDING ON SUCCESS   BUILDING ON SUCCESS

BUILDING ON SUCCESS BUILDING ON SUCCESS

BUILDING ON SUCCESS
BUILDING ON SUCCESS   BUILDING ON SUCCESS
BUILDING ON SUCCESS

the problem The Tourist Authority of Thailand (TAT) and agency Leo Burnett had witnessed remarkable success with the *Amazing Thailand* theme. The challenge was to find new ways to keep the advertising fresh and make it even more compelling.

the strategy The agency wanted to create a uniqueness for Thailand in the new millennium, one that would attract tourists from all over the world. It focused the campaign idea on dealing with change and the added pressures that people face as the world moves further into a technological era. Strategically, Thailand was positioned as the perfect place to escape the stressful, fast-moving work environments of the West.

The creative breakthrough was centred on the idea that people were becoming like robots, and losing touch with their real selves. What if, asked the agency, these "human robots" were to visit Thailand and find themselves reconnected with their human selves?

Thailand's tourism icons — temples, floating markets and enchanting dancers — were woven credibly into the proposition. But the natural charm of the Thais themselves shone through as the true means of turning robots back into real people.

the result Since TAT and Leo Burnett launched the *Amazing Thailand* campaign to overseas markets in 1998, international visitor arrivals have significantly increased. In 1997 arrivals were up by just 0.4% on the previous year. In the year following the campaign launch that figure stood at 10.4%.

IT'S AMAZING WHAT PEOPLE TAKE HOME FROM THAILAND.

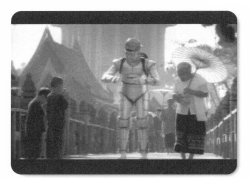

A mystical shot of a Thai temple framed by trees leads us to discover a tourist, in the form of a sad human robot looking at its image in a pool of lotus flowers. An old Thai lady invites him inside where he tries desperately to emulate the graceful movements of people in prayer.

FEMALE VO: *Out here, your neck muscles loosen…*

The robot's jaded taste buds are reawakened by a delicious spread of Thai dishes. Seeing a lady rowing produce to a river market, the robot rows furiously after her. As his interest in life is rekindled, he joins a troupe of Thai dancers, though his movements are still a bit stiff.

FEMALE VO: *Your backache disappears…*

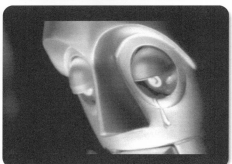

The robot sits meditating with Thais under trees.

FEMALE VO: *Your mind is enlightened.*

The robot's head is bowed. An old Thai lady gently fits a cap onto it. When he lifts his head it is no longer a robot we see, but a handsome young Caucasian. He stands in a Thai boat and gives the traditional greeting to his newly found Thai friends who have helped reconnect him with his real self.

FEMALE VO: *It's amazing what a visit to Thailand can do for life in the next millennium. Amazing Thailand 2000. Enchantment for the next thousand years.*

END LOGO: *Amazing Thailand 2000.*